ARMY FATIGUES

*Joining Israel's Army
of International Volunteers*

MARK WERNER

DEVORA
PUBLISHING
JERUSALEM ◆ NEW YORK

Army Fatigues: Joining Israel's Army of International Volunteers
Published by Devora Publishing Company
Copyright © 2008 by Mark Werner. All rights reserved.

COVER DESIGN: Zippy Thumim
TYPESETTING & BOOK DESIGN: Jerusalem Typesetting
EDITOR: Bonny V. Fetterman
EDITORIAL & PRODUCTION MANAGER: Daniella Barak

Conversations and events in this book are all true. Some names and identities have been changed to protect privacy.

Hard Cover ISBN: 978-1-934440-08-7

E-MAIL: sales@devorapublishing.com
WEB SITE: www.devorapublishing.com

Printed in the United States of America

This book is dedicated to the memory of my father,
Harold Werner, who taught me by his example
that sometimes one must follow the more difficult
path because it is the right thing to do

And to our children, Rachel and David, who make
their parents proud by living meaningful lives

CONTENTS

Acknowledgments vii

Preface ix

Introduction xiii

Chapter 1: The Army Base at Batzop 1

Chapter 2: At Home in Raleigh 63

Chapter 3: On the Border of Gaza 69

Chapter 4: Observing the Middle East from a Distance 125

Chapter 5: Welcome to the Israeli Navy 137

Chapter 6: On the Eve of the Pullout from Gaza 219

Chapter 7: Return to Betzet Tira 225

Postscript 273

About the Author 279

ACKNOWLEDGMENTS

I would like to thank the volunteers I have served with, who have inspired me by their commitment and passion to continue returning to Israel each year to work on military bases. I would also like to thank the young Israeli soldiers who opened up their hearts to my inquiries and whose lives have touched me.

There are two very special people without whose help this book would not have become a reality. I am indebted to my agent and editor, Bonny V. Fetterman, for her sage advice and unwavering persistence in seeing this manuscript published. I am especially grateful to Suzi Wolfe for her professionalism and her willingness to devote many after-work hours to typing multiple versions of this manuscript.

And finally, my love and thanks go to my wife and best friend, Arlene, for partnering with me in all of my endeavors.

PREFACE

I have a habit of keeping a travel log when I visit unusual places. This book grew out of four such travel logs, recording my experiences as an American volunteer on Israeli military bases in the period from 2002 to 2005.

I composed these travel logs to share my experiences with my wife, Arlene, and my two children, Rachel and David. I added an introduction to explain to my children (both in their early twenties) my personal motivations in volunteering. I did not want them to ascribe my actions to a mere impulse associated with my turning fifty. Deep down, I also hoped by my example to positively influence their connection to Israel.

I also shared my travel logs (via e-mail) with the volunteers I had served with during each of my four stints on Israeli bases. Many of my volunteer colleagues had noticed that, during off-hours on base, I spent most of my waking hours writing down my thoughts and observations. I did not keep it a secret that I kept a travel log. Consequently, before departing from each base, a number of volunteers requested a copy of that log and I agreed to e-mail it to them.

The responses I received to my e-mailed travel logs were, in part, unexpected. I expected the notes of appreciation from many volunteers for providing them with a written record, reinforcing their own memories of their experience. I did not expect that, in their notes of appreciation, a number of them would encourage me to turn my travel logs into a book. They knew that I had pushed for more publicity for Sar-el, the organization that enables volunteers to work on Israeli military bases. "What could have greater impact than a book by a Sar-el volunteer?" they urged.

I succumbed to this line of reasoning. One of the best-kept "secrets" of the Israeli military is the army of volunteers that Sar-el brings to serve on Israeli military bases. Since Sar-el's inception in 1982, over 100,000 volunteers from over thirty countries have served on these bases. Both men and women, these volunteers range in age from eighteen to eighty-two and usually have no military background. They don Israeli army uniforms, work side-by-side with Israeli soldiers, live in the same cramped army barracks, and eat in the same army mess halls. This stream of volunteers performs routine but necessary work on Israeli military bases. In doing so, it frees up Israeli soldiers for other duties, including patrolling against terrorism.

What motivates Americans, and volunteers from many other lands, to give up their vacation time or retirement leisure to work on Israeli military bases? It is certainly not the food, lodgings, or scenery on these bases. It must be something more – something that makes Israel a special place.

I knew what my motivations were in volunteering, but I was very curious about the motivations of the other volunteers. On these bases, I asked a number of my fellow volunteers why they were there. I came to appreciate that many of them were on a personal journey unique to each individual. I have tried to describe some of these journeys, starting with my own.

Finally, this book spans an extraordinary period of recent Israeli history – from the height of the second Intifada to the emotionally charged Israeli withdrawal from the Gaza Strip. In combining my travel logs into this book, my aim is to give readers a feel for what life was like for Israelis during this period – both in contending with terrorism as part of their daily lives and in dealing with the political issues of the day. Israelis are outspoken on these issues, whether about the religious vs. secular schism, the political left vs. the political right, or the Israeli-Palestinian conflict. I have tried to include the views of soldiers and civilians as the critical events of this period unfolded.

I hope that in describing the personal journeys of the volunteers I encountered, as well as the Israelis who shared their stories with me, a broad audience of readers will come to understand the importance of Israel as a Jewish homeland. Something draws people from all age groups and walks of life to volunteer for this experience. That special "something" is what has helped the Jewish people to survive for four thousand years – and draws them back to Israel.

INTRODUCTION

I distinctly remember sitting in Mr. Flaim's eighth-grade history class on a hot morning in early June 1967. Despite the fact that Mr. Flaim was one of my favorite teachers, I was not listening to him. Instead, I was thinking about what I had heard on the radio that morning.

War had broken out in the Middle East that day. For months, tensions had been building as Arab armies massed on Israel's borders. Egypt's President Nasser had ordered U.N. peacekeeping troops out of Sinai. Arab leaders promised their people that the destruction of Israel was imminent. When Egypt blockaded the Straits of Tiran, cutting off Israel's southern port of Eilat from access to the Red Sea, war seemed inevitable.

Since political tensions were high for several months, Israel had been forced to mobilize its citizen army. The country's farms and factories were paralyzed for lack of labor and Israel appealed for overseas volunteers. Some young men from my hometown volunteered to go. I wanted to go very badly, but at age fourteen, I was too young to be eligible.

Now that war had broken out, I was worried about the existence of Israel. My family was just as worried. Even before the start of the war, we talked frequently over the dinner table about whether Israel could survive. With the overwhelming numerical superiority of the Arab armies, there seemed to be no way to stop them. Even Iraq had sent an army into Jordan to threaten Israel's eastern border.

Why was I so concerned about a war on the opposite side of the globe? No one else in my eighth-grade class seemed that concerned or even noticed my daydreaming. What made me different from the other fourteen-year-old boys and girls sitting around me? The answer lies in my family's story – and mine.

I grew up on a chicken farm in southern New Jersey. Both of my parents came from eastern Poland. My father immigrated to America after World War II; my mother had come before the war.

My father was the strong, quiet type. His personality was shaped by the two tragedies he experienced in his youth. His mother, whom he rarely spoke of, died of an infection following a miscarriage when he was eleven years old. He was the oldest of six children in a dirt-poor home in a tiny southeastern Polish village called Gorshkov. Unable to feed six small children, my grandfather sent him away from home following my grandmother's death to live with distant relatives. Bounced around from Lublin to Warsaw, my father learned factory work at an early age. Life during the Great Depression in Poland of the 1930s toughened him and, in some sense, prepared him for the second great tragedy of his life.

The "street-smarts" he developed in prewar Poland probably saved my father's life during the Holocaust. During the German occupation, he disobeyed the Germans' orders to assemble for "resettlement" in an undisclosed destination, thus avoiding deportation by cattle car to a death or labor camp. Instead, he persuaded a group of Polish Jews to escape with him to the Polish forests and form a Jewish resistance group. Many of his fellow resistance fighters died from the fierce cold or in gun battles with the Germans. Still, his resistance group grew to the point where they constituted a major fighting force and a thorn in the side of the German military occupation. When the Russian army liberated their area in July 1944, my father's unit emerged from the woods – 400 Jewish fighters protecting another 400 Jewish non-combatants.*

Even though virtually all of his very large family had been killed in the Holocaust, my father tried to make a new life for himself in Poland. He became a policeman under the new Communist regime in Poland. I still have a picture of him, taken in 1946, looking very handsome in his policeman's uniform.

Soon, however, it became clear that there was no future for my father in Poland. Riots broke out in which Polish mobs attacked the few Jews who had survived the Holocaust in the concentration camps or in the woods. These Jews were too few in number to defend themselves from antisemitic mobs that were clearly disappointed Hitler had not killed off every Polish Jew. The new Polish government seemed unwilling or unable to stop these riots.

For my father, the final straw was the attempted assassination by Polish antisemites of the former commander of his Jewish resistance unit, Chiel Grynszpan, who was also working as a policeman in a nearby town. Although the bomb that exploded in a package of flowers didn't kill Grynszpan, but only injured his hands, this attempt signaled to my father that no Jew was safe in Poland, even after the war. Eventually my father found his way to a Displaced Persons (DP) camp in West Germany, reuniting with two of his brothers, the only members of his immediate family who survived the war.

At this point, my father had to make a decision. The DP camp was a temporary stop for Jews who were homeless. Poland was clearly no longer his home. Despite the fact that my father spoke German, Germany was also not an option. Most people in the DP camp had one of two destinations. A large number wanted to leave for Palestine under the British Mandate. Their hope was to establish a Jewish

---

* My father's account of his experience as a Jewish resistance fighter during the Holocaust is recorded in *Fighting Back: A Memoir of Jewish Resistance in World War II* by Harold Werner (Columbia University Press, 1992).

homeland where Jews could protect themselves from genocidal campaigns like the Holocaust. A second group wanted to immigrate to the United States, in the hopes of finding peace and prosperity.

Since the late 1930s and all through the war, the British had restricted Jewish immigration into Palestine in order to appease the Arabs, whose oil reserves were crucial to Britain. Their restrictions continued in the postwar period. Despite this, many groups of Holocaust survivors attempted to enter Palestine illegally in an organized underground movement called "Aliyah Bet." This effort, also called the "clandestine" or "illegal" immigration, attracted worldwide sympathy. This was especially the case following the British storming of the hunger-striking refugees aboard the ship *Exodus* – preventing the refugees from entering the land of Israel and returning them to the DP camps of Europe.

It was 1946 and the refugees in my father's DP camp were desperate to leave. One group decided to attempt entering Palestine despite British restrictions. They traveled to a port in Italy and embarked on a small ship headed to the eastern Mediterranean. Somewhere short of their goal, the ship was intercepted by the British navy and the refugees were sent to an internment camp on the island of Cyprus. Along with thousands of other Jewish refugees, they waited behind barbed wire fences for the British to decide their fate.

The news of what happened to this first group of refugees trickled back to my father in the DP camp. His course of action was dictated by their imprisonment. He had survived the Holocaust because he had never allowed himself to be placed under someone else's control. Even though the British were not exterminating Jews as the Germans had, my father would not trust his fate to a British internment camp. Therefore, he would not attempt to immigrate to Palestine.

Instead, he came to the United States in February 1947. He met my mother in Brooklyn, where he had found factory work in an apparel sweatshop. My father had lost his wartime girlfriend during a German attack in 1943. Similarly, my mother had lost her wartime boyfriend. He was an American soldier who had been killed in the Battle of the Bulge in 1944. Both were looking for a partner. They were married in 1949 at the relatively "old" ages of thirty-two and twenty-nine.

With a $300 loan from his cousin, Simon Honigman, and another $300 loan from the Hebrew Immigrant Aid Society (HIAS), my father bought a chicken farm in Vineland, New Jersey. Many other Holocaust survivors were also attracted to Vineland to become chicken farmers because it did not require a lot of capital, as witnessed by the $600 purchase price for our ten-acre farm. A Jewish agricultural colony had been founded there in the 1880s with the philanthropic support of Baron Maurice de Hirsch, who also sponsored agricultural colonies in Israel. Thereafter, small successive waves of Jewish immigrants settled in Vineland.

The first immigrants who settled in Vineland brought socialist ideals to their new agricultural colony in New Jersey. They established a way of life strikingly similar to the *moshav*, the semi-collective agricultural colonies established in Israel in the same period. As in the *moshav*, property was held privately while other aspects of the community were collectively undertaken. For example, a farmers' cooperative owned the local feed mill and egg hatchery. Farmers sat on the cooperative's board and managed its operations for the good of the community. And the farmers pitched in to help those who suffered misfortune. When Hurricane Hazel ravaged the town in 1954, one physically handicapped farmer suffered the loss of his chicken coop. The other farmers organized the equivalent of an old-fashioned Midwestern barn raising, banding together to rebuild the unfortunate farmer's coop in a single day.*

---

* Twenty-five years later, by happenstance a partner at my first job in a big Chicago law firm mentioned admiringly a community of selfless New Jersey farmers who had rebuilt his uncle's chicken coop following Hurricane Hazel. Feeling a debt of gratitude upon learning that my father had been one of these farmers, this person took a special interest in my early career.

My father worked our farm seven days a week for twenty-five years, without a vacation and without complaint. He was an incredibly hardworking man, leaving the house every day at 5:30 in the morning and returning for dinner twelve hours later. He had learned the virtues of hard work and patience early in life and simply appreciated the opportunity to raise his family in the security of a peaceful environment.

The twin tragedies of his life had robbed him of any firsthand knowledge of what a "normal family" was like. Consequently, he focused on his work, leaving the childrearing to my mother. His early years had also bottled his emotions deep inside. He rarely showed his feelings. Although he was slow to anger, my two brothers (one older, one younger) and I occasionally provoked him. Usually a raised voice or angry look from him was all it took to stop us in our tracks.

My father was the toughest man I ever knew and he was physically very strong. I recall an incident as a young boy when one of the farm workers we hired spent his week's pay on a drinking binge. The worker returned to the farm roaring drunk and came at my father with a sharp edge of a broken whiskey bottle. My father never retreated. He knocked the man down, wrestled the bottle from his hand, and restrained him on the ground until the police arrived.

My father's strength was combined with a steadfast patience to withstand any hardship necessary to support his family. I remember bad winter storms that blocked our rural roads with mounds of snow. When the roads were impassable, he hitched himself to a sled, walked to the distant farms that he had rented, and trudged home again like a beast of burden, pulling a sled-load of eggs through the snowdrifts. No matter what, the chickens had to be fed and the eggs had to be collected.

Despite his toughness and his difficulty in showing emotion, my father tried to connect with his three sons. I remember our surprise the one time he came out to join the three of us after a hard day's work to play baseball. He didn't know how. He gripped the bat with just one hand to swing at the ball. He hit it a mile away anyway. We didn't have the heart to tell him he was holding the bat wrong because we didn't want to embarrass him. We were just delighted that he tried to play with us. We were equally happy when he pulled us on our little sled in the snow. He dearly wanted to do the "father things" and we appreciated when he tried.

Long after my father died, I recall sharing stories with a work colleague whose father was also a Holocaust survivor. What struck me was that both of our fathers saved string. My father kept it in little balls. "You never know when it might come in handy," he used to say. He also saved screws and old nails, teaching his sons to straighten bent nails for re-use rather than throw them away. His Holocaust experience had imbued him with a sense of extreme thriftiness. It also left him with a deep-seated insecurity and the conviction that one needed to be prepared in the event that history repeated itself. He felt that the thin veneer of civilization could quickly crumble into another similar tragedy.

As a child of five or six, I distinctly remember the one time I sensed my parents' apprehension over such a recurrence. It was in the springtime, shortly before Passover. The body of a murdered Puerto Rican girl was found in a chicken coop of one of the Jewish farmers. I overheard my parents' hushed tones as they shared the news of this murder. I learned from the bits and pieces I overheard that all of the Jewish farmers, mostly Holocaust survivors, feared that the girl's body had been dumped in the coop to frame a Jewish farmer. They assumed it was part of the centuries-old "blood libel," which claimed Jews used the blood of a Christian to make matzah before Passover. In Europe, this would have been the pretext for a pogrom against Jews. While American-born Jews probably would not have been afraid of this possibility, my parents and their peers envisioned a repeat of what they hoped they had left behind in Europe. I could sense my parents' fear – and while

I was too young to understand the historical background, their fear made me afraid too.

Luckily, the actual murderer was apprehended. He was not one of the Jews in town. I never learned whether the murderer had dumped the girl's body in a Jewish farmer's coop in order to incite the bigotry of those who actually believed the blood libel myth.

Almost all of my parents' farming friends bore numbers on their arms from the concentration camps they had been in during the war. And like my brothers and me, most of our childhood friends grew up with few, if any, grandparents, not realizing this was unusual.

Growing up, I knew that, in addition to my two uncles, a few other family members had survived the war. They had moved to Israel. My father received their letters written in Yiddish from Israeli towns, such as Petach Tikva and Netanya. He would read the letters aloud to my mother over the dinner table. Since they were in Yiddish, I rarely knew what they said unless he translated them into English. From little bits and pieces of translation, I gleaned that life was very difficult in Israel for our cousins.

My father and mother would periodically prepare a box of used clothes to ship to our cousins in Israel. Sometimes they would also mail a small amount of cash to them. Life on the farm was a poor life and we did not always have much to send.

Our family was strongly Zionistic. Because of what my father had lived through during the war, he understood the need for a Jewish homeland where Jews could flee when endangered. The absence of such a safe haven had trapped Europe's Jews during the Holocaust. Had a Jewish state existed before 1939, many of the victims of the Holocaust might have survived by finding refuge there.

My father wanted to do something to support the new Jewish state, but he was just a poor chicken farmer. In the early 1960s, he decided to help the Israeli economy with what he knew best – chickens. While keeping up our farm, he became a distribution agent for imported Israeli baby chicks. He purchased large numbers of these baby chicks and encouraged other Jewish chicken farmers in South Jersey to do the same. In this way, they could "do their bit" to support the Jewish state. This became a very important industry for Israel. I still have an Israeli postage stamp that was issued to commemorate the export of baby chicks from Israel. I was very proud of my father for leading this campaign.

Unfortunately, tragedy struck this effort. It turned out that the baby chicks were susceptible to a virus to which American-born chicks were naturally immune. Hundreds of thousands of the Israeli chicks died suddenly. My father and the other farmers whom he had persuaded to buy Israeli chicks suffered tremendous losses. Even though my father suffered equally, many of the farmers blamed him for their loss.

Because of the family connection to Israel and our pro-Zionist views, we paid particular attention to what was happening in Middle East politics. So when tensions erupted into the Six-Day War in early June 1967, we worried about the fate of Israel and about our cousins there.

Every night after dinner, we would watch the evening news with Walter Cronkite to learn how Israel was faring in the war. There was no CNN or 24-hour television news service, so if you missed the evening news you had to wait until the next morning to find out what happened. Israel's preemptive strike against the Egyptian air force on the first day of the war was a masterful blow. Within a few days, the Israeli army had defeated its Egyptian foe and reached the edge of the Suez Canal. Then Israel turned its attention to Jordan and Syria, which had also declared war on Israel. It seemed a miracle that in short order Israel had captured the Sinai, the Old City of Jerusalem, the entire West Bank, and the Golan Heights.

The war was over in a mere six days. Our concern over Israel's survival turned to pride over how she had defeated the combined armies of Egypt, Jordan, Syria, Iraq, and Saudi Arabia. This pride was evident even among those of my Jewish friends who previously had not shown any interest in Israel. Suddenly, Israel was a military success, powerful and proud. And, because of this, it was "cool" to be Jewish and identify with Israel.

Starting at age twelve, I spent my summers at a Zionist camp in the Pocono Mountains of Pennsylvania. Camp Galil was run by Habonim, a Jewish organization with a socialist leaning that encouraged connection with Israel and eventual immigration there. Because of its socialist philosophy, my wife still jokingly refers to it as "that Commie camp."

My parents chose to send my brothers and me to Camp Galil because it was cheap and close by. The cost of the camp was low because the campers were expected to do the work required to operate the camp, in addition to sports and other fun activities. Aside from the camp counselors and three cooks in the dining hall, there were no camp employees. So the campers were required to clean their cabins and tents, remove the trash, act as waiters for their fellow campers, and even pick vegetables from the camp's acres of gardens. Because I was big for my age, I was usually assigned to wash pots in the kitchen. These were not the type of pots one would find in a home. Instead, these were large industrial-size pots used by the camp's three cooks. Although they were heavy and unwieldy, I eventually took pride in the fact that I was one of the few campers who could "do pots."

Much of the camp's activities focused on studying Hebrew, singing Israeli songs, and learning Israeli folk dancing. I was a quick learner in all three categories and relished the dancing after Friday night dinner. As soon as the evening meal was over, we emptied the dining hall of tables and chairs to make room for the evening's fun. Israeli folk dancing was performed barefoot and the older campers were permitted to dance for up to four hours on Friday nights on the dining hall's wooden floors.

Hebrew was taught in a very smart way. In addition to daily

language class, it was required that only Hebrew be spoken in the dining hall. So if you wanted to ask someone to "pass the salt," you quickly learned how to say it in Hebrew. Otherwise, meals could be a frustrating experience.

We were told that the camp had played a role in Israel's War of Independence. There was an old barn on the camp premises that we used as a theater for skits and plays. Under the performance stage was a storage area. In 1947–48, the Haganah, Israel's underground defense force, stored weapons there. At night, the weapons would be trucked to a ship waiting in the nearby port of Philadelphia. The weapons would be loaded onto the ship and, all in the same night, the ship would embark for British-held Palestine. All this occurred before the State of Israel was declared in May 1948.

I "topped" out of camp after I turned sixteen. For campers my age, the next summer was to be spent in a Habonim program in Israel, training to become a camp counselor the following year. All my friends went and I had dearly wanted to go with them, but my parents would not allow it, citing the cost. Consequently, I spent the summer of 1970 working on the farm. Much later, my father revealed to me that, while cost had been a factor in their decision, it was not the primary reason. Both of my parents were afraid that if I spent a summer in Israel, I would not return home. I told my father he had been wrong in not letting me go and that it was the only one of their decisions I ever felt had unfairly held me back. Having grown up in a small farming community, I could have greatly expanded my horizons by spending a summer in Israel. For me, it was a missed opportunity.

Fast forward to 2002. In the intervening thirty-two years, I married a wonderful woman, had two great kids, and became a successful lawyer. With my family, I finally got my chance to visit Israel in 1996 and meet my Israeli cousins. My wife and I went on three more trips in 1998, 2000, and 2001. In addition to visiting Israel, we provided financial support for various causes in Israel.

But writing a check was not enough. In 2000, with the encouragement of President Bill Clinton in the waning days of his second term, Israeli Prime Minister Ehud Barak offered the Palestinians an opportunity to build their own independent state on 96 percent of the lands that they demanded. Rather than countering this offer, Palestinian leader Yasir Arafat chose to respond with violence – the second Intifada.

The Palestinian Intifada targeted Israeli civilians. Periodically, the news carried reports of bombings of buses, cafés, and even teenage discos. The Palestinian terrorism succeeded in scaring away Israel's most important source of revenue – tourism. By the time of our fourth trip to Israel in December 2001, we found empty hotels and restaurants, a depressed economy, and a population saddened by the fact that the world seemed to have abandoned them. It was frustrating to feel that there was little we could do to alleviate this situation.

For me, the "straw that broke the camel's back" was the Passover massacre in Netanya in the spring of 2002. Palestinian terrorists had targeted a Passover seder at a large hotel. The attack killed twenty-nine people. I was outraged by this, in the same way I suppose that Christians would be outraged if a terrorist attack targeted people at a midnight mass on Christmas Eve.

Somehow, writing a bigger check was not the answer. I wanted to do more. So I drafted a proposal to establish a program that would send American volunteers to Israel to work on military bases. My thought was that the volunteers could perform routine tasks so that the soldiers could spend more time patrolling the streets.

I e-mailed my proposal to the national president of United Jewish Communities. Shortly thereafter, I received a courteous response thanking me for my commitment, but pointing out that such a program already existed. It was called "Volunteers for Israel" (VFI, or "Sar-el" in Israel), and it placed volunteers from all over the world on Israeli army bases. The volunteers went on three-week stints where they performed basic work at the army bases in order to free up Israeli soldiers.

Three weeks was a long time to take off from work, but I resolved to save up my vacation time. My wife encouraged me to apply for the program. I applied in the fall of 2002 and was scheduled for a three-week stint starting October 21, 2002.

When my kids heard about my plans, their reaction was: "Cool! I'm proud of you, Dad." My supervisor at work, a deeply religious Christian, respected my commitment and made it easy for me to take my three weeks of vacation together. My friends voiced their respect for my decision and were supportive. It was helpful to have this complete support from everyone.

The materials from the VFI office in New York explained that I would be stationed at an Israel Defense Force (IDF) army base, and that I would be informed of the location of the base upon my arrival at Tel Aviv's Ben-Gurion airport. I would live in barracks with other volunteers and with Israeli soldiers. I would be assigned to jobs on the base under the supervision of those soldiers.

My wife and I carefully read the preparation instructions. They made it clear that living conditions would be less than comfortable. The VFI booklet described the Israeli army barracks in the following terms:

> Living conditions on the bases can best be described as austere or primitive.... For example, barracks have no central heat in the winter or air conditioning in the summer.... Volunteers sleep 4–10 in a room.... Electricity sometimes becomes unavailable; more often, hot water is unavailable, and on very rare occasions even cold water is scarce.

Meals were to be eaten on base in the mess hall along with soldiers and other base personnel. Although the booklet promised, "you will not starve," it did warn that "the food may not be what you are accustomed to." Specifically, it described the meals as follows:

> Breakfast and dinner are indistinguishable. They consist of eggs and tomatoes, eggs and cheeses, eggs and bread, or eggs and sweet tea or coffee. Lunch is the substantial meal of the day. It is usually a meat meal.

Clearly, I would be eating lots of eggs. That was not a problem for me, having grown up on an egg farm.

We would be on the same schedule as the soldiers on base. That meant breakfast at 7:00 A.M., followed by a workday ending in the late afternoon. Workdays were Sunday through Thursday. On Friday and Saturday, we would be on our own, to visit family and friends in Israel, or simply travel the countryside.

The instructions warned us not to bring a lot of clothes. We would be issued army fatigues for the workweek, which could be turned in for replacements when dirty. Concerning the fatigues, the instructions advised:

> You may have difficulty distinguishing the clean from the dirty… since many fatigues are grease or paint-stained, but rest assured they are clean. Uniforms are never ironed.

It was apparent that the Israeli army was not obsessed with "spit and polish" cleanliness.

We were also instructed that any civilian clothes we brought would have to be hand-washed. So we were told to bring liquid laundry detergent, a clothesline, and clothespins.

Shortly before my departure, I heard from two other North Carolina VFI volunteers who would be going on the same three-week stint. Frank lived in Wilmington, and it turned out that our wives had met each other recently. While Frank was Jewish, the other North Carolinian going on our stint was not. Bill, a devout Baptist, lived in a small town north of Durham. He called to say hello and share with me his reason for going, namely, his deep religious conviction that the Holy Land was given to the Jews by God as their homeland. His conviction was such that he felt a need to personally help defend that homeland for the Jewish people.

I learned from the VFI office that at least fifty men and women were going on our three-week program from the U.S. I was proud that three would be from North Carolina, although we had no assurance that the three of us would be assigned to the same base.

CHAPTER 1

The Army Base at Batzop

October 20–November 7, 2002

SUNDAY, OCTOBER 20, 2002

After a weekend in New York City with my wife, Arlene, and my daughter, Rachel, I headed for New York's JFK airport. As always, security at El Al Airlines was comforting in its thoroughness. At the first El Al security stop I was asked a series of questions:

Q. "What is the purpose of your trip to Israel – business or pleasure?"

A. "Pleasure."

Q. "What will you be doing there?"

A. "I'll be working on a military base as a volunteer with Volunteers for Israel."

Q. "Then the purpose of your trip is not pleasure?"

A. "It'll be my pleasure."

Q. "Do you speak Hebrew?"

A. "A little, but I prefer we speak in English."

Q. "Where did you learn Hebrew?"

A. "I study it now back home in Raleigh."

Q. "Did you study it as a child?"

1

A. "Yes."

Q. "I see from your passport that you've been to Israel before. For what purpose were these trips?"

A. "To tour the country."

Q. "Do you have family in Israel?"

A. "Yes."

Q. "Where do they live?"

A. "Rosh Ha-Ayin, Netanya, and Pardes Chana."

Then they proceeded with the usual questions about whether I owned my suitcase, whether I packed it, whether it had been in my control, and whether anyone had given me any packages to take to Israel. Unlike other airlines' employees, they were blunt in explaining the reason for their questions: "We ask you these questions in case someone gave you something with a bomb in it."

At the gate, El Al called all passengers on our flight who had come into JFK on a connecting flight and had checked their luggage straight through from their origin to Israel. One by one, they took each such connecting passenger into an adjacent room to identify their luggage before they would take those bags on the plane. Even a little old lady with a walker was required to get up to identify her luggage. Each bag of a connecting passenger was opened and searched.

While waiting at the gate, I struck up a conversation with a man sitting to my right who was also on the Volunteers for Israel program. As a senior citizen, he told me, he did not have a lot of money to give to support Israel, so he was giving his time instead. I felt in good company already.

MONDAY, OCTOBER 21, 2002

The nine-and-a-half hour flight was uneventful. Since I cannot sleep on planes, I stood in the back of the plane for long periods of the flight. As the plane flew into the morning and passengers awoke, the Orthodox Jews on the flight rose for morning prayers, draped in *tallis* and *tefillin*. I watched one Orthodox Jew teach a non-observant Jew to put on *tefillin* and perform morning prayers. Since the non-observant Jew had no yarmulke, the teacher borrowed one from his son's head. The son had to keep his hands covering his head until the yarmulke was returned. El Al must be the only airline where a portion of the passengers stand up every morning for prayers. It is also an airline that you can count on serving bagels and lox for breakfast. And it was good!

Ben-Gurion airport was not overcrowded, but there were lines at the passport control stations because two planes disembarked at the same time. When we had been in Israel in December 2001, the airport had been like a ghost town due to the disappearance of tourism.

I was greeted outside the baggage area by Pamela Lazarus, a petite, attractive, forty-ish woman with a friendly smile and piercing dark eyes. Pamela was a Sar-el representative. (In Israel, Volunteers for Israel is referred to as "Sar-el" – short for the Hebrew Sherut le-Yisrael, which means "Service to Israel.") I later learned that Pamela was one of only two paid employees working for Sar-el, which primarily relies on volunteer staffing.

A native and long-time resident of the Rogers Park neighborhood of Chicago, Pamela had volunteered with Sar-el many times in the 1990s. Following her divorce, she "made aliyah," meaning she moved permanently to Israel. Pending her search for a job, she spent her free time volunteering at Sar-el's office in Jaffa. She was so good at what she did that Sar-el offered her its first paid position as program director. She gladly accepted because she loved the work and loved the organization's purpose. She also enjoyed meeting interesting people from all over the world.

Pamela informed me and the two other Sar-el volunteers on my flight that over one hundred Sar-el volunteers were arriving today. She assigned the three of us to join forty-one other volunteers sent earlier in the day to an army base near Ramle, which is about thirty minutes southeast of Tel Aviv.

A female soldier took us outside the baggage area to a waiting car. The soldier driver of the car laughed at our reservations about how our luggage could possibly fit in his compact car. Amazingly, he fit our three large pieces of rolling luggage into the trunk. We squeezed into our seats with our carry-on bags on our laps and the car scooted out of the airport for the short ride to the base.

The name of the base, Batzop, is a word created from the first letters of the Hebrew words for "commanding equipment base." This base repairs and distributes communications equipment for the Israeli army. Batzop, in turn, is located adjacent to a much larger base called Pikud Ha-Oref, which means "Home Front Command." This larger base is responsible for overall security within Israel (analogous to the Homeland Security Department in the U.S.). Its soldiers wear a distinctive orange beret.

Both bases are situated in Ramle, a mixed Jewish–Arab town of about 65,000 inhabitants. It is a small city whose most prominent feature is a Franciscan clock tower that was used by Napoleon as staff headquarters during his unsuccessful campaign to conquer the area. According to a description we were given, Muslim Ramle was built by the ruler Suleiman Abed El Mulib in 716 C.E. on the site of an earlier Jewish settlement. The name of the city is derived from the word *ramel*, which means "sand" in Arabic.

Upon our arrival at Batzop, we did not immediately meet the volunteers who had arrived earlier in the day. They had already been outfitted in Israeli army fatigues and had been given their afternoon work assignments around the base. Since we arrived later, all that was expected of us this afternoon was to receive our army fatigues, hat, belt, and boots, and unpack.

Two things were immediately noteworthy about our fatigues. First, the pants were difficult to wear; in place of a zipper they bore a series of buttons that take entirely too long to undo. Second, the shirts were very utilitarian; to make up for the wearing of long sleeves in a hot climate, they have slits in the armpits for air circulation. At first, I mistakenly thought that the shirts were torn there.

Nevertheless, we were all very proud of our fatigues. Even though we were not in the Israeli army and the fatigues were ill-fitting and spattered with paint, it gave me a thrill to put them on. Since we were only allowed to wear them while on base, I wore them all the time on the base for the next three weeks, even after dinner, when some of our volunteers changed to civilian clothes to hang out in the compound.

The preparation materials had been honest about the living conditions. I was assigned to a 10′ × 12′ room with three other men. Since I was the last to arrive, I got the only top bunk in the room. There were four such rooms to each trailer. A bare fluorescent bulb in the ceiling lit each room.

A temporary *madricha* (soldier instructor) named Nati gave the three of us our preliminary briefing. We sat around an outdoor table while she cradled her M-16 rifle on her lap. A few minutes later, our permanent madricha, Avigail, joined us at the table and gave us our schedule of work for the next three weeks. Our little compound of trailers was also occupied by Israeli soldiers with M-16s strapped over their backs. They occasionally stopped by to interrupt Avigail or to say hi to her.

By the end of the afternoon, the earlier arriving volunteers trickled in from their work assignments, tired from an afternoon of labor following a long flight. I met my three bunkmates, who were all very agreeable guys. Mike Lowenstein was a sixty-year-old safety engineer from Baltimore. His wife, Elaine, was also volunteering on the base with him. My other two bunkmates, Herb Blank and Don Rutherford, were both from New Jersey. They were long-time friends who first met in grade school in Elizabeth and served in the U.S. navy together. Herb and Don decided to come together to this Sar-el program and, at seventy-two, were among the oldest volunteers. Two out of the three of my bunkmates had been on this program previously. Since I was both the youngest and a "rookie," it was entirely appropriate that I had the top bunk.

Following showers, we ate a quick dinner of eggs, Israeli salad, rice, olives, and bread with the other volunteers. We quickly realized how cosmopolitan our group was. In addition to having volunteers from all across the U.S., our group included volunteers from Canada, Holland, South Africa, New Zealand, Russia, Germany, Sweden, Norway, and Finland. All but the Russian volunteer could speak English, but he quickly struck up conversations with the Israeli soldiers who were originally from Russia.

I was surprised and pleased to learn that many of the volunteers (between a quarter and a third) were not Jewish. The Christians were from many different countries, but most were from Scandinavian ones. I asked them why they had volunteered. Their answers varied, but primarily boiled down to an admiration for what the Israelis had accomplished in turning a desert into blooming, green gardens. They also expressed their admiration for Israel's ability to survive as the only democracy in the Middle East, despite having to fight numerous wars to defend itself. Sadly, the support of these Christians from Scandinavia was not reflective of popular views in their home countries. The Scandinavian media had portrayed Israel so negatively that boycotts of Israeli products were successful at curtailing trade with Israel. One young Norwegian volunteer confided to me that, upon returning home, he could not breathe a word of what he had done in Israel. To do so would risk ostracism by his friends and acquaintances. His honesty was sobering.

After dinner we crowded into the *moadon* (recreation room) to watch the CNN news at 7:00 P.M. on the base's only television. There had been a suicide bombing at a highway intersection north of Tel Aviv near Hadera. A car packed with explosives had rammed a bus, killing fourteen people and injuring over thirty others, including some people in nearby cars. The news especially seemed to impact the Israeli soldiers in our midst, most of whom had been on the same stretch of highway many times.

I called my cousins Bracha and Ruchama to make plans with each of them for my upcoming two free weekends. Ruchama was very upset over today's bombing. She worked near Hadera and had driven through the same highway intersection thirty minutes before the bombing.

Later in the evening, all the volunteers gathered together for a ceremony to award special patches to the newly arrived volunteers. The patches were blue and white striped and were designed to be slipped over the shoulder epaulettes on our army shirts. The ceremony required each volunteer, one at a time, to stand in front of the group. Two previously "initiated" volunteers would stand on each side of the newcomer to slip the patches over the epaulettes. Then the group gave a cheer and our madricha Avigail slapped the newcomer on the back three times. The blue and white patches identified us as volunteers to the Israeli soldiers.

TUESDAY, OCTOBER 22, 2002

For the second night in a row, I couldn't sleep. Perhaps it was a combination of the too-short, too-narrow, too-thin mattress and the change in time zones. In any event, I was awake for the muezzin's call to worship at 4:30 A.M. in nearby Ramle and decided to get up to shower, in case hot water was in short supply. (It wasn't.) A nearby shed had showers and even a mirror. I hung my towel on our compound's clothesline, secure in the knowledge that it would be dry shortly. One of the advantages of being in the Middle East is the lack of humidity.

At 7:00 A.M., the volunteers walked together to the mess hall for breakfast under the bright, nearly blinding sun – as usual, not a cloud in the sky. Breakfast was a repeat of dinner – eggs, Israeli salad, and tomatoes. Large loaves of white bread and pitchers of sweetened hot tea were also on the tables. After each meal, the soldiers and volunteers bused their silverware, plastic plates, and cups into big tubs.

Breakfast was followed every day by a short meeting at 7:45 with our madricha to cover work assignments, make necessary announcements, and to brief the volunteers on the news of the previous day. Avigail gave us details of yesterday's bombing in Hadera.

By 8:15, we joined all of the soldiers on the Batzop base for flag-raising. This was the only time during the day, except for meals, when all eighty soldiers and forty-four volunteers were together. The ceremony was brief. The soldiers and volunteers formed six long lines facing the flagpole. The presiding officer ordered: *Amod dom!* (Attention!) and the flag was raised. There was a moment of silence as the two flag-raisers and presiding officer saluted the flag. Then the officer ordered *Amod noach!* (At ease!) and everyone assumed the "at ease" stance. At that point, the officer walked up and down the columns of soldiers and volunteers for inspection prior to dismissing the assembled body. It was all done in fifteen minutes.

I originally was assigned to a team of volunteers working on the repair of communications headsets worn in Israeli tank helmets. Other volunteers were assigned to install the headsets in the helmets, to repair dents in the helmets and paint them, or assemble and paint the long antennae used on tanks and army radios.

I had previously mentioned to our madricha Avigail that I would like to be assigned to heavy physical work. I did not want this to be a relaxing vacation. Just before we started, Avigail asked me and Philip, a Dutch volunteer, to switch over to the quartermaster's warehouse for heavy work. Under the direction of Elena, a nineteen-year-old female soldier, Philip and I shook out, folded, packed, and stored every blanket and pillow in the warehouse. Many of the blankets had been used in the field and were extremely dusty. We also sorted and shined every pair of army boots stored there. It was dirty, sweaty, dusty work, but at the end of the morning we were able to see progress in the organization of the warehouse. We had done such a good job that Alex, the quartermaster of the base, offered us the job of cleaning the M-16 rifles on Thursday as a reward. He also let us (and only us two) select clean fatigues from the end-of-the-day delivery that we unloaded from a big army truck. For the first time, we had clothes that fit!

At midday, we broke for lunch. This was the main meal of the day and the food was excellent. Several different salads, plus chicken, potatoes, eggplant stew, and chicken soup were the fare. I sat with several Israeli soldiers from the larger "Home Front

Command" base adjacent to Batzop. One of them spoke excellent English. He asked why we volunteers were in Israel. I explained that we had come to show our support and that each of us had committed three weeks of our time to volunteer on Israeli military bases. I added that several hundred volunteers from around the world had come for the current three-week stint and forty-four of us were at this base. He translated my answer into Hebrew for the other soldiers, who expressed their appreciation with nods and smiles.

In the afternoon, Philip and I sorted clean fatigues into big boxes, and sorted and tied the dirty ones into bundles. In sorting the clean ones by size, at first we looked for the labels in each shirt or pants. The sizes were indicated by Hebrew letters: *bet* meant small, *gimel* was medium, *mem* was large, and *mem 2* was extra large. But Elena warned us to disregard the labels because many of them were wrong. After a while, we realized that this was true and we also disregarded the labels. Instead, we simply held up each item and eye-balled its size. In any event, many of them were so old that the labels had been washed out and faded to the point of being unreadable. Some of the clothes had a date stamped in them. My pants, for example, were stamped "1986." And many of the fatigues had been stitched and re-stitched to cover tears. The army made maximum use of these fatigues, as they seemed to do with all army equipment.

During our afternoon workday, we learned of our first serious injury. René, a thirty-two-year-old Dutch volunteer, had been perched high up under the hood of a big army truck. He was tugging on a hose when it suddenly gave way, and he fell backwards off the truck, landing on his back and neck. He was taken to the hospital in an ambulance and later returned to the base with a bandage on his neck. René had previously told me that he had volunteered as a possible prelude to making aliyah to Israel with his girlfriend, who had remained behind in Holland.

The other Dutch volunteer was Philip, my working partner. Philip was one of the few Sar-el volunteers I encountered who had

9

a military background. He had served in the Dutch army and later in the U.S. army. As a rifleman in Thailand during the Vietnam War, he had been wounded and he proudly exhibited his mangled upper right arm. On a U.S. military disability, he had returned to Holland to become an artist. Despite his disability, he kept in shape. He was proud of the fact that he still fit into his U.S. army fatigues, which is what he was wearing when I first met him. With his handlebar mustache and shaved, bald head, he looked every bit like a soldier.

Philip was born in what is now Indonesia; his father worked there when it was still a colony of the Dutch East Indies. He remembered as a young boy the nighttime torch-bearing mobs that rioted in the streets during the Indonesian independence movement of the 1950s. Machete-wielding rioters chopped up anyone who was not a native Muslim. Barely escaping with their lives, he and his family fled to Holland.

Recalling his narrow escape from the Muslim mobs in Indonesia as a child had seared his memory and made him deeply suspicious of Muslims. That memory was brought to the forefront by what he was currently experiencing in Holland. He felt threatened by the large influx of Muslim immigrants to Holland, comprising 10 percent of the country's population. Many militant Muslim youths had formed gangs that attacked Jews and Jewish synagogues.

Now Philip was torn between the twin instincts, whether to fight or to flee. As a soldier by background, he wanted to fight. And having been forced out of his birthplace by Muslim mobs, he did not want to run away again. In fact, he was a leader in forming a Jewish defense organization in Holland. A countervailing factor was his instinct to protect his family. If Holland was going to become an unsafe place for Jews, his instinct was to move his children to Israel. In fact, he had volunteered in Sar-el to explore that possibility.

Later in the afternoon, we heard the sound of many military jets passing nearby. Several of us wondered whether the Israeli government was retaliating against the Palestinians for the terrorist bombing in Hadera. The evening CNN news, however, indicated that Israel was showing restraint in the face of the attack.

Before turning off the lights in our bunk, my bunkmates and I talked about our day's work, our impressions of the soldiers, and why we had come. Mike, an Orthodox Jew from Baltimore, made his first trip to Israel following high school and visited several times as a tourist. Now he felt a need to make a more personal contribution and hoped that volunteering would satisfy this need.

Mike believed in the biblical promise that God had given the land of Israel to the Jewish people. In his view, the Holy Land extended to the Gaza Strip, and therefore any thought of giving up Gaza was sacrilegious. In fact, Mike had been a fundraiser to support Neve Dekalim, a Jewish settlement in the Gaza Strip where he and his wife had friends.

Religion was one of the reasons, but not the only reason for Mike's steadfast support for Israel. Both of his parents had fled Nazi Germany in the late 1930s. His involvement in and support for Israel was strongly influenced by his belief in the need for a homeland for Jews where they could find refuge from antisemitism.

My motivation, I explained to my bunkmates, was not based on religion, but on recent history. As the child of a Holocaust survivor, I feel that the existence of the State of Israel is the only thing that will prevent another Holocaust. Had Israel existed in 1939, many of the six million Jews who were murdered might have been saved. I told them that the Passover massacre in Netanya earlier in the year was the immediate trigger for my decision to volunteer.

Herb was also a longtime staunch supporter of Israel and, like Mike and myself, his sentiments were colored by his close connection to the Holocaust. His parents had emigrated to the U.S. from Poland between the two world wars. His mother's parents, six brothers and sisters, and their many children had remained in

Poland. All perished in the Holocaust, with the exception of one nephew who arrived in Israel during the War of Independence and was promptly handed a rifle to defend the country.

This was Herb's second Sar-el stint. He liked the fact that it provided him with an outlet to physically help the country and an opportunity to meet interesting people. But one of his major motivations was that it gave him "quality time" to spend with his best friend, Don, also from New Jersey. While they constantly bickered over the slightest things, it was the type of friendly ribbing that occurs between two people who have been best friends for sixty-five years.

I was most interested in Don's reasons for volunteering. I was initially surprised to meet a non-Jew volunteering to work on an Israeli army base. Don was quite forthcoming with his reasons. "I really admire Israel and its ability to survive, surrounded by a sea of hostile Arab countries," he said. "It's like David standing up to Goliath and succeeding against impossible odds. And then to turn a desert into beautiful green fields and modern cities is just amazing."

Don explained that Herb had persuaded him to go on his previous Sar-el stint in 1993. His wife, Joan, had joined him and Don insisted that it was the best thing they had ever done together. "When people ask me why a non-Jew would volunteer for this duty, I enjoy telling them how good it makes you feel to contribute your efforts to such a worthy cause," he explained. "And besides, being here and traveling through the country on the weekends gives me a sense of adventure that I don't normally experience." While Don was retired, he had been quite an athlete, according to Herb. He still looked in very good shape.

When it came to politics, Don's view of the Israeli-Palestinian conflict was distinctly hawkish: "The Israelis are always being pushed to give up land for peace. I see them willing to give up land, but I don't see the other side offering peace." Don felt that Americans needed to understand that in the Middle East offering compromise often triggers the opposite reaction you'd expect from a Western country. Concessions, he said, are viewed by the Arabs as a sign of weakness, which encourages them to raise their demands and increase their terrorism to extract greater concessions.

During the course of our time together, we had many interesting conversations, running the gamut from politics, to Israeli food and culture, to our children and families. Often they took place after lights out. These conversations created a durable bond between the four of us.

WEDNESDAY, OCTOBER 23, 2002

Today was a hard workday. After the usual breakfast of eggs, tomatoes, and bread, and the flag-raising, we were given our assignments. Philip and I were assigned to work with two Israeli soldiers on building a concrete and brick walkway from the road to a guard station at the entrance to the base. I learned to combine cement mix, sand, and water to create cement, which we then used to set the blocks and bricks.

During our mid-morning break, we received a short talk from the assistant civilian director of the Sar-el program in Israel. He came to express his appreciation to all of the Sar-el volunteers. He pointed out that last year, Sar-el brought over 4,000 volunteers to Israel. These volunteers had freed up a large number of Israeli soldiers to patrol what he referred to as "the front lines."

In closing, he told us that of the fourteen people who were killed two days ago in the bus bombing in Hadera, four were Israeli soldiers. One of the soldiers, a member of the Druze Muslim religious sect, had just been discharged from a rehabilitation hospital following his recovery from a prior injury. (Since 1956, the Druze community has volunteered to be subject to the same universal military conscription as other Israelis.) While in rehabilitation, he befriended a female Sar-el volunteer who had taken care of him at the hospital. As a token of thanks, he had given the volunteer his combat pin. Now, with the soldier's death, the volunteer asked permission to visit his family to extend her condolences and to return the combat pin to them. In Druze families, men and women are separated during the first three days of mourning. Sar-el therefore arranged for the female volunteer to visit with the family when the initial days of mourning were over.

Over lunch, we again spoke with a group of young soldiers who were curious about us and why we were on the base. They seemed impressed that we left our families to volunteer. I told them I had kids their ages and showed them pictures of Rachel and David. Staring at Rachel's attractive face, they asked if she was a model. One female soldier, noticing David's yarmulke, asked if he attended synagogue. "Yes, he does," I replied. Then, half-jokingly, she volunteered to marry him. The other female soldier sitting next to me explained that a handsome young man who also was religious was held in high esteem, hence her offer.

Our compound was overrun with wild cats – all small, underweight scroungers. One gray cat, the only one friendly enough to come up to us to be petted, had been named "Clinton" by a previous group and the name stuck. Clinton received more leftovers than the other cats because he had such a friendly disposition. A volunteer took some scraps for Clinton as we left the mess hall, although there were rules against feeding the cats; the base commander wanted the cats to keep the base rodent-free.

For the afternoon, Philip and I were switched to two other physically demanding jobs. First, we were assigned to move furniture – metal beds and cabinets – to prepare the compound for more volunteers and more soldiers. The base commander appreciated the volunteers so much that he ordered that we get the best accommodations. Hence, the better metal beds went to the volunteers' rooms and the army cots went to the soldiers' rooms.

Once the furniture moving was completed, we were assigned to clear away underbrush adjacent to a building that housed ammunition. Due to the danger of the ammunition exploding in case of a brush fire, the underbrush had to be cleared away. By the end of the day, we had only completed part of this task.

Before retiring for the night, I reflected on the fact that I had not been concerned about my safety since I had arrived in Israel. But this weekend, Arlene was planning to drive from Raleigh to Philadelphia to visit our daughter for her birthday. Consequently, I had been on the phone with Arlene to help her map out her gas stops in order to avoid stopping along the stretch of highway between Fredericksburg, Virginia, and Washington, D.C. The "D.C. Sniper" was still on the loose and one of his victims included a man filling up his car at a gas station along that highway corridor. In fact, that particular shooting occurred while I was at Batzop. It is ironic that Americans view Israel as a dangerous place, while from an Israeli perspective, it is America that appears dangerous.

THURSDAY, OCTOBER 24, 2002

At the flag-raising ceremony, we began to take notice of customs specific to the Israeli army. First, hats must be worn out of respect for the flag. After the flag is raised, there is roll call for the soldiers. Unlike the U.S. army, however, roll call is usually by first names, especially on a small base where all of the soldiers know each other.

There are other customs that applied to all soldiers and, of course, to all volunteers. First, when not worn, one's hat must be tucked under one's left epaulette. Second, it was emphasized that you never close the top button of your shirt. Doing so is a clear sign that you are so depressed that you may be suicidal and will result in a psychiatric consultation. (Even without this rule, closing your top button in this heat would make me question someone's sanity!) Third, Israeli soldiers don't normally salute officers. There is an easy informality in the Israeli army between officers and enlisted men, with each calling the other by their first names.

After flag-raising, our madricha Avigail gave us the news: Hamas, the Palestinian terrorist organization, had taken credit for the suicide bombing attack against the bus in Hadera on Monday; Israeli forces were active in the West Bank town of Qalqilya to arrest Palestinian terrorists.

Philip and I worked in the quartermaster's warehouse for the third day in a row. Alex, the quartermaster, was a young sergeant from Birobidzhan in Eastern Siberia (the region designated as a Jewish agricultural colony by Stalin in the 1930s). Alex was very muscular and a boxer when not in the army. He clearly appreciated the fact that we were willing to do the dirtiest and heaviest of jobs. To his credit, whenever he asked us to perform a difficult task, he joined us in that task, always picking up the heaviest piece. He spoke Russian and Hebrew and very little English, but between his English and my Hebrew we managed to understand each other.

Elena was Alex's assistant. Originally from Pinsk in Belarus (a former Soviet republic in Eastern Europe), Elena commuted by bus every day to the base from Gilo, a southern suburb of Jerusalem. Gilo had received much publicity for being the target of Palestinian sniper fire from the Arab village of Beit Jala on the opposing hill (a northern suburb of Bethlehem). She told us her fiancé was a pilot-in-training in the Israeli air force, which is considered a very elite role in the military.

Even though she was only nineteen, Elena acted as the "mother" to the volunteers, in terms of meeting our needs for clean fatigues and for tools of all kinds. Round-faced, blond-haired, and blue-eyed, this soldier had a smile for every volunteer. She would visually size up each volunteer bringing in dirty fatigues and come up with replacements of the correct size. If the replacement did not fit, she allowed them to try on others until they were satisfied. Since there was no "fitting room" in the quartermaster's warehouse, she pushed them into the quartermaster's tiny office and shut the door behind them.

Today Alex had us finish the project we started the day before – clearing the underbrush from around the building housing ammunition. In the process of clearing the ground, we came across numerous live rounds of M-16 rifle ammunition, which we handed to Elena. It was very hard work, because we also had to clear the land of rocks, bricks, and concrete chunks. We carried

16

away hundreds of pounds of rocks and debris and hacked away a lot of stubborn thorn bushes.

Elena saw how hot we were and, for our morning work break, asked if we wanted a drink. Of course, we said yes. She brought us steaming hot tea that she made using mint leaves called "nana," grown adjacent to the quartermaster's warehouse. It was very tasty, but hot tea was the last thing we wanted to drink on a 90° day.

Throughout our time working in the base warehouse, breaks for hot tea with nana meant an opportunity to get off our feet and to relax for a few minutes. I soon learned the cultural importance of drinking tea with nana. At break time, Elena offered hot tea and it would be a breach of etiquette to refuse, even if you were hot and sweaty. Our accepting provided the excuse for Elena to pick mint leaves adjacent to the warehouse building and to make the tea with nana that everyone seemed to crave.

During these breaks, Elena, Philip, and I sat together on the warehouse steps under an awning. Conversation often focused around Elena's concerns about life after the army – whether she should go to work or enroll in a university. She worried about her fiancé's chances of making it through his Israeli air force pilot training and hoped he would not be discriminated against because he was Russian.

Elena expressed her own disappointment that her request to be a madricha for the volunteers had been turned down. She assumed that her application had been rejected because her English was "so-so" and laced with a heavy Russian accent. The two madrichas assigned to the volunteers spoke excellent English, which was probably a prerequisite for the job. But Elena showed much more care and concern towards the volunteers than our assigned madrichas and over time, many of the volunteers looked to her for help and advice. I could understand Elena's frustration. She was actually functioning as a madricha, but was not acknowledged as such.

From Elena we learned what life was like in the sniper zone of Gilo. Although her family's apartment didn't face Beit Jala, she had friends whose apartments did. They were forced to live with sandbags against their windows to protect against the unpredictable sniper fire. Many of her friends did not feel they could move away because their apartments were so cheap (no one else wanted to live there) and they could not afford to live elsewhere.

The problem was compounded by the army's difficulty in combating the sniper fire. The Palestinians tended to break into Arab Christian homes in Beit Jala, from which they directed their fire towards Gilo. The Israelis, realizing that the Christians were being held hostage in their homes, were reluctant to return the fire for fear of hitting the human shields. Instead, IDF troops would rush over to the particular Beit Jala home where the sniper fire originated, usually arriving after the Palestinian terrorists had left.

As she got to know us better, Elena shared her concerns over the dilemma that her parents faced. Her father had been an engineer in Belarus before their immigration to Israel. Now, both of her parents had to settle for low-paid, menial jobs. Consequently, they questioned their decision to come to Israel and openly debated whether to return to Belarus. Such a move would pose a painful choice for Elena – would she return with her parents or remain in Israel with her fiancé? My sense was that she would choose the latter course, but Elena did not want to consider the prospect of separating from her parents.

After lunch, we proceeded with additional heavy work. We loaded, delivered, and unloaded a big army truck with material – large tents, metal bars, wooden pegs, field benches and tables. Then we did odd jobs for Alex.

As a reward or thank you, we got to spend the last part of the afternoon cleaning weapons. Alex and Elena showed us how to disassemble an M-16 rifle, clean it, and reassemble it. The process started with placing each rifle part in a tub of kerosene-like cleaning fluid. Then we scoured each piece with a red brillo-like cloth, dipped it again in the vat of kerosene, and wiped it with a clean dry cloth. It took us thirty minutes to disassemble and clean the first M-16, then fifteen minutes to do the second, and ten minutes to do the third. Then we switched to the Uzi submachine gun. The Israeli-built Uzi is a much shorter and simpler gun than the U.S.-built M-16 rifle. It has fewer parts and therefore is easier to disassemble, clean, and reassemble. Alex showed me how to do it once, and I was able to clean two Uzis in the short time left in the afternoon.*

While we worked on the weapons, Elena told us a story from her boot camp training. As part of their weapons training, the soldiers in her platoon were required to take apart and reassemble their M-16s in pitch-black darkness, in their platoon tent with the flaps tied down at night. The smallest part in an M-16 is the firing pin, which is the size of a hairpin. The women had been trained to clip it in their left shirt pocket to avoid losing it. At the end of the exercise, one woman could not locate her firing pin. The platoon stayed up all night until, just before dawn, the pin was located. Otherwise the entire platoon would have been punished.

Almost all the soldiers on base carried either an M-16 or an Uzi. I asked Elena who carried which gun. She explained that the longer M-16 was considered the more "macho" weapon, so the men usually chose that one. The women were usually assigned the shorter Uzis. Even though smaller, the Uzis are heavier in weight because all of their components are metal, while some M-16 parts are plastic. Ironically, the women end up carrying heavier weapons than the men.

Since the soldiers are required to carry their weapons whenever they are on duty, they also carried them into the mess hall. They slid their rifles under the table where they ate. If you sat opposite or alongside them, you had to be careful not to kick their rifles. The soldiers' rifles are not loaded, except when they are on

---

* I learned from my bunkmate, Herb, that the Israeli inventor of the "Uzi," Uzi Gal, moved to the U.S. and recently passed away. The reason he knew this was that Herb had been his accountant.

guard duty or on patrol. (When not loaded, a magazine clip is banded onto the rifle and can be quickly inserted if necessary.) Therefore, there was little danger of accidentally kicking a rifle on the floor of the mess hall and having it go off.

Like any other military, the Israeli army makes its share of screw-up decisions. One of these related to a soldier named Maya. I noticed her the first day I arrived at the warehouse. It was hard not to. She had what we call in America "movie star" looks. Her long, dark hair framed a beautiful dark-skinned face whose most prominent feature was her striking blue eyes. And she had a gorgeous figure that even baggy army fatigues could not disguise.

Maya was one of the two soldiers assigned to work in the warehouse under Alex's direction (Elena being the other). She had a severe allergy to dust. It was so bad that within seconds of entering the warehouse, her eyes welled up and she began sneezing and choking uncontrollably. It made no sense for the army to have assigned Maya to the warehouse. This was a place where dust was constantly in the air. All day, supplies were delivered to and shipped from the warehouse. Often these included used, dirty items such as uniforms, blankets, boots, etc. No amount of cleaning could have eliminated the dust.

Maya had petitioned the army for a transfer to a less dusty job because of her medical condition. The army turned her down. So every day she reported for duty to the front entrance of the warehouse, but did not enter.

Alex did not want Maya to suffer and so did not insist that she come in. But he had no use for her, other than as an occasional "gopher" to walk to another building on the base to deliver a message. Consequently, he placed a small desk and chair in the shade outside the warehouse entrance. All day Maya sat there reading a book with a box of tissues close at hand. Because of her beauty, male soldiers delivering or picking up supplies would constantly stop by to socialize and her desk was often surrounded by them.

Hardworking Elena did not hide her disdain for Maya, or for the army in assigning her to a dusty job. She was clearly jealous of

Maya and the attention that she drew. "I have an allergy to dust too, but they make me work in this dirty place anyway," said Elena. "I don't see why the army should let Maya sit there all day, reading her book and gabbing with all these men!"

Whereas Elena was extremely friendly toward all the volunteers and soldiers, she was barely civil to Maya because of this jealousy. Maya's inability to work in the warehouse doubled the workload on Elena, further fueling her resentment. During work breaks, when Elena, Philip, and I sat outside the warehouse, Elena showed her annoyance whenever Philip or I ever started up a conversation with Maya. I found Maya to be a sweet, rather shy young woman who was simply biding her time in the impossible situation in which the army had placed her.

There was a second soldier on the base named Maya ("Maya II"), who taught me a lesson – not to draw assumptions based on appearance. Maya II was a friendly black woman who occasionally stopped by the warehouse to pick up supplies. On one of these occasions, I mentioned something about her being Ethiopian. She forcefully cut me off, raising her tone: "Don't assume I'm Ethiopian just because I am black. I'm from Ghana." "Well, how did you come to be an Israeli soldier?" I asked. "My father was the Israeli ambassador to Ghana where he met and married my mother," she replied. "After I was born and his tour of duty ended, we returned to Israel where I grew up." It was clear that I had hit Maya II's "hot button." She resented when people assumed, based on her black skin, that she was Ethiopian. In Israel, most Ethiopian immigrants are poor and uneducated. Maya II wanted people to know that she was neither.

Despite coming from so many countries, our group of volunteers seemed to have coalesced nicely. The Dutch and South African volunteers seemed to get along particularly well, perhaps because they both spoke related languages (Dutch; Afrikaans). Over the lunch break, we said goodbye to one of the South African volunteers, Louie, who had completed two months of volunteer work at the base. We also sang "Happy Birthday" to Nate, one of the Canadian volunteers.

One volunteer named Bruce remained apart from everyone. Bruce was a tall, broad-shouldered, twenty-six-year-old carpenter from Indiana. He was already in his fourth month at Batzop. I hardly ever heard Bruce say a word. He tended to quietly do crossword puzzles or read the Bible when sitting at an outside table in the volunteers' compound. The scuttlebutt was that Bruce's grandfather had been an SS officer in Hitler's army. Bruce was a deeply religious Christian who was torn with guilt over his grandfather's Nazi past. He was serving as a volunteer in part to atone for his grandfather's actions against Jews.

The Israelis nicknamed Bruce "The General." This was actually a term of respect. Bruce had served on the base so long in the radio disassembly area that the Israelis had given him the run of the place. In turn, Bruce directed the newer volunteers assigned to that area. The Israelis saw this function as "giving orders" – hence, he was "The General."

After dinner, we were offered the option of spending the evening in nearby Ramle. Our madricha, Avigail, and assistant madricha, Shira, offered to join us, not as chaperones but as "protection" (Avigail's description), because Ramle is a mixed Jewish–Arab town. I was so tired from the heavy lifting of the last three days that I declined this trip, which I otherwise would have been interested in taking. Besides, with our workweek ended, I needed to pack for my weekend at the home of my cousins, Bracha and Menachem.

I very much regretted not having gone to Ramle when I heard what had happened there from Carol and Sara, two of the volunteers who had gone. Perhaps I could have helped. Avigail and Shira had walked into Ramle with four female volunteers after sundown. Avigail had her M-16 rifle, but Shira was unarmed.

They entered a small café and purchased falafel sandwiches. It was about 8:30 and darkness had already fallen. On the nearly deserted main street of Ramle, the six of them sat down at an outdoor table in front of the cafe. The only other table was unoccupied. Avigail sat at the table with her gun on her lap and the gun strap slung across her back.

Suddenly a hooded man seemed to appear from nowhere, behind Avigail. In a single motion, he slammed Avigail's head down onto the table, yanked the gun strap from across her back, and ran off around a corner with the gun. It all happened in a matter of seconds.

Avigail sat up and screamed: "My gun! My gun!" Instantly, their army training kicked in. In one voice, Avigail and Shira yelled to the volunteers: "Get inside! Get inside!" All six of them rushed into the café. Avigail and Shira shoved the volunteers down to the floor behind the counter. Then the two madrichas flung themselves across all four volunteers. No one knew whether the hooded assailant would return and start firing Avigail's rifle. If that happened, the two madrichas were prepared to act as human shields to protect the volunteers. Once they were all were positioned on the floor, Avigail and Shira pulled out their cell phones and called for help.

For the first few moments, confusion reigned inside the small café. The female café clerk and the two patrons who happened to be inside at the time yelled: "What's happening?" They immediately reacted to Avigail's and Shira's terse responses by crouching below the windows, waiting for the police to arrive. Avigail continued to cry out mournfully: "My gun! My gun!"

Once the police came and it was clear that the assailant had left the area, the danger was over. Then the impact of what had happened hit both madrichas. They started crying hysterically, sobbing to the volunteers: "We're sorry! We're sorry!" Carol and Sara tried to comfort them, saying, "It's okay. We're alright." But Avigail and Shira felt they had failed in their duty to protect the volunteers. They had allowed the volunteers to be put in danger and felt they had let them down. There was no consoling them.

Both madrichas were in shock. Avigail slumped down into

a corner, shaking. Shira was also very upset. The enormity of the danger they had been in had sunk in. Had the hooded assailant inserted the magazine clip into Avigail's rifle and opened fire, they could have all been killed.

Beyond the physical danger, Avigail had added reason to be upset. It is a crime in Israel for soldiers to lose their weapons or to allow them to be taken from them when not properly held. Avigail realized she faced the possibility of going to jail for allowing her weapon to be taken from her.

The police called an ambulance for Avigail, but once it arrived the medical personnel simply calmed her down and decided there was no need for her to be transported by ambulance. The volunteers who had been at the café table were very complimentary of how quickly, professionally, and courageously the two soldiers had reacted at the time of the attack. The two nineteen-year-olds had offered their lives to protect the volunteers in their charge. All six of them spent until 1:00 A.M. at the police station. They were individually questioned about the attack and finally satisfied the police that Avigail had been carrying her weapon properly at the time of the incident. (My cousin Bracha later gave me the article in Saturday's *Maariv* newspaper about this attack.)

FRIDAY, OCTOBER 25, 2002

Sar-el madrichas often arrange a short field trip as a "thank you" to the volunteers at the end of the workweek. After a rushed breakfast, we boarded a bus to Latrun, located about ten miles southeast of Ramle. Avigail and Shira sat in the left front seats, directly in front of me, and two additional armed soldiers sat on the right. They were both chastened and quiet from the events of the previous night. Avigail seemed mechanical in her effort to keep her emotions under control. Her puffy eyes revealed she had been crying. One of the additional armed soldiers tried to ask Avigail about the attack. She just waved him away; she didn't want to talk about it. Clearly, she was tremendously embarrassed to have had her rifle taken from her.

Our first stop was the museum at Latrun in honor of the Israeli Tank Corps. Latrun is an old British army fort on a hilltop overlooking the Valley of Ayalon. According to the Bible, this was the site where Joshua defeated the Amorites. Over a thousand years later, Judah Maccabee defeated a Greek-Syrian army in the same place to help win Israel's independence in 165 B.C.E. This victory is celebrated in the holiday of Hanukkah.

In 1948, the departing British turned over this strategic fort to Jordan's Arab Legion. It overlooks the only road connecting Jerusalem to Tel Aviv. During the War of Independence, Israeli forces tried to take Latrun in order to break the Arab blockade that was threatening to cut off and starve the Jewish population of Jerusalem. The Israelis launched five attacks in attempting to take the fort. You can still see the pockmarks in the fort's walls from the bullets and shells fired in these battles.

Because the Israelis were unsuccessful in taking the fort, they devised an alternate plan. They discovered a small shepherd's trail in the hills around the fort and at nighttime they surreptitiously built a steep and perilous road along this route to supply Jerusalem. The story of the failed attempts to take the fort and the building of this alternative roadway is recounted in the movie *Cast a Giant Shadow.* In this movie, Kirk Douglas played the real-life American colonel, Mickey Marcus, a West Point graduate who had advised the Israelis during this effort. Tragically, as the alternative supply route neared completion, Marcus was killed accidentally by an Israeli sentry who failed to recognize him in the dark.

The museum is housed in the old British fort. Outside the fort is the "Wall of Remembrance," listing the names of the men who died in the Tank Corps during all of Israel's wars since 1948. There are 4,886 names engraved on this long wall, which is similar to the Vietnam Veterans Memorial in Washington, D.C.

The museum's walls and floors are made of steel to represent the tanks in which the men died. Inside the museum, we entered a room called the "Gates of Bravery," in which pictures of the men who died are constantly flashed on the walls. On the anniversary of each one's death, their picture is displayed for a long time, and not just flashed up for a few seconds like the others. There are also seventy "blanks" in the total display. These represent the individuals killed in the War of Independence who, because they were the only survivors of the Holocaust in their families, had no one to supply the museum with a picture.

We watched a short but very emotional movie about the sacrifices made by the men who fought in the Tank Corps. This included remarks by a tanker blinded in battle to his daughter on her fifteenth birthday, crying over the fact that he had never seen her face.

Our group broke into applause when we first saw a tanker in the movie wearing a helmet headset. These were the same helmet headsets that many of our volunteers had been repairing and assembling over the past week. This made an impression on us and we felt a special connection to the Tank Corps.

Surrounding the Latrun museum is an amazing outdoor array of ninety real tanks from various stages of the Tank Corps. They start with the tiny two-man Hotchkiss tank, made in France and used by Israel during the War of Independence. This tank looks like a toy, standing barely higher than my head and weighing only 12 tons. The tanks also include the American-built Patton tank, the mainstay of the Tank Corps in the 1960s. Finally, they include the more modern Israeli-built Merkava tank, versions Mark I, II, and III. The Merkava Mark III is a sleek monster, weighing up to 85 tons when fully loaded. It carries a 120 mm cannon and three machine guns and can travel up to 60 km/hour (approximately 37 miles/hour). All of the tanks on display are real and are available for children (and adults such as us) to climb on.

After touring the museum, our group started to split up. Our bus dropped off many of our group at the main bus terminal in Jerusalem and then turned around to drop off the rest of us in Tel Aviv.

From the Tel Aviv bus station, I took a cab to the home of my cousins, Bracha and Menachem, in the Tel Aviv suburb of Rosh Ha-Ayin. By 1:00 P.M., I was at their house. Both of them had left work early on this Friday afternoon to meet me.

Spending the weekend at their home allowed me to taste a little bit of everyday life in Israel. Menachem is a tall, well-built man in his early fifties. He drives fast, cannot sit still, and has the high energy level of a man half his age. He retired from the Israeli air force as a lieutenant colonel after twenty-five years of service, and most of his and Bracha's social acquaintances are from his days in the military. Since leaving the air force, he had tried two businesses. The first was a restaurant, which he sold when the downturn in tourism due to the Intifada forced many restaurants to close. The second was an effort to establish a chain of used car outlets in Israel, equivalent to what CarMax is in the U.S. This used car business had four locations and Menachem was planning more. He is an ambitious, hardworking man and has a very direct, outgoing personality.

Menachem's wife, my cousin Bracha, provided the grounding for his entrepreneurial streak. She spent most of her working life as a teacher, then as a principal of a school. When I had first met her, she had just received an award as the best school principal in Israel. It was presented to her by then-Prime Minister Ehud Barak on national television. Looking for a new challenge, she recently changed jobs to work as the director of a boarding home for at-risk children. These children, ages six to eighteen, had to be taken away from parents who were drug-users, alcoholics, child-abusers, or were in jail. They lived at the boarding home, a large house in downtown Tel Aviv, and attended public school nearby. After graduating from high school, most went into the army. Bracha worked very hard at her job, often coming home at a late hour.

Bracha and Menachem's home, in a government subsidized housing development for retired military officers, was located in a beautiful new suburb of Tel Aviv. Since their two sons were both married and lived elsewhere (in the U.S. and in Netanya), there was plenty of space in their house. They made me feel very welcome.

We talked about the latest news of their sons, Amit and Itay. Their oldest, Amit, moved to Maryland several years ago to work in an Israeli wholesale diamond business. Amit and his wife, Liat, had two little girls, whom Bracha and Menachem adored. Unfortunately, given the long distance, it was hard for them to see Amit and his family and they realized that it was unlikely that Amit and his family would be returning to Israel in the near future. "Amit drives a Lexus and has a big house in the U.S.," Menachem said. "He knows he could not have that lifestyle here."

Since they had come home early to meet me, we had a bite to eat and then did what is common in Israeli families when they are not working: we took a mid-afternoon nap. Around 7:00 P.M., we went to Menachem's former restaurant for dinner. It was billed as an "Eastern restaurant" and its style was reminiscent of Darna, my favorite Moroccan restaurant in Jerusalem. The multi-course meal was delicious and whatever weight I might have lost from the prior week's work on the base, I was sure I gained back in this one meal.

Straight from dinner, we drove twenty minutes south to the city of Rehovot to Bracha and Menachem's once-a-month singing club. This was a group of about 200 people, mostly former military friends of Menachem and teacher friends of Bracha, who had been singing together for over ten years. On the performing stage of a mid-sized theater, a man played piano. He led the audience seated in the theater in singing older Israeli tunes, whose words were displayed on the movie-size screen in front of them. The songs were Israeli favorites from the 1950s, 60s, and 70s. The crowd clapped and swayed to particular favorites, and Bracha and Menachem were in heaven singing songs from their youth. I sang along, as I could catch the pattern of most tunes quickly and, except for the fastest songs, I could keep up with the Hebrew on the screen in front of us. A couple of the tunes were Yiddish songs I remembered from my parents, or Hebrew songs I learned in Camp Galil as a teenager. In the middle of the hour-long session, the piano player announced that their singing club had been named the third best such club in the country. The crowd applauded enthusiastically.

After a short break for hot tea and pastries, the singing club crowded back into the theater to listen to a special performance by David D'Or, one of Israel's most famous singers and composers. As part of his introduction, it was announced that he was scheduled to sing for the Pope at the Vatican the next day, only the second Israeli singer ever invited to do so.

David D'Or lived up to his billing. He had a tremendous, pure, high-octave voice. One of the songs he sang was about a farmer who worked very hard all his life, but died before he reached his goal. The song had come out at the same time as the 1995 assassination of Prime Minister Yitzhak Rabin by an Israeli extremist. It had become popular because the farmer came to symbolize Rabin to the public. The crowd became very emotional, singing along with David D'Or about the farmer.

The performance ended at 12:45 in the morning. Instead of heading home (I was already tired at this point), Menachem and Bracha were just "warming up" for their Friday night. We went to a friend's house in Rehovot where a group of twelve of their friends from their singing club had congregated. The conversation was in fast Hebrew and I could not follow most of it, especially because at this hour the part of my brain that translates had shut down for the night. Menachem obligingly translated for me from time to time. At about 1:00, a meal was served, consisting of fruit, cheese, bread, wine, salads and cake. We finally returned home at 2:40 A.M.

This schedule was a typical one for Menachem and Bracha. They worked hard during the week and on the weekend they "partied hard," not appearing to require much sleep (other than their mid-day nap). I felt like I was holding them back because I was not used to staying up as late as they did.

SATURDAY, OCTOBER 26, 2002

This morning, Menachem and I headed for the beach in north Tel Aviv, just ten minutes away. The Mediterranean was flat, with few waves, and the sand was very fine. Menachem is very fitness conscious, so he asked if I wanted to exercise. I was happy to, so he took me through a series of bending and stretching exercises at the edge of the water. It was a good fifteen-minute workout, which ended with a refreshing swim in the sea. Afterwards, we walked for a couple of miles, noticing other men exercising on the beach as we had.

Thirty years ago, Menachem told me, the Israeli cities along the coast constructed a series of jetties to trap the sand from the sea. In this way, the beach gradually grew instead of eroded. Much of the sand is silt emptied into the Mediterranean by the Nile River. After Egypt completed the construction of the Aswan Dam along the Nile, the level of sand accumulation slowed but still continued. Menachem joked that while the Arabs were busy trying to push Israel into the sea, the Israelis were busy trying to extend Israel into the sea.

We returned home for the midday meal and an afternoon nap. This evening, Bracha and Menachem went to Bracha's high school reunion in Hadera. Although I was invited to join them, I declined. I needed more rest from yesterday's late night partying.

SUNDAY, OCTOBER 27, 2002

While Saturday had been a day for rest and relaxation with my cousins, Sunday was a work day. We were up early. By 6 A.M., I had said goodbye to Bracha and was heading off with Menachem for a quick workout at his fitness club. Later he gave me a lift back to Ramle.

We immediately hit stand-still traffic on the highway. The authorities had set up a roadblock and were checking each vehicle. Menachem explained that Rosh Ha-Ayin is just south of a major east-west highway that comes into Israel from the West Bank. Whenever the authorities have an inkling of a terrorist attack, they set up roadblocks on the highway to intercept the terrorists. (I found out later that the authorities' suspicions had been well founded. The evening news reported that a Palestinian terrorist had blown himself up at a gas station in Ariel, a West Bank town on the east-west highway about twelve miles east of Rosh Ha-Ayin. He killed three soldiers and wounded nine other people. The Al Aqsa Brigade, an arm of Yasir Arafat's Palestinian Authority, claimed credit for the killings).

After Menachem dropped me off at the base, I unpacked my bags, donned my army fatigues and went to work by 10:00 A.M. Work today was all outside. Three other volunteers and I prepared the ground in front of a guardhouse in order to construct a brick sidewalk. It was back-breaking work – clearing the ground with a pick ax and shovel, carrying away buckets of rocks, bringing back buckets of fine sand, and placing the bricks just so. In the process, we learned from a volunteer named David how to carefully prepare ground for installation of a brick sidewalk. David was an engineer, born and educated in the Ukraine. He now lives in New Jersey. A skilled problem-solver, he was also creative in making use of whatever materials were laying around. Most importantly, he was good at teaching others to take over various parts of the building process. We worked well as a team.

David was a perfectionist. He insisted on tearing out the small amount of brick sidewalk that had been sloppily laid the week before by Israeli soldiers. The soldiers whose work had been torn out looked on glumly as their officer lectured them on the need to take as much pride in their work as the volunteers did. David was insistent that any work done by the volunteers be done right. It showed in the finished product, of which we were rightfully proud. By the end of the day we had finished about a quarter of the brick sidewalk.

After work, the volunteers compared notes on how they spent their weekend. Philip, my Dutch work partner, had a particularly noteworthy experience. On Thursday, he went to Efrat, a city of 35,000 people in the West Bank just south of Jerusalem.

He visited a friend in this community of Orthodox Jews who are primarily immigrants from the U.S. With his friend, he went to the Jerusalem neighborhood of Gilo the following morning to visit the family of Shiri Nagari. I had read an article about her in *Newsweek* over the summer. Shiri was a very pretty twenty-year-old girl who had been in a bus bombing on June 18 of this year. She had few visible injuries, so she let the other injured passengers go ahead of her to be treated. When the emergency medical personnel finally got to her, they realized she had massive internal injuries. Although she was operated on for hours, the doctors could not save her. The surgeon working on her, who had seen many gruesome injuries from terrorist bombings, broke down and cried when she died. Her family had posted her picture on a website and Philip had seen it. He was an artist and felt compelled to paint a portrait of Shiri for her family. He presented the portrait to the Nagari family on Friday and they were very grateful for this special present. They insisted that he join them for the Sabbath, which he did.

My bunkmate Mike and his wife Elaine visited Kibbutz Saad near the Gaza Strip. The purpose of their visit was to see the Israeli family that had "adopted" Mike when he had spent time there in 1959, when he was seventeen. Mike mentioned to me that he had also visited Kibbutz Lavi in northern Israel during his 1959 stay in Israel. I told him that I had visited Kibbutz Lavi last December and spent a very pleasant evening talking with Mr. and Mrs. Orbaum, two of the kibbutz founders. Mrs. Orbaum was a *Kindertransport* survivor, sent as a child from Germany to England in 1939. While in England she met her husband and the two of them moved to Israel to help found Kibbutz Lavi in 1949. Since they were farmers and I had grown up on a farm, we had a lot in common to talk about. It turned out that Mike had also met this couple when he visited Kibbutz Lavi in 1959. The reason he remembered this meeting was that Mr. Orbaum had pulled out his glass eye and tossed it to Mike, scaring him no end.

After dinner, we listened to a lecture from Avigail about the origins of the Israel Defense Force. Avigail also announced that, given the theft of her rifle in Ramle, none of the volunteers would be permitted to leave the base during the workweek.

MONDAY, OCTOBER 28, 2002

For the first time, there was a chill in the air in the morning at about 6:00 A.M. This made a difference in the shower hut, which was also chilly. It was simply an enclosed building with a corrugated roof and fixed screened windows.

At our 7:45 A.M. announcements, Avigail reported that the IDF had been active in Jenin yesterday and had arrested forty-one terrorists. Two were in the process of leaving to go on a suicide bombing mission. She also informed us that the Labor party was threatening to quit the coalition government, thus throwing the country into early elections. At issue was the large amount of money budgeted by the right-wing Likud party to support the Jewish settlements on the West Bank. The Labor party was demanding that much of this money be re-allocated to social welfare support rather than for West Bank settlements.

Today I was assigned to the quartermaster's warehouse again. By now, this was very familiar territory for me. I had started reading all of the signs in order to improve my Hebrew. I knew, for example, that *Chomer dalik asur la-ashen* next to the outdoor vat of kerosene meant "Flammable material – smoking forbidden."

We spent the entire morning cleaning the warehouse's inventory of gas masks. These were not the gas masks that the soldiers used in the field and were required to carry in their field packs. Instead, these were gas masks used to train new soldiers. By constant usage, they had gotten dirty and our task was to clean, pack, and box them, which we completed by lunchtime.

For the first time since we arrived, dessert was available at a meal. It was dry, hard cinnamon cake, but both the volunteers and soldiers seemed to enjoy it. They served the same cake at dinner, only it was even drier and harder by that time.

Observing the soldiers at every meal was always interesting.

They sat together with us, sliding their weapons under their seats. Most of them were eighteen to twenty years old and, although they were in uniform, they could not help but act like eighteen to twenty-year-olds. This meant that a lot of socializing went on between the boys and girls, just as you would expect of high school seniors in the U.S. The girls wore tight uniforms to look as attractive as possible to the guys, and the guys were also careful about their appearance.

Today, I ate lunch with a tall thin man in his late twenties who was on base to do his once-a-year reserve duty. His name was Yossi, and he was the youngest of eleven children. His parents were immigrants from Morocco and Egypt. Yossi was a truck driver who had been out of work for a month. Once he finished his four-week reserve stint in the army, he expected he would still be unemployed. While he had no wife or children to support, he was nonetheless discouraged by his situation. All he wanted was a job, but the Israeli economy was in recession and his prospects for employment were not good.

The afternoon started with a tour for the volunteers. We were shown through the communications lab, where the electronic equipment was repaired and refurbished. Some of the volunteers worked in the lab, although most of the people working there were soldiers. In the course of our tour, we were shown the multi-step processes for the three primary communications repair tasks performed on the base: radio repair, tank antennae construction, and refurbishment of tank helmet headsets.

After our tour, I spent the afternoon doing various manual labor projects in the quartermaster's warehouse. Because the day had not been as tiring as the previous one, I was able to close the afternoon with a healthy two-mile run around the base with another volunteer, Nancy, a forty-year-old mother and housewife from Philadelphia. She was a long-distance runner and, after I pooped out at two miles, she continued her run.

Walking back to my bunk, I recalled an amusing exchange with an elderly female volunteer earlier in the day. She said she had heard some of the other women, assuming I was single, discussing who to match me up with. "But I noticed that you wear a wedding ring," she said. "What gives?" I told her I'd been happily married for twenty-six years and I didn't need or want to be matched up with anyone. I asked her to convey that to the women who had been talking about me. I asked her whether I had done anything to lead these women to think I was single. "No," she said, "but they're all Jewish grandmothers who like to be matchmakers. They assumed you were single because most of the other male volunteers came with their wives."

After dinner, Avigail made two announcements: First, there would be an inspection tomorrow of our living quarters by the deputy commander of the base. Second, on Wednesday we would be sending twenty of our volunteers to a base in the south to assemble gas masks with a large number of volunteers.

TUESDAY, OCTOBER 29, 2002

We all cleaned our quarters and swept, washed and "squeegied" our floors after breakfast to prepare for inspection. We were warned that the inspecting officer would check for dust on the door and windowsills. In fact, he did this in our room. He would not fail volunteers' bunks, but he was not pleased with our bunk because our floor was not spotless. (Someone had walked on our floor after we had squeegied it, leaving a boot print.) He asked whether we were satisfied with our living arrangements and we gave him a couple of suggestions (access to current newspapers; coffee with breakfast in the mess hall). He listened politely, but noncommittally, and I had the sense that he really didn't want to hear our suggestions. Then he moved on.

This morning after inspection, we received a visit from the military director of Sar-el. He explained what had happened at Ariel on Sunday with the suicide bomber. A tragic error by a soldier had set off the bomb. About thirty soldiers had surrounded the bomber and then shot him after confirming he wore a bomb belt. The soldiers walked away, assuming the bomber was dead.

35

However, one soldier shot him a second time to be sure he was dead. The second shot hit the bomb belt and set off the bomb, killing three soldiers.

Avigail's morning announcements were brief: Yesterday, the IDF had removed some hilltop outposts (not even amounting to settlements) established by Jewish right-wing zealots on the West Bank. The IDF had arrested eight Palestinian terrorists in Shechem and two more in Qalqilya. And a terrorist bomber had been apprehended on his way into Israel from the West Bank.

Morning work in the quartermaster's warehouse consisted of wrapping and storing eight large, folded sets of camouflage netting. The netting was very heavy and bulky, requiring two people to lift it. It took us the morning to complete this task.

After lunch, Avigail arranged a meeting for us with three young female Israeli soldiers. We asked them what the base soldiers thought about the volunteers. One soldier chuckled and said: "We think you are all crazy. We serve in the army because this is our country and because we are required to serve. Why do you leave your families and homes to do this hard work?" At that point several of the volunteers replied that we also felt strongly about Israel and that many people outside of Israel feel the same way. The three soldiers seemed moved by these remarks.

We also met with Sergeant Shmuel, a seventeen-year army veteran who was in charge of worker safety at the base. He expressed his thanks to the volunteers and said that the base had come to rely on the volunteers for essential work. As an example of this, he mentioned that there had been no Sar-el volunteers in Israel this year between the Jewish holidays of Rosh Hashanah and Sukkot. As a result, there was a shortage of tank helmets with the headphones, which the volunteers customarily repaired for the Tank Corps.

The sergeant lived in the West Bank settlement of Quarne Shomron, a town of about 1,300 families. The town suffered an attack last year in which a Palestinian terrorist broke in and killed a mother and her four children. Sergeant Shmuel carried the bodies of the four children, all of whom he knew, out of their house. "Stories about not being able to sleep after witnessing a traumatic scene are true," he observed; he had trouble sleeping for a long time afterward.

Back at work, I helped Elena with her once-a-month document shredding. For security reasons, it is a crime in the Israeli military to throw away any piece of paper that has a soldier's name or identification number on it. The quartermaster's office had many such documents. Rather than keep track of which documents contained sensitive information, the people staffing the quartermaster's warehouse treated them all the same, tossing them into a giant plastic bag. Elena was responsible for disposing of this plastic bag which, when full, was almost the size of a person. I carried this giant (and heavy) bag to the base commander's office where we occupied the shredding machine for about two hours. The shredding machine was ancient, jamming whenever we fed it more than two pages at a time. By the end of the afternoon, we had reduced the plastic bag of paper to a mass of confetti.

The evening routine in our compound for the soldiers was predictable. After dinner, a number of them headed out in small groups for their night guard duty on the perimeter of the base. The remainder stayed in the compound, playing cards or board games, watching television, or just talking and smoking. (A very high percentage of these young men and women smoke, consistent with the Israeli population at large.)

The youngest of our volunteers, Vicki, was an eighteen-year-old Swedish girl who was here with her Aunt Margit. Margit was a friendly Norwegian woman who, throughout our three week Sar-el stint, conducted a series of interviews with Israelis for an article she was writing. Neither Vicki nor Margit was Jewish and, for that reason, were especially appreciated by the Jewish volunteers.

Vicki was a very attractive blond, and the male Israeli soldiers were almost comical in falling over each other for a chance to talk to her. At meals there was usually jostling among a number of the male soldiers over who would sit next to her. Vicki was a sweet and friendly girl who didn't seem to mind the attention; after all, the soldiers were her age and were very handsome fellows.

Two of my roommates, Don and Herb, walked into Ramle in lieu of dinner (eggs plus spaghetti). They reported that the kosher pizza and beer at the Ramle bus station had been a refreshing change. It appeared that Ramle was no longer off-limits for the volunteers.

WEDNESDAY, OCTOBER 30, 2002

Our compound was quieter than usual this morning. Twenty volunteers had been selected at random to join a group of 150 volunteers assembling gas masks at a base in the south. The ones chosen left early in the morning for a two-hour bus ride to a base close to the port city of Ashdod.

Morning announcements were brief: At a Jewish settlement named Hermesh, about four miles south of the Arab town of Um-Al-Fakn, a terrorist had killed three people and injured three others before he was shot dead. I learned that Um-Al-Fakn, with its population of 40,000 Arabs, was a source of terrorist activity even though the town is not in the West Bank, but is in Israel proper. Avigail also announced that two tunnels were discovered coming from the Egyptian border into the Gaza Strip and presumably had been used to smuggle arms from Egypt to the Palestinians.

At flag-raising, as if on cue, Israeli fighter planes thundered overhead just as we were standing at attention. A number of us craned our heads upwards to follow their flight. I wondered whether these planes were part of a retaliatory strike for the murders at Hermesh yesterday.

This morning I joined four other volunteers to work on tank, truck, and jeep radios, which had been brought to Batzop for repair. Soldiers and volunteers separated the radios from their bases and volunteers took the bases apart, removing wires and shock absorbers for testing. Then we scraped the paint and dirt off the radio bases and sanded them to a smooth surface to ready them for painting. In the meantime, the radios were sent to the lab for testing and refurbishing. The Israelis saved everything! Used but serviceable shock absorbers, wiring, and screws were reinstalled on the radio bases once they were spray painted, and then the refurbished radios were installed on the bases. There was a large volume of work here for the volunteers and it was important work.

After lunch, I switched over to another assembly line. Helmets from tank crews were sent to our base for maintenance. Along with other volunteers, I removed the inside webbing, which was sent to the laundry, and the radio headphones, which were taken to the lab for testing and repair. We checked the bare helmets for dents, then sanded and painted them. Other volunteers installed fresh webbing and refurbished headphones in the newly painted helmets. There were many steps to this process and the volunteers performed all of these steps either by themselves or together with the soldiers.

Our twenty volunteers returned from the south by dinnertime, looking quite tired. They had spent the day in a giant hangar-type building with a large number of Sar-el volunteers from other bases. Having assembled and packed 2,800 gas masks by day's end, they were justifiably proud of this accomplishment.

This evening, we gathered around the television in the *moadon* to catch the news on CNN. Israel's Labor party had just resigned from the Unity Government, in opposition to the government's planned budget that provided significant funds for settlements in the West Bank. It was now likely that the country would be compelled to have early elections because Prime Minister Sharon's Unity Government had lost its majority. The only alternative to new elections was if Sharon's Likud party was able to fashion a new coalition majority with one or more of the right-wing religious parties.

While the Israeli soldiers preferred to watch this breaking news in Hebrew, several sat with us through CNN's broadcast in

English. The soldiers seemed to take in stride the fact that the co-alition Israeli government was on the verge of crumbling. Perhaps their blasé attitude towards the news broadcast reflected the fact that Israeli politics is frequently punctuated by coalition realignments and crises.

To end the evening, Avigail arranged for a dance instructor to teach us Israeli folk dances. We danced under the lights in the plaza where flag-raising was held. I was familiar with most of the dances from my teenage years at Camp Galil. The only dance that was new to me was the equivalent of aerobics set to Israeli music. After an hour of jumping around, we were tired and sweaty, but we had had a good time.

THURSDAY, OCTOBER 31, 2002

We got up earlier than usual today to be ready for a field trip to Jerusalem. About a quarter of our group would be going home from Jerusalem, having stayed only two weeks, while the rest of us would return to base on Sunday morning. Sar-el asks people to stay a minimum of three weeks, but apparently allows two-week stints as well.

I walked back from breakfast with Vicki, who would be flying back to Stockholm tomorrow. I asked her if she was happy that she had come. She very enthusiastically said yes, that she had had a good time. She especially liked the time she spent with the soldiers, who were roughly her age. Through that interaction she felt that she had learned a lot about Israeli society.

In addition to the usual two armed soldiers, a female army guide named Avital joined our bus (not to be confused with our madricha Avigail). On the road to Jerusalem, we passed the burned-out trucks on the side of the highway, left as a memorial to the effort to supply Jerusalem between 1947 and 1948. I noticed that next to each burned out hulk was a rock bearing the date when the truck was destroyed.

Our first stop was Ammunition Hill in East Jerusalem, where we visited a museum dedicated to Israel's re-capture of the Old

City of Jerusalem during the Six-Day War. During the War of Independence in 1948, the Old City had been besieged and the Israelis had been forced to surrender it to Jordan's Arab Legion. As I listened to our guide, I began to appreciate how traumatic the loss of half of Jerusalem had been for Israelis at that time. Between the ceasefire of 1949 and the Six-Day War of 1967, Jerusalem had been divided between Israel and Jordan, with Jordan holding the Old City and barring Jews from its holy sites. This museum honored the soldiers who perished in the battle to re-take the Old City in 1967.

Avital described the situation facing Israel in 1967 just prior to the Six Day War. Egypt and Syria had formed a union called the United Arab Republic and declared their intention to destroy Israel. After Egyptian President Nasser illegally closed the Straits of Tiran, blocking Israel's southern port of Eilat from access to the Red Sea, he evicted the u.n. peacekeeping forces from the Israel-Egypt border area in the Sinai Peninsula. With the u.n. forces gone, he moved an enormous invasion force in their place.

Although a war with Egypt and Syria seemed inevitable, that was not the case with Jordan, which controlled the West Bank, including eastern Jerusalem and the Old City. Israel pleaded with Jordan to stay out of the conflict, but once the war had started, King Hussein of Jordan gave in to Nasser's urgings. Jordan attacked Israeli-held western Jerusalem by invading its demilitarized zone and taking over the u.n. High Commissioner's Building. The Israelis responded by launching an attack on eastern Jerusalem and the entire West Bank.

Ammunition Hill was Jordan's most heavily fortified stronghold in Jerusalem. The Israelis had to take it in order to open the road to strategic Mount Scopus and re-capture the Old City. A company of about a hundred paratroopers was assigned the task to storm the hill at night. They were successful, but at a high cost. Thirty-seven of the paratroopers were killed and many others were wounded. At the top of the hill is a large memorial listing the names of the men who fell in the attack. The memorial also lists the names of other men from the same company who died fighting for Israel in subsequent wars. Almost half of the company lost their lives in the various wars. This company of the paratroopers' brigade, known by its number (66), is famous in Israel.

The day before the attack, the men of Company 66 took time to write final letters to their wives and parents, in case they didn't survive the battle. Many of the letters of the deceased soldiers have been donated by their families to the museum that we visited at the base of Ammunition Hill. One excerpt from the famous "Letter from Ofer" is displayed near the museum's entrance. It expressed a young soldier's feelings after seeing pictures of Jews in German concentration camps and being struck by the hopeless look on their faces. This made him realize what he was fighting for – so that Jews would never again be placed in such a helpless situation. Ofer died in the assault on Ammunition Hill. His letter is read annually from the rostrum of the Knesset (Israel's parliament) on Yom Ha-Zikaron, Israel's Memorial Day.

Many years after the Six-Day War, the Israelis invited the commander of the Jordanian forces that had defended the hill to visit the site, to honor the Jordanian soldiers who had perished there. The Jordanian commander made a speech at the memorial topping the hill. He said that his men had fought like lions but the Israelis had fought harder, like men willing to die for their cause.

The paratrooper brigade, which had taken Ammunition Hill and played a major role in the 1967 conquest of the Old City, is considered a very elite force within the Israeli military. For each graduating class of paratroopers, their final 90 kilometer march (about 56 miles) ends on the summit of Ammunition Hill, where they receive their distinctive red berets.

Our next stop was the Haas Promenade, which provided us with a breathtaking view overlooking all of Jerusalem. To our right was the u.n. High Commissioner's Building, which is still used by u.n. personnel. By attacking this building in 1967, Jordan's King Hussein had declared war on Israel. I recalled that, shortly before he died, King Hussein acknowledged in a television interview that the greatest mistake in his life had been to give in to Nasser's pressure and attack Israel in 1967. Israel trounced Jordan, gaining back the Old City of Jerusalem as well as the entire West Bank from Jordan.

As we stood on the promenade, gazing out at the panoramic view, we suddenly heard the muezzins from mosques in the Arab portion of Jerusalem calling their faithful to prayer. Hundreds of chanting Arabic voices came at us as if in stereo. The echoes against the surrounding hills lent a strangely eerie dimension to these voices.

Just before we left the Haas Promenade, our two madrichas handed out Sar-el tee-shirts and pins to those volunteers who were leaving today. Then we boarded our bus and headed back into the New City, passing the Inbal Hotel, the Moses Montefiore Windmill, and the King David Hotel, which housed British officers during the mandate period. The bombing of this hotel in 1946 by the Irgun, the militant Zionist group headed by Menachem Begin, is recounted in the movie *Exodus*.

Our bus dropped us off for lunch in Jerusalem a few blocks from Ben Yehuda Street, the famous pedestrian shopping area of the city. I was heading towards Ben Yehuda Street with two volunteers, Marc and Nancy, when Nancy suddenly stopped and expressed her concern about walking on a street that had frequently been a target of terrorist bombings. Marc and I said we were not as concerned and, in any event, would not miss an opportunity to have lunch on Ben Yehuda Street. Nancy relented and agreed to accompany us. It was a gorgeous fall day. We bought falafel and shawarma sandwiches and savored them at one of the outdoor café tables.

With only a few minutes left, I checked to see whether my favorite Israeli stamp store was still there. It was at the base of Ben Yehuda Street on Zion Square and its windows had been blown out several times in bombings at this square. The shop was still there and Mrs. Ross, the kindly old lady sitting behind the counter, remembered me. Last December she had told me to bring a list of Israeli stamps I needed for my stamp collection, but I had forgotten to bring the list on this trip. Her daughter, standing next to her, asked me what I was doing in Israel. I explained that I was a Sar-el volunteer working on an Israeli military base. Skeptical that volunteers would be put to serious work by the army, she asked specifically what I did. "Well," I said, "yesterday I worked on rebuilding helmets used by the tank crews." Her skepticism melted into a smile as she replied, "In that case, I give you double thanks – one from me and one from my son in the Tank Corps. He has never complained about your helmets." The volunteers received many "thank you's" from Israelis, but for me this one was by far the sweetest.

As I was leaving Ben Yehuda Street for our bus, I heard a little thunder and then it rained for about three minutes – just enough to wet the pavement. This counts as a rain in Israel, a country where rain is rare.

Our field trip in Jerusalem continued with a visit to the Underground Prisoners Museum. Constructed in the nineteenth century as a hostel for Russian pilgrims, it had been converted into a prison when the British General Allenby conquered Jerusalem from the Turks in 1917. In the British mandate period, the building served as Jerusalem's central prison and many of the Jewish freedom fighters captured by the British prior to 1948 were incarcerated there.

The museum docent walked us through the prison exercise yard where those prisoners who were not in solitary confinement were given thirty minutes per day to walk around. The final stop in the prison was the cell that had housed two Jewish freedom fighters, Meir Feinstein and Moshe Barzani, both nineteen, who were sentenced to be hanged in 1947 by the British. The Jewish underground managed to smuggle a hand grenade hidden in an orange to them. At their hanging, the two men planned to blow themselves up and take a few British guards with them. But the night before, the prison rabbi visited them. They learned that the rabbi planned to accompany them to the hanging to give them comfort. Not wanting to kill a Jewish holy man, they changed their plans. After the rabbi left that night, they sang "Adon Olam" and exploded the grenade between them, killing them both.

It had been a long day and we had seen a lot. We dropped off half of our contingent at the Jerusalem bus station and then got back on the highway, heading for Tel Aviv. As we left Jerusalem, I felt a twinge of sadness. It is one of my favorite places in the world and I would not see it again until some future trip.

The Tel Aviv bus station was busy Thursday at evening rush hour. I bought some pastry and a drink, which I quickly consumed, and a bouquet of flowers for my cousin Ruchama, whom I was visiting this weekend. She lived in Netanya, which is normally about a thirty-minute taxi ride from Tel Aviv, but in rush hour traffic that is doubled.

Ruchama works until 8:00 on Thursday nights, so she gave me instructions to get to her mother's apartment. I arrived at about 6:00 P.M. to find a tiny, smiling, white-haired woman welcoming me at the door. I offered my flowers to Ruchama's mother, Yael. She introduced me to Ruchama's sister, Bracha, and Ruchama's daughter, Shani, a three-year-old Shirley Temple look-a-like with blonde ringlets. Shani was absorbed in watching cartoons on the television. Yael offered me some tea and cake and we settled down in her living room to wait for Ruchama.

Since she spoke not a word of English, and I had declined her offer to speak in Yiddish, she spoke in Hebrew and I only gleaned about half of what she said. She was visibly very happy to meet me. She talked about the one time my parents had visited her in 1981. She mentioned that one of the partisan fighters who had been in my father's resistance unit during World War II lived in Netanya and my father had met with him then.

Yael was very concerned about the political situation with Iraq. She was afraid of Iraqi Scud missiles and worried about the safety of her only grandchild, Shani. I recalled that some of the Scud missiles that the Iraqis had fired into Israel in 1991 during the first Gulf War had hit Netanya, so her fear was quite understandable.

I was having trouble understanding Yael, who became emotional as she spoke about the Scuds, falling into a too-fast Hebrew for me to follow. I was very relieved when Ruchama's brother, Michael, showed up around 7:00. Michael, who speaks English, is in his early forties, and is single. He helps out his mother and sister Bracha, who is mentally handicapped. A short, burly, mustachioed man, he was a senior sergeant in the Israeli navy and quartermaster for the Israeli submarine force in Haifa.

Michael was also interested in talking about politics, especially the tensions between the U.S. and Iraq. Like almost all Israelis, he viewed Saddam Hussein as a madman who would not hesitate to use chemical or nuclear weapons against Israel. The only reason that deterred Saddam from doing so, according to Michael, was his fear that Israel, itself possessing nuclear weapons, would respond by using them on Iraq. Although he did not share his mother's fears of another Scud attack, we both agreed that Israel's new Arrow anti-missile missile was a great improvement over the U.S.–built Patriot missile and would be more effective in shooting down Scuds.

I was interested in Michael's work with the Israeli navy and he obliged by giving me a brief history of Israel's submarine force. He said that plans for an Israeli submarine force were scrapped in 1968 when a British-built submarine, the *Dakar*, was lost at sea. The Israeli crew bringing it to Israel from Britain on its maiden voyage disappeared with sixty-nine men aboard. This was a very traumatic event for the families of these men and for the whole country. After that, Israel had no submarines until the 1990s.

In 1991, in preparation for the First Gulf War, the U.S. and its allies formed a coalition force that included various Arab countries that wanted to liberate Kuwait from Iraqi occupation. The U.S. and its allies realized that, upon the outbreak of hostilities, Iraq likely would fire Scud missiles into Israel. Saddam Hussein was counting on the fact that Israeli retaliation would force the Arab members of the U.S.-led coalition to step down, for fear of fighting on the same side as Israel. Anxious not to play into Saddam Hussein's plan, the western allies came up with a strategy to keep Israel out of the war.

As part of an inducement to the Israelis not to retaliate against Iraqi Scud attacks during the impending hostilities, Germany offered Israel a "submarine package." The Germans would build two new submarines for Israel at no cost, provided Israel bought a third one from Germany. Israel accepted and the submarines were delivered in the mid-1990s. These three submarines constitute the entire Israeli submarine force. As the quartermaster for this force, Michael was responsible for supplying all of its logistical needs.

At this point, Ruchama arrived. An active, bushy-haired, forty-three-year-old single mother, she hastily gathered up Shani and drove us to her apartment, about a ten-minute drive from her mother's home. After putting Shani to bed, we ate a light dinner at about 9:30 and caught up with each other's lives. Ruchama told me about her job as a psychotherapist working with a team of professionals treating people with psychological problems. Every morning she dropped Shani at a nearby *gan* (kindergarten or daycare center). If she had to work late Shani stayed with her mother, Yael.

By this time (about 11:00 P.M.), I was very tired and went to bed. Ruchama had to work the next morning, so I had the luxury of sleeping late and sleeping on a real mattress.

FRIDAY, NOVEMBER 1, 2002

I woke up after 9:00 A.M. and watched the busy street outside. Across from Ruchama's apartment is a *gan* (not Shani's *gan*) and I watched as parents dropped their children off. The *gan* was surrounded by a high metal fence. The entrance was a heavy door of metal bars. The door was kept padlocked at all times. The parents waited at the entrance until someone from within came to open the door and take their children. There have been random attacks on Israeli schools by Palestinian terrorists, so each *gan* or school has to take precautions, which often includes having an armed guard at each facility.

The smell of cooking food wafted throughout the neighborhood and into the apartment. It was the same smell of Eastern European Jewish cooking I remembered from my grandmother's apartment in Brooklyn forty years earlier. It was Friday morning, and many households were cooking chicken soup or cholent (a slow-simmered stew) in preparation for the Sabbath.

Ruchama returned from work shortly after one on Friday afternoon. After a quick lunch, it was naptime. As I had seen the previous weekend, Israelis like to take a nap on Friday and Saturday afternoons. This is what allows them to stay up late on Friday and Saturday nights.

For secular Jews like my cousins, Friday night is a time for family get-togethers. Yael had cooked a festive meal; she and her two other children, Michael and Bracha, brought it to Ruchama's apartment in big pots. It was a delicious, traditional Friday night dinner – homemade gefilte fish (like they made it in Poland, according to Yael), chicken soup, kreplach, and chicken. During and after dinner, Shani monopolized her Uncle Michael, who doted on her. We all relaxed over a real Sabbath feast.

SATURDAY, NOVEMBER 2, 2002

Saturday morning I woke to the smell of cholent, which Ruchama had started cooking the day before. It is a stew composed of meat, potatoes, beans, onions, and various vegetables, which is put in a big pot over a very low flame on the stove on Friday afternoon. It cooks for about eighteen hours and the smell is wonderful. In honor of my visit, Ruchama had made a cholent, something she does very infrequently, and invited some friends for the main meal on Saturday.

Ruchama spent the early part of the morning in "quiet time" with Shani. Saturday is the only morning that Ruchama is free to spend with her daughter because Sunday is a workday. Consequently, this time is very precious to both of them. In Shani's bedroom, Ruchama sang songs in a low tone to Shani and Shani sang along with some of them.

Before lunch we took a drive to buy some flowers for the house. Because it was the Sabbath, all stores were closed in Netanya, so we drove north to a mall midway between Netanya and Hadera. The mall was not that different from a small mall that one would find in the U.S. It even had a food court with a McDonald's. The difference was that a guard checked each car driving into the mall parking lot and another guard, posted at each mall entrance, checked bags and handbags. At the parking lot entrance, I saw a sign that Ruchama translated for me. It read *bitachon bor*, which means "security hole." Ruchama explained that such a hole in the ground was now common in Israel at mall parking lots. It was used to dispose of suspicious packages that could be bombs. She referred to it simply as the "bomb hole."

We drove back to Netanya along the scenic coastal road. Netanya has a beautiful beach along the Mediterranean that has attracted a lot of development. The beachfront apartment buildings reminded me of some areas along south Florida's Atlantic coast just north of Fort Lauderdale.

Ruchama's friends started arriving around 1:00 P.M., along with her brother Michael, and the meal commenced. She served a delicious variety of Israeli appetizers, such as cooked eggplant, chopped liver, pickled beets, and challah and wine. I could have filled up just from that. But this was followed by cholent and kishke, and finally, chocolate mousse for dessert. This heavy food was delicious, but acted as a sleep-inducing agent. By the time her friends left a few hours later, I could barely keep my eyes open. We all napped until almost evening.

Earlier in the day, I had asked Michael if he would take me to a hardware store. The quartermaster on our base had a warehouse full of tools, but not a single large ax. In clearing the land around the building that housed ammunition, we had encountered a large tree stump. We tried unsuccessfully to cut this down with the small saws they had in the warehouse, but they were inadequate. I wanted to buy a large axe to finish the job and then donate it to the warehouse.

Michael suggested that we go in the evening, when the crowds of shoppers had thinned. The large crowds at the mall on a Saturday afternoon, he noted, made it a potential target for terrorists.

On the way, we talked about Michael's two favorite subjects: cars and sports. Michael is an avid soccer fan and spends his free time following television or radio broadcasts of Israeli soccer matches. He even recently traveled to Cyprus to watch an Israeli team take on one of England's best soccer teams, Manchester United. The European soccer league does not allow any of its teams to play in Israel due to security considerations, so any match against an Israeli team had to be played outside Israel.

Michael also explained why the government provides free bus transportation to soldiers. Up until about ten years ago, soldiers usually hitchhiked to and from their duty stations. When Palestinians started kidnapping and killing isolated, hitchhiking soldiers, especially female ones, the government had to do something. It decreed it a crime for soldiers in uniform to hitchhike and instead offered them free bus transportation. Now I understood the long lines of soldiers waiting for buses for their weekend leaves. Unfortunately, this also means that whenever there is a bus bombing, many of the victims are teenage soldiers traveling to or from their duty stations.

At Netanya's shopping mall, Michael pointed out a guard stand at the entrance where an incident had occurred almost a year ago. The guard had stopped a terrorist who exploded his bomb right there, killing both of them. Not finding a hardware store in the mall, we drove further into Netanya. At the entrance to a hardware store, we were "wanded" by armed guards with a metal detector. The store did not have a large axe, so we returned to Ruchama's apartment empty-handed.

We got back in time to catch the local Israeli news reporting the events of the day. IDF forces in the West Bank had received information about an impending terrorist bombing. They surrounded and arrested the terrorist bomber in Shechem, a city in the West Bank.

I switched to the CNN news, which carried nothing about the arrest of the suicide bomber. Instead, it carried a story about the economic plight of the Palestinians in the West Bank. The background of the story was that Prime Minister Ariel Sharon was trying to shore up his coalition government, after the Labor party had resigned from it, by attempting to induce some right-wing parties to join. The Palestinians viewed this potentially new more hard-line government as boding more trouble for them. The CNN story irked me, with its portrayal of Palestinians as victims and Israelis as oppressors. It seemed one-sided and biased to me because it left out the whole context of the ongoing Intifada. When the previous Israeli prime minister, Ehud Barak, and then-President Clinton had tried to negotiate a peace leading to the withdrawal of Israeli forces from the occupied areas and the establishment of a Palestinian state, the Palestinians rejected the offer and answered it with a wave of violence. This resulted in increasingly hard-line Israeli governments. Here in Netanya, staying with my relatives, I saw the impact that the constant threat of violence had on everyday life.

SUNDAY, NOVEMBER 3, 2002

My cab ride back to the base was uneventful. I showed the guard my army ID, and said in my best Hebrew: "I'm a volunteer with Sar-el at the Batzop base," and he let me in. I felt like I was returning to my home away from home. By now I felt like I fit in at the base and the surroundings were very familiar to me.

Today I was assigned to the "road crew" again. We spent the entire work day, under David's direction, planning and installing an extension of the brick sidewalk we had built the previous week.

The four of us acted as a team in assembly line fashion and by the end of the day we were about 80 percent done. Most of my efforts went into carrying pails of fine sand, mixing cement, and laying the cement around the perimeter of the bricks. It was very hard work, but the weather was warm and sunny and I enjoyed the exercise.

From time to time, one of the officers on the base stopped by to view our progress. This young man wore sunglasses all the time, so you couldn't see his eyes, and always seemed in a rush. He was tall and thin, with a narrow, tanned face and close-cropped curly hair. We called him "Scarface" because of a knife-wound across his left cheek. Scarface would tell us, "The soldiers hate me because I push them. They call me an S.O.B." He was very pleasant to the volunteers though, especially those of us on the road crew, because we worked hard and he could use us to shame his soldiers into working harder. Scarface was especially respectful of David (we now called him "David the Engineer") and occasionally checked in with him as to our need for tools or additional bricks.

After dinner a loud siren suddenly went off. Our madricha came running to inform us that we were having a drill simulating an attack on the base. All the volunteers were ordered into the *moadon* (the recreation room) while the soldiers on guard duty ran through their security routines. We sat there and watched "Friends" with Hebrew subtitles until the "all clear" notice was given.

MONDAY, NOVEMBER 4, 2002

The morning news from our madricha was all negative. She reported that a survey in Israel showed that one out of four Israelis was thinking of leaving the country. Unemployment in Israel continued to rise – it was already at double-digit levels. Finally, Israel had discovered that the Lebanese were dumping sewage into one of the three tributaries originating in Lebanon that feeds into the Jordan River. Through the U.N., Israel had protested this upriver pollution, but expected little help from the international body.

On a lighter note, I learned from my roommate Mike that the military was serious about enforcing its rule against being in the rooms of soldiers of the opposite sex, even the volunteers. He was in his wife's room at about six o'clock yesterday evening and was sitting on her bed talking to her. Our madricha Avigail happened to walk by the open door with the base discipline officer. Afterwards, she took Mike aside and scolded this sixty-year-old for sitting on his wife's bed. Men are not allowed in a woman's room, and vice versa, even if they are husband and wife.

While we were on the subject of fraternization between the sexes, Edith, another volunteer, recounted a funny story. One evening after dinner, she saw a boy and girl, both soldiers, walking hand-in-hand. As they approached his bunk, they stopped and kissed goodbye. He entered the bunk. A few moments later, the girl looked around and, thinking no one saw her, followed him into his bunk. But while breaking military rules by going into a man's bunk, she kissed the *mezuzah* on the doorway as she entered. Military rules could be broken, but religious rules could not!

Work this morning in the quartermaster's warehouse started out with sorting, folding, and storing uniforms. When we finished, Philip and I cleaned guns used by the base sentries. By now I had become very proficient at taking them apart and reassembling them. I could break down an Uzi or assemble one in about fifteen seconds. Cleaning each one, of course, took a lot longer.

As usual, lunch was delicious and I ate too much. Lunch was not only the best meal of the day, it was also the most crowded. At breakfast and dinner the volunteers outnumbered the soldiers, but at lunch, the soldiers greatly outnumbered the volunteers. That was because many of the soldiers lived within commuting distance and were allowed to live off base. Each morning at flag-raising, the presiding officer collected the passes from the commuters that gave them permission to leave at night. Even the commuters, however, had to stay on base when their turn came for nighttime guard duty.

Work in the afternoon was varied, which I liked. Philip and I started by cleaning m-16s. Just as we finished, a truck deposited a large volume of supplies in front of the main warehouse. We spent the rest of the afternoon sorting and storing these supplies in one of the warehouses.

By the end of the afternoon, we were tired but satisfied that we had put in a full day's work. The hardest part for me was washing the kerosene smell off my hands and arms before going to dinner. Despite my best efforts, I was not successful in completely getting rid of the smell.

Late this afternoon, the base commander stopped by to chat with some of the volunteers. In addition to the output of communications equipment (radios, tank helmets, antennae), he seemed pleased with the physical improvements the volunteers had brought about at the base, specifically the gardening and the building of the sidewalks. In an effort to persuade the volunteers to return to his base, the commander promised that he would build new bathroom facilities for our compound.

The commander also asked the volunteers whether they needed anything, and several of them quickly answered: tools. The base was short on tools: the fine tools needed to assemble the strands of wire in the antennae, tools to install the earphones in the tank helmets, gardening tools, and tools for sidewalk construction. Many of the tools on the base were very old or refurbished; Israelis don't throw anything away. The commander promised to purchase more tools.

After dinner, we heard a rumor that there had been another Palestinian suicide bombing that day. So we all crowded into the television room to learn that a Palestinian had set off a bomb in a shopping mall in Kfar Saba, killing one person and injuring twenty. Kfar Saba is a town just northeast of Tel Aviv, about twenty miles directly north of our base.

The news also reported that an Israeli helicopter had blown up a car carrying a leading Hamas terrorist leader today in the West Bank. The Palestinians, of course, protested the attack. But

Israel has a right to go after the terrorists proactively – or else they end up killing Israeli civilians, as they did today in Kfar Saba.

TUESDAY, NOVEMBER 5, 2002

Avigail provided three items of news at our 7:45 A.M. meeting. The Kfar Saba terrorist bombing had now claimed two lives and left nineteen wounded. The two people killed were a seventeen-year-old boy, who was buying a birthday present for his mother, and the security guard who stopped the terrorist. Both were recent immigrants from Argentina. The military declared a high state of alert in the central portion of the West Bank, having received a tip about impending terrorist activity. And Prime Minister Sharon had cobbled together a new coalition government by getting some small rightist parties to join his coalition, so it looked like his government had survived the walkout of the Labor party.

Flag-raising was special for the volunteers today. As a "thank you" to the volunteers, two of them were chosen to raise the flag. Reggie and Bracha, two of our female volunteers, were thrilled to raise the flag and then, together with the two presiding officers, salute it.

We were working in the quartermaster's area when the skies darkened suddenly, thunder rolled, and it started to rain. Then it started to pour. The smell of the rain falling onto dry desert-like land was delicious. At first, the soldiers smiled and some of them danced outside in the rain. Then when the downpour intensified, everyone began to worry about the water, which leaked through the roofs of a number of workplaces.

Elena told me that this was the first major rain in nine months, since the rainy season last January/February. Since it rains so infrequently, the Israelis are not prepared for it. They have no umbrellas or raincoats. As the downpour continued, the gutters on top of the quartermaster's main warehouse overflowed and the water streamed past the warehouse. Elena, René, and I worked furiously with squeegees to push the water downhill from the entrance and succeeded in keeping the water out of the warehouse.

Then, suddenly, as if on cue, the rain stopped at noon and we were able to walk to lunch.

On the way back from lunch, I made a point of checking the brickwork we had laid adjacent to one of the guard stations. At the edge of the brickwork, David the Engineer had designed a cement channel to direct water away from the guard station to the road. It had worked just as planned and I felt a great deal of satisfaction in this.

By 1:00, the heavy downpour returned and we retreated indoors. Many of the volunteer crews could not work – the gardening crew, the road crew, the battery-testing crew, even the helmet painting crew (due to the smell of the oil-based paint, this work had to take place outside). Then, again suddenly, the rain stopped and the outdoor work resumed.

Even during the downpour, David the Engineer had found a way to be constructive. He went around the various warehouse rooms to look for leaks. He marked each leak with chalk on the ceiling. After the rain stopped, he climbed onto the roof and repaired each one. It was slippery work because the roof was still wet.

This morning, Mike and Alex the quartermaster went to Ramle to buy needed tools for the volunteers' work. The base commander had agreed to fund the cost of new tools, however, the IDF ended up getting tools for free. One of our volunteers had brought money donated by some of her friends in San Diego. The money was originally supposed to go to a needy Israeli soldier but she agreed to use the money to pay for the tools. It was just enough to cover the cost. One of our group's lasting impacts, in addition to the work we had done, was ensuring that future groups of volunteers would have better tools than we had.

After dinner, Elena gave us a presentation on the 1973 Yom Kippur War. She emphasized that the Israelis were ill prepared for the surprise Egyptian–Syrian attack on the most holy of Jewish holidays. As a result, almost 3,000 Israeli soldiers were killed, a catastrophic number for such a small country.* Even though Israel eventually defeated Egypt and Syria, Prime Minister Golda Meir and Defense Minister Moshe Dayan were blamed for the country's being completely surprised by the attack. Dayan resigned his position and Golda Meir was defeated in the next election, after which she retired from politics.

Elena's presentation struck a surprisingly resonant chord with me. At seventeen, I had wanted to spend a summer in Israel, but my parents opposed the plan because they were afraid that I would decide to stay in Israel. I always wondered whether my parents had been correct in their assumption. If they had let me go and if I had remained in Israel, I would have been in the third year of required service in the Israeli army at the outbreak of the war. I wondered whether I would have survived the Yom Kippur War or if I would have been one of its many casualties.

A number of volunteers from our original group were leaving tomorrow, including two of my bunkmates, Don and Herb. I was sorry to see them go. The four of us had gotten along well together, despite the potential friction that can arise from living in cramped quarters. We all had pretty easy-going temperaments and had been considerate of each other's needs and feelings. We enjoyed our nightly discussions, sharing our experiences and observations. And we were all serious about getting the work done – that's why we were here.

WEDNESDAY, NOVEMBER 6, 2002

Yesterday's rain brought cooler weather, at least at night. This made for a chilly morning shower. The news at our morning meeting with Avigail was chilly too. She reported that overnight all roads to Ben-Gurion Airport had been blocked, based on information of a possible terrorist attack there. And in fact, Israeli security forces captured three terrorists on the highway near the airport.

---

* This is roughly equivalent to a country the size of the U.S. losing 350,000 soldiers.

Fortunately, Don and Herb were not planning to leave until after the awards ceremony this evening.

At flag-raising, the volunteers were again chosen to raise the flag. This time two other volunteers, Sara and Carol, did the honors and were very excited about it.

Carol had been interviewing Israeli soldiers as part of a project for her cultural anthropology class. Today, she interviewed a soldier named Yochanan, who had immigrated to Israel from Ethiopia as a young child. He and his family came to Israel as part of Operation Solomon, a 36-hour airlift rescue to Israel of over 14,000 of Ethiopia's Jews during the civil war there in 1991. Yochanan told her that his parents had never seen a plane before and were afraid to board it because of the noise it made. In fact, they had lived in such a remote mountainous part of the Gondar region of Ethiopia that, upon the first visit of an Israeli to their village, they were astounded to learn that not all Jews were black.

Alex was on vacation today and so Elena was in charge of the quartermaster's warehouse. It turned out to be a very hectic day there. The army unit stationed at the Batzop base would be traveling north tomorrow for a day-long trip and on short notice we had to prepare the necessary supplies. This ran the gamut, from medical packs and water coolers to tables and utensils. It also included handing out guns to the soldiers who would do guard duty while the unit was traveling. Elena handed out the weapons.

In the midst of the pressure of all of these preparations, Elena pulled her back in mid-morning and so was in severe pain for the rest of the day. To minimize her pain, she directed and I lugged supplies. We finished all the preparations and had all of the supplies packed and prepared by 5:00 P.M. Despite her back pain, Elena was very happy at the end of the day. She just heard from her fiancé that he had passed his final exams in officer training school as a pilot in the Israeli air force. Even with a bad back, she made hot mint tea for us to celebrate.

Our awards ceremony took place after dinner. The volunteers

who were departing that night and the next day received a Sar-el certificate of appreciation signed by the base commander, along with a Sar-el tee-shirt, cap, and pin. I said goodbye fondly to my roommates Don and Herb, who headed for Ben-Gurion airport immediately afterwards.

Our final activity of the night was another session of Israeli folk dancing with the same instructor we had before. What made it different this time was that, with some coaxing from the volunteers, some of the soldiers on base joined in. Since they are required to hold onto their weapons at all times, they slung their M-16s over their backs to dance with us. Israeli folk dancing is foreign to these eighteen to twenty-year-olds, because it was more popular in the early days of Israel's statehood. It was hilarious to see them bumping into each other as they good-naturedly joined in with the volunteers.

Upon my return to our bunk, now occupied by only Mike and me, I learned the secret of how to get a good night's sleep on our too-thin mattresses. Don and Herb's empty beds revealed multiple mattresses. That was why they had been able to sleep so soundly! I took one of their mattresses, slipped it under my own, and had a very restful sleep that night.

THURSDAY, NOVEMBER 7, 2002

The army unit that staffed the Batzop base left this morning for a fun trip to Caesaria, a seaside resort famous for its Roman ruins. With the exception of those soldiers chosen to carry weapons and guard the group, the unit was not in uniform. As they boarded the buses in civilian clothes, they looked and acted like a group of high school kids going on a class trip, with the older sergeants and officers looking like their teachers. That was not surprising, given that the great bulk of the soldiers were still teenagers.

Only a small contingent attended flag-raising. The volunteers outnumbered the few remaining soldiers who remained on base after the buses departed. Because most of the army unit had left the base, there was only about an hour's work at the quartermaster's warehouse. After that, I returned to my bunk to get the presents I had bought for Alex and Elena while I was in Israel. I had a Leatherman knife/pliers set for Alex and various Ahava skin products for Elena.

They seemed moved, by both the presents and the thoughts I expressed as I delivered them. I told Elena that she and Alex were good soldiers and that Israel needed more good soldiers like them. I asked her to tell Alex that, since he spoke very little English. She replied that Israel needed more American friends like me and she hoped I would return. Having listened to her pour out her heart about her trials and tribulations in the army and her aspirations in life and with her fiancé, I had tried to give her good advice. In turn, she had plied me with hot mint tea. I felt somewhat fatherly towards her and knew that I would miss her.

Philip finished painting a Sar-el poster that the base commander had requested of him. It was on a 3′ × 3′ piece of plywood, and Philip's rendition of the bright blue and yellow Sar-el emblem was excellent. It would be posted outside the entrance to the volunteers' area and hopefully would be the first thing that future Sar-el volunteers would see when they arrived at their compound in the Batzop base.

Shortly before we left, we had the opportunity to hear from retired General Aharon Davidi, the founder and civilian commander of Sar-el. He was a tall man of seventy-six years with a white beard and ramrod straight posture in his military uniform. General Davidi had been the commander of the Israeli paratroopers and had led the assault on Sharm-el-Sheik (the southernmost point of the Sinai Peninsula) during the Six-Day War. Normally, Israelis refer to their officers by first name, but because of his fame and reputation in Israel, General Aharon Davidi was referred to simply as "Davidi."

General Davidi thanked the volunteers for coming, emphasizing the morale boost our presence provided to Israelis. He described how Sar-el was founded twenty years earlier. At that time, Israel was involved in a war in Lebanon; the PLO, recently forced out of Jordan, had taken up positions in Lebanon and was shelling towns in the north of Israel. The war in Lebanon created an acute labor shortage and Israel put out a call for volunteers throughout the world, primarily to work on its farms. Six hundred and fifty volunteers, mostly from the U.S., answered the call for a minimum two-month stint. At the end of the two months, then-retired Colonel Davidi, with the enthusiastic support of the volunteers, decided to organize Sar-el as an ongoing program. He continued as the civilian head of Sar-el ever since then.

After General Davidi's remarks, we loaded our luggage into the belly of a bus parked adjacent to our compound. Then we mingled outside for a few final, tearful farewells with our madrichas, with Elena, and with each other. A lot of bonding had occurred over the course of three weeks of hard work and living together.

It was tough for me to say goodbye to Elena. I am certain that she had witnessed the departure of other volunteer groups from the base, but over the course of three weeks we had developed a bond of friendship. I gave her a hug and a kiss, and asked her to promise to keep in touch. As the bus pulled away, I saw Elena standing there, alone in the compound, looking forlorn as she waved with one hand and brushed aside tears with the other.

Once we were able to check our luggage at Ben-Gurion Airport and proceed to the El Al gate, we joined up with Gary and Kathy, who had been among the group of twelve volunteers who left our base after the first two weeks. They had spent their third week in Israel driving around the north of the country: Haifa, Safed, Tiberias. At Rosh Hanikra, the northernmost part of Israel along the Mediterranean, they stopped at an army post guarding the border with Lebanon. They were thrilled to see soldiers at the post using radio backpacks with "their" antennae – ones that they had assembled at Batzop.

CHAPTER 2
At Home in Raleigh

Returning home to Raleigh was like entering a different world. I slept away most of the weekend, appreciating more than ever our comfortable bed. When I recovered from the jet lag, I discovered that my Sar-el experience had a beneficial mental and physical impact on me. I returned in a relaxed state that I had not experienced in over a decade. The manual labor had been difficult, but it had cleared my mind of the routine concerns of everyday life. I also came home about ten pounds lighter. While I had eaten like a horse during my stay in Israel, apparently the full days of physical work had burned off more calories than I had consumed.

Getting back to work on Monday was more difficult than I had expected. My colleagues had done a magnificent job of taking care of things in my absence, but it was hard for me to focus on my work. My mind kept wandering back to the Batzop base – to Alex and Elena in the quartermaster's warehouse or to "David the Engineer" and our "road crew." I remembered various conversations I had with soldiers in the mess hall. And I recalled how proud we felt, lining up in our uniforms for flag-raising every morning. These thoughts would flood into my mind, making it difficult to concentrate.

I followed the news in Israel much more closely, reading the *Jerusalem Post* online several times a week. Each terrorist bombing affected me more deeply, making me gloomy on days when the morning radio news carried a report of an attack. This was especially the case when I heard of bus bombings, because I knew that many of the victims were young soldiers like those I got to know at Batzop.

I tried to keep in touch with Elena. She had given me her address in Jerusalem. The letters I sent her were returned "addressee unknown." I worried about her safety because she commuted by bus everyday to the base. I wondered if she had moved back to Belarus with her parents or moved in with her fiancé. There was no way to find out and that frustrated me.

I also kept up with many of my Sar-el colleagues by e-mail. Philip reported that a gang of Muslim teenagers in Holland had physically attacked one of his young daughters. Now he was more determined than ever to move to Israel with his children.

Immediately upon my return, I busied myself with "spreading the word" about Sar-el in Raleigh. I wrote a newspaper article about my Sar-el experience and also gave presentations locally. In response to numerous requests at work, I even gave a lunchtime talk about Sar-el and about life in Israel in general. For many of my work colleagues, my remarks helped to dispel their impression that bombs were blowing up on virtually every street corner in Israel.

II

In early 2003, the Second Gulf War began. The U.S. bombing of Iraq, as a prelude to the American invasion of that country, set off fears that Iraq would respond by firing Scud missiles into Israel, as it had done in the First Gulf War. I read with close interest that Israelis were back to carrying gas masks against the possibility that Iraqi Scuds could contain chemical gas. I wondered how Yael, Ruchama's mother, was taking the heightened tensions over possible Scud attacks. I wrote to Ruchama and wished her and her family well during these anxious times.

The opening invasion of Iraq was accompanied by a quick seizure of the western Iraqi desert, which is the only location from which Scuds could be fired into Israel. In a few short and dramatic days, Iraq was conquered and the threat to Israel of Scud attacks had passed. I learned through my e-mail grapevine that in March, with a call-up of Israeli reserves due to the tensions over Iraq, Sar-el had contacted certain volunteers who had previously indicated their availability to come on short notice. Two of the volunteers in my group had responded.

The Second Gulf War precipitated considerable criticism from Arab nations. Those countries demanded that President Bush intervene to negotiate a solution to the Israeli-Palestinian conflict. In response, on April 30, 2003 President Bush unveiled his "Roadmap for Peace" in the Middle East, developed in coop-eration with Russia, the European Union, and the United Nations. The Roadmap's goal was a two-state solution: Israel existing side-by-side with an independent and democratic Palestinian state.

President Bush's Roadmap for Peace was predicated on both sides making preliminary concessions. Israel would pull out of new settlements established in the West Bank over the previous two years, and Israel would release Palestinian prisoners from their jails. At the same time, the new Palestinian prime minister, Mahmoud Abbas, committed to disarming the Palestinian ter-rorist groups and ceasing all terrorist actions against Israel. The Roadmap was initiated by both sides agreeing to a six-month moratorium on terrorist attacks by the Palestinians and on Israeli military actions against the Palestinians.

Almost from the outset, the Roadmap seemed doomed to failure. Although Israel started to release Palestinian prisoners and to dismantle some West Bank settlements, the level of Palestinian terrorism lessened but did not stop. Prime Minister Abbas an-nounced that, contrary to the terms of the Roadmap, he would take no actions to disarm or dismantle the terrorist groups. In the absence of concrete action to eliminate these terrorist groups, the Roadmap appeared to require Israel to implement its concessions without any implementation of concessions on the Palestinian side. It was obvious that Israel would not countenance a one-sided peace plan. I was not optimistic that the situation would lead to a peaceful resolution.

III

In July, Arlene and I attended a mini-reunion of my former bunkmates and their spouses, hosted by Mike and Elaine at their home in Baltimore. We had a very relaxing weekend at their home, enjoying a traditional Sabbath in their Orthodox Jewish community.

On Saturday night, Mike showed us a short video about Neve Dekalim, the Jewish settlement in Gaza that he supported. While we declined his gentle solicitation for financial support for that community, I respected his commitment to the Neve Dekalim settlement. Unlike Mike, I supported a pull-out of the Israeli settlements from Gaza, because the logistics of defending 7,500 people living in the midst of over a million hostile Palestinians was militarily untenable. Mike knew my views from our days as bunkmates and did not try to engage me in a political debate.

They had also invited about a dozen Sar-el veterans, who were members of their congregation, to join us later that evening. It was very interesting to learn about their experiences on other Israeli military bases. Listening to their stories made me more eager than ever to plan another trip to Israel.

My plans were complicated, however, by a change in my job situation. A promotion in August put me in charge of a much larger group of people at my company, half of whom were in Philadelphia and half in Research Triangle Park, North Carolina. This required me to commute every week between the two locations. Learning the basics of my new job responsibilities would also require a lot of time, making it hard to get away for a three-week stretch in Israel.

IV

The U.S.-sponsored Roadmap for Peace was dealt a fatal blow in August 2003. First, Prime Minister Abbas' refusal to dismantle the terrorist organizations allowed them to re-arm and prepare new actions. In August, a massive bombing of a double-decker bus in Jerusalem by a Palestinian suicide bomber killed twenty Israelis and wounded over a hundred. The bus was leaving the area of the Western Wall loaded with religious families, so many of the victims were children. Hamas took credit for the attack. The bombing triggered the inevitable Israeli response – the killing of Hamas leaders. The Palestinians charged that Israel had broken the ceasefire and therefore they would no longer honor it either. They did not acknowledge that the bus bombing of innocent civilians, for which Hamas took credit, had precipitated the Israeli retaliation.

A second blow to the Roadmap for Peace occurred in September. Yasir Arafat refused to place the Palestinian military under the command of Abbas' military head, Mohammad Dahlan. Instead, Arafat named a new military head, loyal only to himself, to ensure that Abbas would take no action against the terrorists. Without any true control, Abbas submitted his resignation. Arafat completed "cleaning house" by replacing a number of cabinet members with his own cronies. With these changes, it was clear that Arafat had rejected the U.S.–sponsored Roadmap for Peace in favor of his continued support for terrorism.

A series of suicide bombings followed. On one September day, two bombings took place, one in Ariel and the other in Rosh Ha-Ayin. I called my cousins Menachem and Bracha in Rosh Ha-Ayin to see if they were okay. Menachem told me that they were fine, but that the bombing in a grocery store around the corner from their home had killed an Israeli father who had gone there to buy milk for his children. Although I was relieved that my cousins were unscathed, my frustration grew with each report of a new terrorist bombing.

V

The massive Jerusalem bus bombing and the Rosh Ha-Ayin bombing near my cousins' home affected me like the 2002 Passover massacre in Netanya. I resolved that I had to do something to help.

My new work schedule was such that I could only identify two weeks that I could reserve for a "vacation" to Israel in the latter part of 2003. I contacted Sar-el's Pamela Lazarus and told her that I could only offer her a two-week stint. Pamela responded that, although three weeks was preferred, they would be happy to take me for only two. I sent her my registration materials and booked my flight on El Al.

In the meantime, the Palestinian violence continued. In early October, on the eve of Yom Kippur, a female suicide bomber blew herself up in a crowded restaurant in the port city of Haifa, killing nineteen and injuring sixty. Haifa has a long tradition of peaceful relations between Arab and Jewish residents. What was particularly ironic about this bombing was that the restaurant co-owner was a Lebanese Arab and many of the victims of the bombing were Arabs as well. The victims also included a number of young children. Rather than worrying about Israel from a distance, I increasingly felt the need to be there.

CHAPTER 3

On the Border of Gaza

October 30–November 12, 2003

THURSDAY, OCTOBER 30, 2003

It was hectic at work in the morning, as I tried to tie up loose ends. I had arrived at my Philadelphia office at 6:00 A.M. because I knew there was much to do before leaving in the early afternoon to catch a plane to New York. By the time I arrived at the El Al counter at JFK Airport, however, thoughts about my work had receded in my consciousness and I started to relax.

Work seemed far away as the El Al "interrogator" put me through her series of questions:

Q. Do you speak Hebrew?

Q. Where did you study it? Why?

Q. What are your plans in Israel? Do you have relatives there?

Q. Describe your Sar-el program. What did you do the last time you did this program?

I told her that at my base last year I cleaned rifles, laid brick sidewalks around sentry posts, and repaired tank crew helmets. After this answer, she softened her tone and apologized for having to ask me further questions about Sar-el, my luggage, and my family in Israel.

Two El Al flights were leaving for Tel Aviv within two hours of each other, so the terminal was filled with the sound of Hebrew. To test my beginner's skills, I strained to understand snippets of the conversations around me. In addition to Hebrew and English, many passengers spoke Russian.

I noticed an El Al employee walking through the passenger waiting area. Her eyes were on the luggage, looking for any unattended baggage or any suspicious-looking packages. She even inspected the public pay phone kiosks, checking under the seats to make sure nothing was taped to them.

As we settled down in the plane, the on-screen television displayed pictures of nature, with quiet music in the background. The scenes were of Machtesh Ramon (Ramon Crater), Israel's equivalent to the Grand Canyon. The crater floor resembled the surface of the moon. It reminded me of the time our family toured Machtesh Ramon. My son David was the only one in our tour group able to identify the 300-million-year-old fossil that the guide had picked off the crater surface while we were walking. We were very proud of him for this.

FRIDAY, OCTOBER 31, 2003

After eight hours of flying time and at most an hour's sleep, I woke up at 9:00 A.M. (Israeli time). What woke me was the smell of warm bagels being served as part of breakfast. We were over the heel of Italy, about two hours from Ben-Gurion Airport.

Over breakfast, I watched a particularly funny episode of the television sitcom "Frasier." Frasier and Lilith's son was preparing for his bar mitzvah. Frasier decided to make a speech in Hebrew from the pulpit to conclude the bar mitzvah service, though he did not understand a word of Hebrew. To retaliate against Frasier, a co-worker fed him the wrong speech, so Frazier spoke to his son in "Klingon" (a Star Trek language) instead. I recall seeing this episode previously, but it was even funnier watching it surrounded by a plane full of people who spoke Hebrew.

Our smooth landing at Ben-Gurion Airport was welcomed by the applause of the passengers. As the passengers from our plane queued up in the passport control lines, I noticed that about three-quarters went to the lines for Israeli citizens while the remainder went to the "foreign" lines. The small percentage of passengers from our plane in the "foreign" lines was indicative of the dearth of tourists visiting Israel these days. Most of the passengers were returning Israelis.

I took a taxi to Bracha and Menachem's house in Rosh Ha-Ayin, my first destination in Israel. They welcomed me warmly, but I could tell from Bracha's face that she was unhappy. And it did not take long for her to explain why. Her older son, Amit, had moved his family to Maryland several years ago to work in the diamond business. Now, her younger son, Itay, had just announced that he was leaving his law practice in Ramat Gan, on the outskirts of Tel Aviv, to take a job in Charlotte, North Carolina. Bracha was not happy about her sons "deserting" her, and there was not much I could say to give her solace. It would be sad for her to be so far from her children and grandchildren.

Itay, his wife Liat, and three-month-old son, Omer, joined us for a beautiful Sabbath dinner, along with Bracha's father, Nathan. I was especially glad to meet Nathan, who was a first cousin of my father and had grown up with him in Poland. In 1939, Nathan was deported from the Soviet-held part of Poland to Siberia and eventually found his way to Soviet Central Asia. He met and married Bracha's mother, a Bukharian Jew, in Uzbekistan. The family immigrated to Israel in the early 1950s. Since Nathan only spoke Hebrew and Yiddish, our conversations were assisted by Itay. Nevertheless, he was happy and talkative; Itay could barely keep up. His pet peeve was the *Haredim*, ultra-Orthodox Jews who refused to serve in the Israeli army. I agreed with him that exempting the Orthodox from military service did not seem fair, since they too were protected by and benefited from the State of Israel.

Itay and Liat had lots of questions about North Carolina, and I tried to respond to them all. Neither of them had ever been to Charlotte. Omer was a very cute baby with big, expressive eyes. His parents and grandparents doted on him, passing him from lap to lap throughout the meal.

Liat asked me about Sar-el. Like most Israelis, she hadn't heard of it before. When I explained what its volunteers do, Itay joked that I had joined the ranks of the *miluim*, Israel's army reservists. I denied this, since the reservists serve a mandatory four weeks of military duty every year, while I was just an unarmed volunteer working on military bases. In response, Itay dubbed it "mini-miluim" instead. Nathan commented that, to volunteer in Sar-el, I must be an idealist like my father, which I accepted as a compliment.

Much like her mother-in-law, Liat was a very level-headed young woman and she and Bracha got along extremely well. She came from a politically prominent Israeli family. Her grandmother had been the head of Meretz, one of the leftist political parties, and a member of the Israeli cabinet. Liat had spent a year in Newport, Rhode Island as a teenager and so her English was very good. Prior to the birth of Omer, she worked in the advertising business in Tel Aviv. She had planned to return to that job shortly, with her mother and Bracha splitting the child care duties. However, upon their move to Charlotte early next year, she was resigned to giving up her professional career to stay at home with Omer.

Itay and Liat's impending move to the U.S. was not the only change in the family's situation. Menachem had left his CarMax-like company a month ago and had been staying home while he prepared for his next venture. Ever the optimistic and energetic entrepreneur, he planned to start yet another new company in Israel.

About the only person who was not in a changing situation was Bracha. When I had visited last year, she was just starting as the director of a boarding home in Tel Aviv for at-risk children who could not live with their parents. I could see that by the end of the week, she was exhausted from the long hours she devoted to her job. Even though the school's assistant director lived at the school, Bracha frequently received after-hour calls that required her to drive back to Tel Aviv to take care of emergencies.

Bracha was also tired because she had been preparing all week for a Saturday afternoon party for about thirty of their friends from their monthly singing group. Every few months this group of friends had a Saturday afternoon party, rotating at different homes. Tomorrow was Bracha and Menachem's turn. Bracha had been preparing all the food in the Bukharian style she had learned from her mother. Bukharian Jews are known in Israel for their colorful woven yarmulkes (which are also popular in the U.S.; my son David has one) and for their special, spicy meat and rice dishes. While Bracha enjoys cooking, the food preparation, combined with her heavy workload at the school, was a burden for her. Liat promised to arrive early Saturday morning to help her set up for the party.

SATURDAY, NOVEMBER 1, 2003

True to her word, Liat arrived at 8:00 A.M. with Itay, Omer, and Grandpa Nathan in tow to help prepare for the party. By the time I got up, tables and chairs had already been set up for the expected guests. To get the men out of the way of the food preparation, it was suggested that Menachem, Itay, and Nathan take me to the sea to show me the marina in Herzliya. We walked along the new and beautiful boardwalk, one of only three such boardwalks in Israel on the Mediterranean, and admired the boats anchored in the marina. After a light lunch at the boardwalk's restaurant, we walked through part of the adjacent mall. The mall was not crowded because many of its stores were closed for the Sabbath. All the entrances to the boardwalk, restaurant, and mall were manned by armed security guards who wanded each entrant for weapons and explosives. The Israelis seemed to take this security in stride, since it was normal everywhere. In fact, my guess is they would be uncomfortable if the guards were not there.

By the time we returned, Menachem and Bracha's friends had already started to arrive. Bracha's Bukharian foods were a big hit, especially her desserts. I spent a good deal of the time talking with Gadi, whom I had met when I visited last November. Gadi worked in the business development side of the medical devices industry and was very well traveled. His English was excellent and I was interested in hearing his opinions on the two favorite subjects of Israeli conversations – the Palestinians and the Israeli economy. Although the Oslo peace talks had failed, he still believed that a political resolution could be reached along the lines of the deal that President Clinton and Prime Minister Ehud Barak proposed in 2000. As for the creation of an independent (and non-belligerent) Palestinian state, he felt this was not possible until Arafat left the political scene. On the second subject, he was optimistic that the improvement in the worldwide economy, especially in the U.S. and Europe, would help to alleviate Israel's currently suffering economy (11 percent unemployment). However, he acknowledged that tourism, a major part of the Israeli economy, would not fully recover until the violence of the Palestinian Intifada ended.

I asked Gadi whether the Israel population had changed its behavior in response to the Palestinian terrorism. He talked about the security precautions in place, but said it was very important to Israelis that terrorists not "win," in the sense of making Israelis live in constant fear. It was important for them to maintain their normal lifestyle. They still took public buses and visited shopping malls. Gadi believed that, in order to maintain their sense of normalcy, Israelis compared the risk of a terrorist incident to that of a traffic accident. Since Israelis do not live in fear of traffic accidents, they do not live in fear of the bombings. Gadi's explanation was a plausible one, but I'm not so sure that all Israelis would agree with his assessment.

When the guests had left and the dishes and pots were cleaned, Bracha suggested that we all settle down for the traditional (but later than usual) Sabbath nap. I woke up at 7:30 P.M. refreshed from my nap and finally felt acclimated to Israeli time.

Menachem and Bracha were already up and watching the television news. The Israeli news reported that the European Union had just released its list of the most dangerous places to visit. Israel topped the list, followed by North Korea, Iraq, and Iran. The U.S. was lower down on the list. Immediately afterwards, the news showed footage of the actual shooting of a Los Angeles lawyer by his client outside a California courthouse. Apparently, the client was unhappy with the estate work that the lawyer had performed and decided to kill the lawyer. Menachem commented on the irony of this juxtaposition – how the Europeans perceived Israel to be a dangerous place, while the Israelis watching the television news perceived the U.S. to be a dangerous place.

Soon we were ready for our evening plans – a visit to Bracha's brother Mickey in Kfar Saba. Located about twelve miles northeast of Tel Aviv, Kfar Saba is a city of about 75,000 people. During the Six-Day War, Kfar Saba suffered attacks from the neighboring Arab city of Qalqilya – located less than five miles away. Kfar Saba continues to be a target of Palestinian terrorist attacks, such as the one during my Sar-el stint the previous year.

Driving out of his neighborhood, Menachem pointed out the grocery store around the corner from his home where a suicide bomber had killed one Israeli and wounded six others this past summer. Menachem had been driving in the neighborhood that day, had spotted the smoke from the explosion, and called Bracha to check on her. He speculated that the reason that the terrorist had targeted Rosh Ha-Ayin was the ease of entry; the major east-west road from the West Bank connects with a major north-south highway just north of Rosh Ha-Ayin at an Israeli Arab village called Kfar Quesen. The Israeli Arabs in this village were friendly with Israeli Jews and Menachem knew many of them from shopping there. Nevertheless, the terrorist had traveled from the West Bank and stopped at Kfar Quesen before proceeding to Rosh Ha-Ayin.

We arrived at Mickey's house after a twenty-minute drive and were met outside the house by a huge German shepherd. He recognized Bracha and Menachem, and so let us proceed to the front door. I later learned that this dog, named Boxey, was actually very friendly and gentle, and was only aggressive when it came to cats. I liked the dog instantly.

Mickey and his wife, Orna, greeted us at the door. Orna introduced me to three of their children: Effi, Omri, and Elona. Their oldest daughter, Sharon, lived nearby with her husband and two children. Effi, a beautiful dark-eyed young woman with long, black curly hair, was studying to be a lawyer; she introduced me to her husband, an officer in the Israeli border guard. Their son Omri, at seventeen, was four months away from commencing his army service, where he intended to join the intelligence branch of the military. In doing so, he would be following in his father's footsteps. Mickey had risen to the rank of lieutenant colonel in the Israeli military intelligence before he retired.

I instantly regretted having forgotten to bring my camera. Mickey bore a remarkable resemblance to my deceased father, which was not surprising given that his father Nathan and my father were first cousins. It was strange sitting next to him while we spoke. I felt like I was sitting next to a version of my father at my current age; (Mickey and I were both fifty). Not only was Mickey's appearance and build similar to my father's, so were his mannerisms. I had an instant flashback to the scene in the movie *Field of Dreams*, in which the main character had the opportunity to play catch with an image of his deceased father as a young man.

Mickey was the first Israeli civilian I met who already knew about Sar-el. He said he had heard about it on television and knew that a lot of people participated in this program. He explained it to Orna, who responded with a warm *Kol ha-kavod!* – a Hebrew expression that roughly means "Bravo!"

After talking for a while, Mickey pulled out the family tree chart that my brother Robert had compiled and sent to our relatives in 1990. From that chart, Mickey showed his family how he and I were related. We both agreed that Robert needed to update the chart to include the children born since 1990.

Afterwards, we watched a special moment on Israeli television. It was a commemoration of the eighth anniversary of the assassination of Prime Minister Yitzchak Rabin. To honor Rabin, a gathering had been announced in the Tel Aviv square where he had spoken at a peace rally in 1995. Immediately following his speech, Rabin had been killed by an Israeli religious zealot.

I had last seen this square, now re-named Rabin Square, with my wife on Christmas Day of 2001. The tour guide pointed out the modest memorial plaque marking the spot of the assassination. Directly across from the square was a giant poster with an American flag, expressing Israel's support for the U.S. three months after the attack on the World Trade Center and the Pentagon. It read:

SEPTEMBER 11 – THREE MONTHS AFTER
WE'RE STILL WITH YOU

I recall comparing this Israeli show of solidarity for Americans, struggling to recover from this traumatic attack, with the Palestinian reaction to the same event. Immediately following the September 11 attack, the news media broadcast the scene of thousands of Palestinians dancing for joy in the streets of Gaza City to celebrate the deaths of so many Americans. As the Palestinians paraded in the streets, they held aloft pictures of Bin Laden. Arafat was embarrassed over the fact that this spontaneous celebration revealed the Palestinian hatred towards America and identification with Al-Qaeda. He had his security force clamp down to halt this exhibition of glee and warned news cameramen not to film it.

Now, crowded together with Mickey's family on their living

room sofa, we watched the somber television broadcast as tens of thousands of people crammed into Rabin Square to hear speeches and songs honoring Yitzchak Rabin. We heard Rabin's daughter speak, as well as former Prime Minister Shimon Peres. David Broza sang a song about peace, followed by Aviv Geffen singing the song he had sung at the peace rally the night Rabin was killed. It was very emotional for the crowd. As the television panned the people in the square, you could see that many young people were crying. Menachem explained that, in life, Rabin had not been popular with younger Israelis, but in death, Rabin had become very popular with this generation because he died for his pursuit of peace. Watching a video of Rabin just before he was killed at the peace rally heightened the emotion of the crowd. A moment of silence in Rabin Square was also observed in Mickey's home at the end of the commemoration. Rabin had been very much respected in both Bracha's and Mickey's families.

SUNDAY, NOVEMBER 2, 2003

The morning began with a 5:30 A.M. wakeup. Before leaving with Menachem, I promised Bracha that I would try to find people in Charlotte to reach out to Itay's family once they moved to the U.S.

We dropped my luggage off at Menachem's fitness club, changed, and drove towards the Mediterranean. By the sea, we walked briskly from the northern Tel Aviv beach up the coast to Herzliya and back. Menachem greeted passers-by, as he was familiar with the weekday society of exercise enthusiasts along the beach. He was clearly in his element. After our walk, we did push-ups and sit-ups at the edge of the water. Then, characteristic of his high energy level, Menachem and a swimming buddy swam out into the sea for 500 yards and back. I passed on the swimming. The final part of his routine was a shot of vodka with his swimming and walking partners in the parking lot at the beach. Then we returned to his club to shower. Menachem and his buddies sang together as they shaved and showered. They clearly enjoyed life.

Menachem got one of his friends from the fitness club to

drive me to the Sar-el office in Jaffa. It was located in a non-descript, circa-1930s building on Jaffa's main boulevard. The front door of the antiquated and unmarked building was locked, with a note to walk around the corner to the back door. The back entrance was guarded by two armed soldiers. Upon showing my passport, I was invited in to meet a smiling Pamela Lazarus, who was very busy making arrangements for all of the volunteers who were arriving that day.

Pamela introduced me to Etty, the nineteen-year-old madricha in charge of my group of ten volunteers. Etty (short for Esther) had beautiful green eyes that matched the color of her uniform. She had been selected as a madricha because of her intelligence and her fluency in English. Later in the day, I came to appreciate her responsiveness to the volunteers' needs and resourcefulness in solving problems.

A number of other volunteers were admitted through the back entrance, at which point Etty gathered us together to tell us where we would be going. We were assigned to a base called Zikim, which is the biblical word for lightning. Zikim was a very large base south of Ashkelon, about 200 yards north of the Gaza Strip. It functioned as a boot camp for new recruits in the Israeli army. The base housed between one and two thousand soldiers at any one time, divided into eight companies. Seven are always going through basic training, while the eighth – called *mifkadah* or headquarters – was the only permanent company, providing logistical support for the base. We would be assigned to work in the logistical support company.

We all crowded into a beat-up van and headed south. Along the way, we dropped off two Sar-el volunteers at the Batzop base in Ramle, where I had volunteered the previous year. As we drove through Batzop, I proudly pointed out to my volunteer colleagues the brick sidewalks we had laid the previous year around the sentry posts. And I noticed that Philip's Sar-el sign still graced the entrance to the volunteers' compound, albeit somewhat faded by the sun.

We made one more stop on the way. Etty had been in touch with the base by cell phone and had learned that the army had no pillows for the volunteers' bunks. So we stopped at a mall along the way, located a Cosmos (the Israeli equivalent of WalMart) and purchased beautiful down pillows and pillowcases for a bargain price of $5 per bed.

After a two-hour ride south into an area of desert sand dunes, we reached Zikim. It was a nearly treeless base with numerous low, block-like buildings in the middle of a desert wilderness. As we drove in, we saw groups of soldiers marching or running to their sergeants' cadence calls. It was a base with a high energy level, generated by the new recruits.

Etty brought us to a meeting with the base officer in charge of the volunteers, Karine, a pretty but no-nonsense young woman. She pointed out the rules of the base – how to act at flag-raising, how to dress during the day (always in uniform), etc. Karine assigned us to three types of jobs: warehouse supply, weapons cleaning in the armory, and kitchen duty. I drew warehouse supply for the next morning's assignment. Karine also warned us that the new recruits would be conducting war games at night or marching to their own loud cadence calls. Finally, she noted that occasionally an announcement of a *hakpatzah* would be made, an "alert" simulating an attack on the base. In that event, we were to rush to the nearest building while the soldiers went through their simulation assignments. We were to stay inside and keep our heads below window level until the all-clear signal was given.

Karine also addressed any concerns the volunteers might have in being so close to the Gaza Strip. She pointed out that although we were only 200 yards from the northern edge of the Gaza Strip, the northern tip of the "Strip" was occupied by some small Jewish settlements. Gaza City, which is the main Palestinian population center of the Strip, was about a five-minute car ride away. From the base watchtower, one could see the lights of Gaza City in this flat, sandy terrain. She assured us we were in no danger, surrounded by barbed wire and guard stations, and accompanied by eight companies of Israeli soldiers, albeit mostly trainees.

Warming up a bit, Karine told us how much our presence benefited the base, because it served to improve the morale of the soldiers on the base to see volunteers from other countries working to support Israel. Moreover, each volunteer on the base replaced a soldier from the *miluim* (army reserves) from being called up. Not only did it allow the reservist to stay home with his family and stay on his job, it also saved the Israeli army the cost of calling up a reservist.

After lunch, the afternoon was filled with logistical work – picking out our uniforms and hauling mattresses and chests of drawers to the volunteers' residence area, which had not previously been set up for volunteers. We were soon drenched with sweat in the heat of the desert afternoon. We were housed in small un-air-conditioned cabins, each with two 10' × 12' rooms, with three or four volunteers assigned to a room. It was crowded, but tolerable. Our cabins were at the very back (southern) edge of the base. About twenty yards behind the cabins was a barbed wire fence with occasional watchtowers and beyond the fence were large sand dunes (over twenty feet high) for about 200 yards, separating the camp from the border with the Gaza Strip. That border had a double-electrified fence and was heavily guarded by a separate unit of the Israeli army.

We still had it better than the recruits, who lived in large tents crammed with cots. After dinner, we settled into our bunks to unpack, listening to the tramp-tramp of units going through their paces outside our window. The watchtower just outside our cabin occasionally flashed its big spotlight in the direction of the Gaza Strip as units of soldiers headed into the sand dunes on night exercises.

I showed my two bunkmates how to get rid of the mosquitoes in our room, using a technique I learned on last year's Sar-el stint. Turning on the fluorescent ceiling light at night highlighted the mosquitoes against the white walls and ceilings. This made them easy targets to swat with a newspaper or magazine. Once the mosquitoes were eradicated, the door had to stay shut, except when people entered or exited the room.

Although my room held two double-decker beds for four, only three volunteers (including me) were assigned to it. Mike Perloff was a fifty-seven-year-old public school teacher from Cherry Hill, New Jersey. Active in local Jewish civic activities and well connected to local police enforcement organizations, Mike had been on two Sar-el stints prior to this one. The thing that made this one unique was that it marked his retirement from a long teaching career.

The same was true for my second bunkmate, Rob Fuller. He had just retired at age sixty-two from his job in a New Zealand electric power company. (Accordingly, he eyed the twin smoke stacks of the Ashkelon power plant, just north of us, with interest and curiosity.) Because of his active lifestyle, Rob was in excellent physical condition – undoubtedly in better shape than any of the other volunteers. He and his wife Elsie were two of the three Christian volunteers in our group.

Rob and Elsie were also notable for another reason. They participated in a New Zealand free hostel system for the many Israeli youths who typically take a year to travel after their army service. For many years, they opened their home for free to young Israelis traveling through New Zealand. Although already a committed supporter of Israel, Rob said he volunteered for Sar-el because he wanted to do something to support Israel besides getting angry at "the rubbish they broadcast about Israel on the BBC." This was his second Sar-el stint, but the first time that Elsie had come with him. They planned to spend an extended time in Israel after their three weeks in Sar-el, visiting with various Israeli families who insisted on reciprocating for their hospitality to their sons and daughters.

Rob's reason for volunteering went deeper than simply an angry response to the anti-Israel bias of the BBC news. It was based on his deep religious principles and his study of the history of Christianity. "For almost 2,000 years, terrible things have been done to Jews by Christians under the banner of religion," he explained. "In fact, using religion as an excuse for killing Jews was a corruption of the true principles of Christianity, which is a religion of peace. I'm here to atone for the crimes that have been committed against Jews in the name of my religion."

His remarks took me back to Bruce, the grandson of a Nazi SS officer, who had volunteered at Batzop last year to atone for his grandfather's crimes against Jews during the Holocaust. While Rob's motivation was also atonement, it was not for persecution committed by a family member. It was a more general atonement for all Christians throughout history who had massacred Jews in the name of their religion. I was deeply moved by the moral basis of his faith. Rob also impressed me with his ability to cite chapter and verse of the Bible, finding passages applicable to every situation we encountered.

MONDAY, NOVEMBER 3, 2003

My alarm went off at 5:30 A.M. It wasn't necessary. At 4:45 the troops in basic training were awakened and by 5:00, the non-commissioned officers (i.e., sergeants) began to drill their units. The sergeants barked out their orders and their units shouted out responses in unison. The most commonly shouted out order was *Chamesh Shniah!* – an ungrammatical command that loosely translates as "Five-second warning!" or "Be ready to receive your commander in five seconds!" The volunteers' bunks were squeezed between Company Eight (men) and a women's company, so we enjoyed the stereo "surround sound" of shouted orders from both units. Sleep was impossible once the drilling commenced.

Stepping outside the bunk door, I was greeted by a shivering small brown Chihuahua-type dog sitting in front of the volunteers' bunks. By 6:45, the soldier trainees took a break next to their tents for coffee, bread and *loof* (which is canned beef equivalent to American Spam, but kosher). The dog sat nearby hoping for some scraps. The Chihuahua and a second larger dog were rewarded with the bottom of the *loof* cans to lick clean. (This was appropriate, given that *loof* looks and tastes like dog food.) The volunteers later named the larger camp dog "Colonel Be-seder"; *be-seder* is Hebrew for "everything's O.K." or "in order."

Breakfast consisted of hard-boiled eggs, cheese, bread, carrots, red peppers, and olives. We were warned that dinner would be the same food. Even though I don't normally eat hard-boiled eggs or cheese, I ate them now because I needed the protein.

Walking to our first flag-raising, Etty explained that all of the trainee soldiers were required to have six hours of sleep daily; therefore their commanders mandated that the trainees went to bed early. Each tent was required during the six hours of sleep time to post a guard, who rotated hourly. The sixth guard each night woke up his tent at 4:45 and the soldiers had to be ready in fifteen minutes for drills.

Flag-raising was a little different than at the Batzop base. Because Zikim was such a large base, flag-raising was done separately by each company. We joined the logistics company, since we would be working with them. Unlike at Batzop, the men and women stood separately from each other. We were ordered in Hebrew: *Adom noach!* (At ease!) and *Adom dom!* (Attention!), and then the flag was raised by a soldier. Afterwards, Karine, the deputy company commander, made a few announcements. One announcement informed the company that the group of volunteers lined up behind them had arrived to work on the base. Karine encouraged the soldiers to help us with our work and to talk with us, practicing their English. She also asked them to make sure the volunteers drank enough water.

Etty then took us to our work assignments. I was assigned to the *machson*, the warehouse, which was actually a complex of several large warehouses. I worked with Ben, a young soldier who liked to play American oldies music very loudly on his radio, especially Madonna and Motown. That was fine with me. Together with Sam, a volunteer from Harrisburg, Pennsylvania, we worked on various warehousing jobs – stacking forms, packing sleeping bags, and sweeping the floors.

Lunch was the first meal we ate apart from the seven trainee companies. Instead of eating in the main dining area with the trainee companies, we joined the logistics company in their separate (and nicer) dining area. It was nicer because the plates were ceramic instead of plastic and cleaner, the tables were already set with side dishes, and there were napkins available. After lunch break, we continued the warehouse work. I found myself drinking much more water than I normally do because of the hot desert weather.

Shortly before 4:00, the volunteers gathered together to receive our distinctive blue-and-white striped Sar-el patches for our epaulettes and then to meet the base commander, Eyal; (Israeli soldiers address their officers by their first names). Since Eyal spoke little English, he delivered his remarks in Hebrew and Karine translated. He expressed his appreciation for the volunteers coming to his base to work and wished us success in our stay at his base. After he left, Karine told us that the base commander had opened his base to the volunteers because he believed that programs like Sar-el were very beneficial to Israel.

At the end of a sweaty workday, I took a run around the base just as the beautiful red sun was setting into the dunes separating us from the Gaza Strip. The soldiers were still drilling in small groups – some doing hand-to-hand combat practice and some practicing use of their rifles in close combat. After my run I headed for the showers. Although there was no hot water, the cold water felt great and washed away the desert dust and sweat.

On our way to dinner, we passed numerous units marching to the mess hall. These units had to wait in line outside the mess hall while their drill sergeants either lectured them or berated them (after all, it's the army) about the day's activities. Each sergeant barked out questions and the soldiers, in unison, shouted their responses until their sergeant was satisfied and let them enter for dinner. After getting their food and sitting down, some of the units were still required to shout out answers to their sergeant's questions. Finally, their sergeant would bark out *Be-teyavon!* (bon appetit) and with one voice the unit would respond: *Be-teyavon!* Only then they were allowed to eat.

Some of our volunteers had worked in the kitchen that day, peeling potatoes by use of a large machine and unloading boxes of food delivered by truck. They reported that the kitchen was kept remarkably clean. We saw the product of some of the volunteers' work at the dinner table. We had diced potatoes mixed with tuna fish, along with the usual tomatoes and olives. It was very tasty.

Walking back to our bunks after dinner, the darkness rang out with groups shouting *Chamesh Shniah* as their sergeants put them through after-dinner drills. By the end of a day of eighteen hours of heavy exercise and drilling, I imagine that these soldiers were exhausted.

Etty gave us an after-dinner talk about what it was like for Israeli teenagers to be inducted into the army. She described the process the army goes through in testing the skills of all the eleventh-graders in order to best assign them to different branches of the service when they graduated high school. She also described the tears and trauma of the female trainees at the first shock of boot camp, which she herself now looked back on with humor. Finally, she explained how she managed to get assigned to Sar-el, in part to avoid being assigned to the "dreaded" (her word, half-jokingly) military police, which polices the bases.

TUESDAY, NOVEMBER 3, 2003

At 5:00, *Chamesh Shniah* began to ring out loudly around us, and so sleep was no longer a possibility. I discovered that if you ran the water in all the showers long enough, hot water was available. This was a big plus because the temperature had fallen into the sixties by early morning, so there was a slight chill in the air.

We came late to breakfast because some of our volunteers were slow risers today. I sat with Richard, a first-time volunteer from Baltimore. He was unusual in that he was forty years old and had young children. Not many people at that stage of child-rearing had the time to volunteer for Sar-el. When I asked him about this, he said the same thing that other volunteers had told me last year: "I wanted to support Israel in a more personal and tangible way." He went on to say that he had gotten two different sets of reactions from his friends at home when they learned that he was going to be a Sar-el volunteer. Some congratulated him for his commitment. Others – including most of his Israeli friends in Baltimore – told him he was crazy. They had all done their three years of service on these bases and knew it was no vacation.

Etty promised us harder work today and she was true to her word. She assigned Sam, Rob, and me to a warehouse detail with a soldier named Raz. We spent all morning dragging piles of brown and green camouflage netting into the warehouse parking lot, untangling each one, and then folding, tying, and storing it. Each netting was large (about 30′ × 30′) and very heavy, requiring two people to handle it. After lunch, Raz and the three of us were assigned as a work detail with rakes and heavy-duty hoes to chop out and clear brush around the warehouse complex of buildings. It was grimy, dusty work, but by the end of the day you could clearly see the improvement in the appearance of the area.

Raz was very friendly and liked to talk, but he had a disconcerting way of saying hello. His right shoulder had been severely damaged in a training explosion. The explosion had damaged his shoulder socket so badly that his arm had much greater flexibility than normal. As a prank, when a person would offer a handshake, Raz would wrap his right arm behind his back and extend his right hand out from his left side. He liked the shock value this produced.

Later Raz introduced us to several of his friends in the warehouse buildings and in the adjacent motor pool garage of trucks. I asked one of the motor pool soldiers where he was from and he answered "Uzbekistan." I mentioned that my cousin Bracha in Rosh Ha-Ayin was from a Bukharian family, which produced an immediate "Aha!" along with a handshake and a hug. Excitedly, the soldier announced to the other soldiers in the motor pool that I was related to a Bukharian Jew. Apparently, most of the soldiers in the motor pool also came from Bukharian families. I was immediately greeted like a long-lost relative, surrounded by soldiers slapping me on the back and shaking my hand. Bukharian Jews are a close-knit group, and they welcomed me like family. I felt like an instant celebrity.

After a long day's work I was dog-tired. Etty had promised me yesterday that the work she would assign me today would be so hard that I wouldn't have the energy to run again after work. (I think it bothered her that I ran after work yesterday.) In the face of that challenge, I knew I had to go running, no matter what. After the run and a hot shower, I felt great.

I felt that the day's work had been productive work that had to be done by someone – if not a volunteer, it would have required a *miluim* soldier. Others in the group felt the same about their work. Mike had spent the day in the base bunker with Max, a volunteer from Canada, sorting different types of bullets (regular bullets, tracers, and long-distance tracers). It was a long and tedious task, involving the trainee soldiers as well, but by the end of the day they had sorted all of the bullets. Similarly, the volunteers working in the kitchen commented that they could see the fruits of their labor at every meal. They were helping to feed almost 2,000 soldiers a day.

As the evening approached, shouts of *Chamesh Shniah* and cheers from various units rang out in the darkness. At times, so many units were shouting out responses that it seemed like they were answering each other. As we walked to the mess hall we watched different units of men (in dark green uniforms) and women (in off-white) march to the front entrance of the mess hall with their M-16s. At the entrance, they lined up at attention and shouted responses to their sergeants' barked out orders. As we had seen the previous evening, in effect, each unit had to stand outside the mess hall to "sing for their supper."

Walking back to the volunteers' bunks, we heard sporadic small arms fire coming from the direction of the area just west of the base, bordering the Mediterranean Sea. We had heard the same shooting late in the afternoon. The recruits were taking target practice at the nearby firing range.

For our evening activity, we were given a presentation by Raz, the soldier in charge of my work detail today. Raz, a tall, broad-shouldered nineteen-year-old from the port city of Ashdod, spoke about why he became a combat soldier. When he was sixteen, he was in a Jerusalem bus that was blown up by a suicide bomber. The Palestinian bomber sat in the front seat and Raz happened to sit in the back, so he survived the bombing. Twelve people died, including two people sitting three seats in front of him. He suffered glass cuts to his arm, which still bears the scars, and was deeply affected by seeing people torn apart in front of him. Because of this experience, when Raz entered the army, he asked to be assigned to a combat unit.

Many people apply to become combat soldiers, Raz explained, but most do not make it. Out of every 500 Israeli teenagers who apply, the army screens out 300 by testing physical stamina as well as mental ability to solve problems and work under pressure. The remaining 200 teenagers enter a four to five-month basic training course (versus the 30-day basic training course for the non-combat trainees at Zikim). The combat basic training course is extremely rigorous. Instead of the three meals a day and required six hours of sleep at the Zikim base, the combat soldiers' basic training course permits only two meals a day and no more than four hours of sleep daily. Discipline is imposed for the slightest infraction. On average, 25 percent of the soldiers in this basic training drop out, leaving 150 of the original 500. After graduation from basic training, the combat soldiers go on to an additional four months of training. In total, combat soldiers constitute only about 10 percent of the Israeli army. The rest, such as the soldiers trained in Zikim, play a support role to the combat units.

Because of his bus bombing experience, Raz chose to enter

the Hondasa Kravit regiment. This regiment of combat engineers specializes in bombs and mines. Unfortunately, during his advanced training in this regiment, a defective c-4 mine exploded, injuring his shoulder severely and knocking him unconscious for four days. After an extensive rehabilitation period, he was told that he would be unable to function in a combat unit. Accordingly, he was re-assigned to the logistics company in Zikim. For ten months, he fought the army doctors, petitioning to return to his regiment. Finally, last week the doctors changed their minds and notified Raz that he could re-join his unit in two months. Raz was overjoyed.

Raz talked about the close bond that develops between members of a combat unit. They spend more time together than apart, entrusting their lives to each other and to their unit commander. The running joke in the army is that once you join a combat unit, your unit commander becomes your mother and father and your rifle becomes your girlfriend. In fact, two months into his basic training, Raz's girlfriend dropped him because he couldn't find time to see her.

It was clear from his remarks that the morale of the combat units is very high. Raz proudly passed around his unit's pin, which was awarded to him in a special ceremony at Masada. He recalled that he and his friends cried when he received his unit pin.

Raz emphasized that the combat soldier's basic training stresses that innocent people are not to be harmed. When there is the slightest doubt that an innocent civilian might be in harm's way, they are instructed not to fire. Once, when his unit was on patrol in the West Bank city of Ramallah, a rocket-propelled grenade was fired at one of their vehicles. They surrounded the building from which the grenade was launched, but did not open fire. First, they emptied out the building of all of its residents, except those in the top (fourth) floor apartment from which the grenade was fired. Other army troops arrived with blankets and hot soup for the Palestinian residents, who were led out to the street in the cold weather. Those residents told Raz's unit that the fourth floor apartment was occupied by four Hamas terrorists. The Israeli soldiers knocked on the door of the apartment and were told that the occupants were holding a hostage whom they would kill if the soldiers attacked. The soldiers could have just opened fire, but instead delayed until they could question the residents on the street further and were able to verify that the hostage story was a fake. Then, instead of risking soldiers' lives with a frontal attack on the apartment, the unit blew up the building and killed the four terrorists. It turned out, by happenstance, that in destroying the building, they also destroyed the basement, containing the largest terrorist factory in Ramallah making c-4 explosives. Raz was very proud to tell his mother the next day that his unit deserved the credit for the newspaper headlines about the destruction of the bomb factory.

The residents of the destroyed building, Raz made a point of telling us, were paid compensation by the Israeli government, enabling them to live elsewhere because they were innocent civilians. I wondered whether this humanitarian part of the story had been covered when the international news reported that the Israeli army had blown up a Palestinian apartment building.

WEDNESDAY, NOV. 4, 2003

It's 5:00 A.M. and the soldiers are marching and calling out responses to their sergeants in unison. I have started to pay more attention to the shouted responses from the soldiers. Aside from *Chamesh Shniah*, the next most common response was *Cain Mefakedet*, which means "Yes, Commander," addressed to a female officer. Many of the drill sergeants were young women. Etty explained that very few female drill sergeants were assigned to train the combat units; most were assigned to drill the non-combat trainees at bases like Zikim. I had gotten used to the sight of no-nonsense female drill instructors berating a unit of male trainees, often meting out punishments such as push-ups for minor infractions. Raz had mentioned last night that there were also women who successfully competed for assignment to female combat units. These female combat units were not sent to places like Ramallah or Gaza City, but sent instead to guard highly sensitive areas such as Israel's nuclear reactor plant in Dimona or to serve in border patrols.

As usual, Etty gave us an eclectic set of morning news following flag-raising. The Egyptians announced they were attempting to start a new roadmap for peace between Israel and the Palestinians. Egypt was insisting that Israel had to first stop targeting the Palestinian terrorist groups. However, Egypt was not insisting that the Palestinian terrorist groups stop killing Israelis. (Seemed a bit one-sided to me.) Separately, today was the first showing in Israel of the movie *Matrix III*. And finally, the weather would cool off today to 28° C (82° F).

Today was a heavy workday under Raz's supervision. We started out by finishing the folding and storage of the camouflage netting. We stored all of the netting on a barn-like upper shelf of one of the warehouses. Since the shelf was about eight feet off the ground, getting these heavy and bulky nettings up to this storage place without a ladder was no easy job. It took four volunteers, plus Raz standing up on the shelf, to accomplish this. After the nettings, we stored the folded-up tents which each house a 22-person platoon during basic training. The tents were even heavier than the nettings.

Work after lunch was completely outdoors and therefore very hot. Tomorrow would be an inspection day for the entire base, so many of the soldiers were assigned to jobs cleaning up the base. Our assignment was to clear out more of the underbrush around the warehouses. We cleared out so much underbrush that by the end of the day we completely filled up the back of a big army truck with branches and debris. Avitan, the sergeant in charge of our work detail, did not appreciate how full the truck was. He asked me and Mike to get into the truck to help him empty it outside the base. It was late in the day, but he promised it would only take us ten minutes. We were skeptical.

We drove out of the southern gate of the base in the direction of the Gaza Strip. From the high vantage point of the truck we could see the Mediterranean to our right, bordered by swampy marshland. After driving only about fifty yards, I saw the tops of some buildings ahead in the distance and asked the sergeant what it was. "Gaza City," he answered. Then he pulled the truck over and backed it towards a gully that bordered on the marshland. We took a half-hour trying to empty the truck's contents into the gully and completed less than a quarter of the task. Avitan realized his error in thinking this would be a quick job, stopped us from proceeding, and drove us back into the camp with the truck still mostly full. He did not want to make us late for an afternoon program involving the entire base – a special commemoration of the eighth anniversary of the assassination of Prime Minister Yitzhak Rabin.

The commemoration was held in a big assembly hall. When the soldiers were seated, the base commander entered and the soldiers were ordered to attention in their seats. I had never seen a "sitting attention" before. It required the soldiers to sit up straight, with their feet on the floor in a "V" position and their hands clasped behind their back. It looked to me like a "sitting attention" was the sitting version of a standing "at ease."

The program portrayed Rabin's lifetime of service for the State of Israel. The audience of young people was somber, serious and paid attention. Various soldiers came up to the podium to speak. Then Karine, accompanied by a guitarist, sang a beautiful and mournful old Israeli song. Karine, the tough assistant company commander, had a magnificent voice! Up to this point, the entire program had been in Hebrew. Now, out of respect for the volunteers, Karine arranged for one of us to be part of the program. We were honored that Richard was asked to read, in English, a portion of Rabin's Nobel Peace Prize acceptance speech. The base commander closed the session with a few remarks and then the audience rose to sing "Hatikvah." I could see out of the corners of my eyes that some soldiers were craning their heads forward to see whether we volunteers knew Israel's national anthem. Of course, most of us did. I never sang a song with greater mouthing motions than that "Hatikvah," just to show the troops we were with them.

After dinner, Mike and I asked Etty if we could speak with Karine. We wanted to request permission to speak to the trainee soldiers as a group. Etty arranged this meeting, and Mike and I shortly found ourselves in Karine's very crowded office. Karine was on the phone. Already there when we entered were two sergeants from the Israeli base of combat soldiers who guard the northern border of the Gaza Strip. One was about six-foot tall, with a face bronzed by the sun and the broad, muscular build of a boxer. He was in charge of base discipline. The other one, Moshe, was slim and shorter. Moshe was in charge of the soldiers checking all vehicles traveling from the Gaza Strip into Israel for explosives and weapons. This is a checkpoint called the Erez Crossing. Moshe's wife was expecting their first child imminently and while we waited for Karine to get off the telephone, he explained that he was concerned over whether he could get to his wife in nearby Ashdod fast enough when she went into labor.*

When Karine got off the telephone, we tried to speak with her but were cut off repeatedly by the sergeant in charge of base discipline. He sat next to us, cradling his m-16 across his knee. The telephone kept ringing for Karine and, after every call, this sergeant continued to interrupt us to "shoot the breeze" with Karine.

---

* Two months later, in mid-January 2004 a female Hamas agent, who dressed so as to appear to be pregnant, approached the Erez Crossing seeking to travel from the Gaza Strip into Israel. The Israeli soldiers at the checkpoint avoided humiliating Palestinian women who set off the metal detector by not frisking them in public (as they did to the Palestinian men). Therefore, when this female Hamas agent set off the metal detector, the soldiers permitted her to walk indoors to be examined by a female soldier. Upon entering, the Hamas agent blew herself up, killing four soldiers. I checked the list of victims and Moshe's name was not on it.

(This was not to flirt with her, as Karine made it well known on the base that she had a steady boyfriend.)

This went on for about fifteen or twenty minutes, and I became angrier and angrier over his rudeness. I was tired from a hard day's work and wouldn't tolerate this behavior from my kids, so why should I tolerate it from this same-aged soldier? Finally, I barked at him: *Sheket!* (Quiet!). He scowled, rose half out of his chair, and raised his fist in a threatened punch. I rose to face him – six inches from his face – with an angry look. We glared at each other for a tense instant. Then his face broke into a grin, his body relaxed, and he opened his clenched fist to shake hands. We shook, and he sat back and quietly said: "Go ahead." He remained silent after that.

Mike and I expressed to Karine that one of the major reasons the volunteers served on military bases was to boost the morale of the soldiers. While the volunteers made an effort to chat with individual trainee soldiers, some seemed shy due to the language barrier. Mike and I suggested that we could have a greater impact if we could arrange to speak to some of the trainee soldiers as a group about Sar-el and the presence of volunteers at their base. Karine agreed to try to set up a session for the volunteers to meet with an audience consisting of five trainee soldiers from each of the seven different training companies at the base. She warned us, however, that it might be hard to get the agreement of the seven trainee company commanders, given how tightly packed their training schedule was.

As we walked down the steps from Karine's second floor office, Mike whispered to me regarding my near altercation with the Israeli discipline sergeant: "You're crazy! That guy could have taken you apart!" "He was disrespectful," I responded, not sorry at all. This was the closest I came to seeing any violence on my trip – and it would have been with an Israeli sergeant!

THURSDAY, NOVEMBER 5, 2003

Chamesh Shniah! Our 5:00 A.M. wake up call was so reliable that

I didn't know why I had been setting my alarm clock. As I walked the few steps to the bathroom, I could see the outlines of columns of trainee soldiers, in full packs, ready to move out in the foggy morning. I have had a tough time sleeping. Based on my experience with one thin army mattress last year, on our first day on the base I had insisted that we arrange for each volunteer to have two mattresses. Nonetheless, even with the two thin army mattresses, I'd been staying up to 3:00 or 4:00 every morning until I fell asleep. My discomfort was compounded by a sore throat and full-blown cold that developed yesterday. Rob was kind enough to give me some Vicks lozenges, which helped my throat during the day, but did not help my sleeping problem. By this morning, I had big dark rings under my eyes from lack of sleep and my voice was down to a whisper. I knew I could have gone to the base infirmary earlier, but was fearful the doctors would have checked me into it. I hadn't come to Israel to lie in an army hospital bed.

After breakfast, we got to the flag-raising area early – so Etty gave us the news before flag-raising. She reported that Prime Minister Sharon had seventy-two hours left to persuade a majority of the Knesset to support a proposed prisoner exchange with the Palestinians. Under the terms of the proposed prisoner exchange, Israel would release 400 Palestinians prisoners who were within two years of the end of their sentences and did not have "blood on their hands," (i.e., had not murdered Israelis). In return, the Palestinians would turn over the bodies of three Israeli soldiers captured and killed last month and would release an Israeli businessman they had kidnapped.

As flag-raising ended on the parade grounds, a number of female and male trainee units headed toward the area. It was a rehearsal for their graduation ceremony later in the day. The female units marched smartly onto the field in their off-white uniforms with their M-16s held across their chests. In contrast, members of the male units straggled into the area to form up. As we were leaving for our work assignments, we heard each unit shouting out responses to their sergeants. It soon became apparent that the sergeants of the female units were directing them to shout out in response to the male units as if in a cheerleading competition for who was the loudest. It was clear that the different units had developed an *esprit de corp* during the course of their basic training. I had to admit that, if this were a competition, the women would have come out the winners, judging by their loudness and spirit.

Our first work assignment was to unload a truckload of old furniture for disposal. We noticed that some of the furniture was still usable and decided to "liberate" it for the volunteers' bunk area, since we had no common area in which to sit. In return for our emptying the truck, the truck driver agreed to drop off a table and ten chairs, which we arranged in the sand outside the volunteers' bunks. It was a cheering site when the volunteers returned to their bunks after lunch to find this welcome addition to our environment. Some of our female volunteers "finished" the table by decorating it with a bunch of yellow wildflowers propped up between several small rocks.

My next work assignment was with a young soldier named Ilya in one of the warehouses. Rob and I were assigned to help Ilya load a truck with tied-up packages of dirty army fatigues headed for the laundry. We were assigned by Bobby, a career army man and a master sergeant.

Bobby was an interesting fellow. He was about six feet two inches tall, very hefty with a wide bull neck, topped by a mustachioed Saddam Hussein look-a-like face. Bobby and Avitan (the sergeant we had worked with yesterday) were the two master sergeants in charge of the warehouse complex of buildings. Meeting him for the first time, Bobby would appear to be very menacing, especially because he would bellow his orders across the warehouse compound. However, he was quite concerned about the welfare of the volunteers and I heard him shout more than once that the soldiers needed to encourage the volunteers to take breaks for water. Bobby was at least 250 pounds; he was also extremely strong. We formed a line to toss the heavy bundles of laundry to each other to load the truck. Although he didn't have to do it, Bobby joined the line. We heaved bulky packages of laundry down the line with great effort. When it came to Bobby, he caught each package with one hand and then flicked it to the next person as if tossing a rag doll.

After disposing of all of the laundry, Bobby assigned me to work with Ilya to help organize and clean up one of the warehouse rooms. Ilya worked on one part of the room and I folded and stored sleeping bags nearby. Some were brand new from the U.S. and Germany. Others were very beat up and had obviously been used by trainees on the base.

Although we worked steadily for the rest of the morning, Ilya was very sociable and was happy to tell me about himself. He was a slimly built, impressive twenty-one-year-old, square-jawed, handsome, blond, and very gentle in manner. Ilya had emigrated from Kazakhstan when he was sixteen, leaving his parents behind. After two years of religious high school to learn more about Judaism, he entered the army. Under the army's "Lonely Soldier" program, he was paid more than a regular soldier because he was the only member of his family in Israel. (A private's pay is not enough to live on, which is why most Israelis doing their army service continue to live with their parents.) Ilya spoke five languages – Kazakh, Russian, Ukrainian, Hebrew and English – and played three musical instruments, including piano and folk guitar. He had his own band. And he had already been accepted to Tel Aviv University after the army to study to become a journalist. His parents allowed him to move to Israel because there were no opportunities for young educated people in Kazakhstan. They were unwilling to join their only child in Israel because they had good jobs in Kazakhstan and had no assurance they could do as well in Israel. So Ilya was waiting for another ten years to pass, until his parents retired at age sixty-five. At that point, he planned to try to persuade them to join him. His face brightened as he told me that his mother would be visiting him in a week – only the second time she had visited him since he left Kazakhstan five years ago.

It must have been hard for a sixteen-year-old boy to move to a new country by himself and learn a new language. He did not go to an *ulpan* (Hebrew language class), but instead simply picked up Hebrew in high school and in the army. The pressure of doing this on his own may have led to his one major shortcoming. He smoked incessantly, even more than the average Israeli, to mask a nervous insecurity. He always had a cigarette in his mouth and his speaking was frequently interrupted by a heavy hacker's cough that one wouldn't expect in a person so young. While he planned to persuade his parents to move to Israel when they retired, I hoped he wouldn't make himself sick before they came.

Ilya gave me his view of the volunteers. He thought it was great that we paid our way to come to work in the army. He said it helped the morale of his unit to see the volunteers work hard alongside the unit soldiers. Just as we stopped working for the lunch break, he came over to me and said he would like to give me a present. He took off his Israeli army watch protector and placed it on my watch. He obviously wanted to express his gratitude in a personal way. I was touched that this young man thought to do this, and thanked him. I wore the watch protector proudly for the rest of my stay at the base.

After lunch, we headed back to our bunks to admire our new table and chairs. As we reached our area, we heard bursts of machine gun fire just south of us in the direction of Gaza City. It clearly was not coming from the direction of the firing range just west of the base. Then we heard some loud explosions; seconds later we heard (but barely saw) Israeli warplanes streaking north, apparently returning from an action over the Gaza Strip. Etty promised to read the papers tomorrow and report back to us on Sunday what had happened.

After a hot shower to erase the morning's sweat, we changed into our "civvies." Then we packed for a weekend off the base and relaxed in our compound until the 4:00 military bus would take us to the Ashkelon bus station.

While we waited, three companies of soldiers, who had completed their basic training and had packed up their gear, marched by our compound. They were in their dress uniforms and marched smartly. Many of us waved and took pictures as they marched by; several of the male soldiers waved back. None of the women did – they were "all business."

Shortly afterward, we heard the strains of military music coming from the direction of the parade grounds. We rushed over to watch the graduation ceremony and came upon a festive scene. All three companies were lined up in front of three tables bearing rifles and Bibles. The parade grounds were surrounded by families of the new soldiers – proud parents, grandparents, brothers and sisters – all taking pictures. A number of senior officers made speeches, including the base commander. Then each soldier was called up to salute his officer and receive his rifle and Bible. It was just like a high school graduation, except these soldiers still had three years (for males) or two years (for females) left to serve in the army.

It was all very stirring. Three companies of Israeli soldiers were leaving a place they hoped never to return to, but about which they would speak proudly for the rest of their lives. The ceremony closed with the singing of "Hatikvah," followed by applause from the audience. Then cheers rang out from the ranks of the soldiers for their drill sergeants as the soldiers broke ranks to join their families.

The volunteers headed back to our compound, picked up our bags, and led by Etty walked to the front gate to board the bus to Ashkelon. We were lucky to get seats because the bus filled up rapidly. Even the aisles were crammed with soldiers from the base going home for the weekend.

Because of the stream of cars leaving the graduation, the bus crawled its way to Ashkelon through the semi-desert surroundings. The soldiers' minds seemed to be on where they were going for the Sabbath, mostly home to their parents, but many of them used the time to socialize. Some were couples, holding hands as they sat next to each other. And others engaged in quick banter with members of the opposite sex, as if this had been a bus full of twelfth-grade high school students in the U.S.

The bus drove through an old part of Ashkelon to the central bus station. Ashkelon is the southernmost Israeli city on the Mediterranean. In this part of the city the buildings seemed very utilitarian and straight out of the 1950s – old four-story walk-up apartment buildings with people's wash hanging out their windows and balconies. The central bus station was a small two-story building. The volunteers all wished each other a good weekend and then we split up to go our separate ways.

I caught a taxi to Netanya to visit my cousin Ruchama. The driver was an Algerian Jew who spoke Hebrew and French, but little English. What would normally have been a trip of slightly more than an hour was doubled due to the typical Israeli rush hour traffic. My cold had gotten worse over the course of the day and I was at the stage where I was non-stop coughing and sneezing with a constant runny nose. The taxi driver first offered me bags of snacks from his front seat and then, seeing my condition, took pity on me and handed me his box of tissues. By the time we reached Netanya, I had used up his entire box and was feeling worse than before. I slept during parts of the trip because I was extremely tired.

Ruchama met me at the door of her Netanya apartment and sized up my condition. She served me a quick dinner, followed by two enormous mugs of hot tea with lemon. I fell asleep the moment I laid down.

FRIDAY, NOVEMBER 6, 2003

I woke up three hours later than usual (8:00 A.M.). It was great to sleep on a real bed and to sleep so late. I was still sick when I woke up, but I felt much better than I had during the cab ride.

Ruchama's four-year-old daughter, Shani, still had her blond Shirley Temple appearance, but had grown since last year. As I woke up, Ruchama was leaving for work and had to drop Shani off at her kindergarten. She made me more hot tea, invited me to help myself to the contents of her refrigerator and left.

It was a very quiet and peaceful Friday morning. As in the previous year, I stared out her front window for a while at the kindergarten across the street. I watched as parents walked their children to the front entrance and the guard opened up the barred door to let the children in. For the rest of the morning, the sounds of children's voices and an occasional passing car were all that broke the peaceful silence.

Ruchama's brother Michael picked me up by mid-morning so that I could exchange more dollars for shekels. He drove me to Herzl Street, the main shopping road in Netanya. Because it was impossible to find parking in the area, he explained, he would have to drop me off and gave me directions for the ten-minute walk back to Ruchama's apartment. I expected him to drop me at one of the many banks dotting Herzl Street, but instead he suddenly pulled over to the curb. "Him," he said, pointing to a man standing on the street. "He will exchange your money." Then he drove off as the man came over and shook my hand. "What is your exchange rate for dollars?" I asked. He quoted me a rate that was comparable to the rate I had gotten at the Currency Exchange at Ben-Gurion Airport, so I exchanged dollars for shekels.

I welcomed the opportunity to walk back to Ruchama's apartment. It was a mid-Friday morning and many people were doing their pre-Sabbath shopping. Herzl Street was crowded with people speaking Hebrew and Russian, strolling past the many small shops. Musicians played instruments, sitting on low stools on the sidewalk, hoping for coins tossed by passersby. I saw a violinist, a guitarist, and an accordionist; the latter was singing in Russian. I bought some Sabbath flowers for Ruchama and got lost only once on the way back to her house.

After a quick bite, Ruchama, Shani and I drove to a nearby shopping mall for groceries. I sat slumped down in the back seat and read to Shani from a storybook. Shani and I were so engrossed in the story that I didn't notice that we had stopped until the trunk suddenly opened, startling me. We were at the entrance to the mall and the guards were checking cars before allowing them into the parking lot.

The Tiv Ta'am (Quality Taste) grocery store was very large and clean, but nonetheless different from American grocery stores. The most prominent difference was that Ruchama's bag had to be checked and we had to be wanded in order to enter the store. The store offered cooked meats and pastries, all prepared in front of the customers. The place smelled delicious. Ruchama bought a long hot dog for Shani at the store's sit-down indoor café and left Shani and me at a table while she shopped.

Halfway into her hot dog, Shani announced she had to go to the bathroom – so we left the food to go through the store to find Ruchama. The store was huge and, after a few minutes of searching unsuccessfully for Ruchama, I realized I had better find a bathroom for Shani. It had been a long time since I had to take a little girl to the bathroom. I knew that Shani had never been in a men's bathroom because she didn't have a father. I also knew I couldn't take her into the ladies' room. So I led her to the entrance to the latter, pointed out an empty stall, and sent Shani in that direction hoping she could do her business without assistance. I stood just outside the ladies' room within eyesight of Shani, with my back to her. Luckily, she could take care of herself. She came out, gave me her hand, and we walked back to the indoor café. Crisis passed!

Returning to Ruchama's house, we all laid down for a pre-Sabbath nap. By 3:00, people had finished their pre-Sabbath shopping and the street outside of Ruchama's apartment fell silent. Even though she did not live in a particularly religious neighborhood, passing cars became a rarity and the sidewalks were empty. It was as if the world had gone to sleep.

At 4:00, a few people started to appear in the neighborhood. Most were caftan–clad bearded men heading with their sons to the Orthodox synagogue across the street. I had previously gotten the address of the Masorti (Conservative) synagogue in Netanya off of the internet and had decided to go there for Friday night services.

I took a taxi to Beth Israel Synagogue on Yehuda Ha-Nasi Street, walked up one flight of steps, and entered the main sanctuary.

A young rabbi speaking Hebrew with an American accent was leading services. He led the Friday night service in both Hebrew and English, as many of the congregants were Conservative Jews from the U.S. The service was easy to follow, not only because the rabbi announced the page numbers in both Hebrew and English, but also because the prayer book was the same one used in Conservative synagogues in the U.S.

After the service, the 25–30 congregants went to a *kiddush* (reception) in the social hall for refreshments. In chatting with the rabbi, I learned that he was from Brooklyn and had gone to the Jewish Theological Seminary in New York City. As part of the curriculum, he was required to spend a year of his studies in Israel. He fell in love with the country and, after graduation, moved to Israel. The Masorti movement in Israel assigned him to this Netanya congregation of 250 members about a year and a half ago. I also met his Israeli wife, a beautiful dark-featured young woman who had prepared the *kiddush*.

As I was turning to leave, a man introduced himself to me. Morrie was an American and the president of the Beth Israel Synagogue. He and his wife Lenore offered me a ride back to Ruchama's apartment. On the ride back, he explained that he and Lenore had moved to Israel about two years ago from Rockville, Maryland to be closer to their two daughters in Israel and their three grandchildren. Their daughters had each been educated in Jewish day schools and had spent a year in Israel as part of the curriculum. They felt a strong connection to the country, moved there after college, and married Israeli men. Morrie and Lenore had merely followed them. They told me that they were very happy with their decision.

SATURDAY, NOVEMBER 7, 2003

I awoke to the sounds of early morning Sabbath services coming from the synagogue diagonally across the street. It was 8:00 and the congregants were singing.

We took Shani to an outdoor playground to meet with her friend, Avishag, and sat with Avishag's mother on a nearby bench while the children played. The playground was very crowded because it was the Sabbath. A woman sitting next to Ruchama heard us speak English and said hello. Her name was Helen and she had moved to Israel seventeen years before from Birmingham, England. She was watching her two children by herself because her husband was traveling in Brazil on business. We spent a pleasant morning talking with her about Israel. She mentioned that her husband, an immigrant from South Africa, attended synagogue every Friday night, but that was unusual for Israelis. Israelis view their options for religion as one extreme or the other – either Orthodox or no religion at all. I mentioned to Helen that I had gone to services the previous night at a Masorti synagogue, which presents a middle position between Orthodoxy and secularism. "Do they allow women and men to sit together?" Helen asked. "Yes," I said. "Well then I would be uncomfortable in such a place," she said. "I was raised Orthodox in England and would not want to sit with the men."

We dropped Shani and Avishag off at Ruchama's apartment with Avishag's mother, who agreed to watch them while Ruchama and I paid a call on her friends, Eli and Sara. We knew this would be a sad visit. They had two sons, Lior, who was eight, and Elan, who was almost three. Two years ago, both boys were tentatively diagnosed with a rare and terminal neurological disease. Late last year, after returning from my first Sar-el stint, I had received an e-mail from Ruchama about the dilemma faced by this family. They knew that the leading medical expert on this disease was working on a treatment at Johns Hopkins University in Baltimore, but they were having difficulty in arranging for the doctor to treat their sons. As luck would have it, I had bunked with a Sar-el volunteer, Mike Lowenstein, whose wife Elaine had worked as a nurse at Johns Hopkins. Even more fortuitous, she knew the doctor's head nurse very well. Elaine was able to arrange for the family to come to Baltimore to have the doctor examine the two boys. These caring people went one step further – arranging for the family's food, lodging, and car transportation to and from the hospital in Baltimore.

Unfortunately, the doctor concluded that the experimental treatment was unlikely to help the older boy, though it could possibly help the younger one. The doctor's predictions turned out to be accurate. Lior continued to deteriorate, while Elan seemed to be stable.

When we entered their home, we were ushered into their very spartan living room. Lior lay on his side on the couch half curled up in a fetal position, not moving. Although he was over five years older than his brother, he had shrunken so much that he was only slightly larger than Elan. His arms and legs looked like sticks. His eyes were sunken in their sockets and, although occasionally open, they seemed glazed and unseeing. Eli sat with him throughout our two-hour visit, keeping his hand on his son. The only movement from the sick child was the flutter of his eyelids and a very slight heaving of his chest. His parents were waiting for him to die.

We spent the visit talking about Sar-el, Israel, or anything else to distract them. Occasionally Lior would start breathing heavily, almost choking. His younger brother would come over to the couch from the puzzle he was working on with Ruchama, touch his head gently, and then kiss him on the forehead. It was a very poignant scene. I knew when we said our good-byes that Lior would pass away very soon.

We drove away in silence; there was nothing to be said. When we returned to Ruchama's apartment, we picked up Avishag and her mother and drove them home. Then we ate a big lunch and laid down for the traditional Sabbath afternoon nap. The world was asleep around us and soon so were we.

The street woke up as the Sabbath ended and the noise woke everyone from their nap. Michael came over and took me and Shani to the Netanya Mall. I wanted to buy small gifts for some of the soldiers I had gotten to know and Shani was coming along for ice cream.

Michael commented that the mall was not very busy this evening, which he attributed to the bad economy and high unemployment: "Israelis have little money to spend, so they are going less and less to the malls," he said. In his view, this was in part due to terrorism. The threat of terrorism necessitated guards at the mall and restaurant entrances and that drove up the cost of everything. The terrorism had also killed tourism in Israel, which he recognized was a major factor in Israel's economic deterioration. He said that the police do a good job in Netanya in capturing most of the terrorists, but in open areas that cannot be protected by guards there was little that could be done to stop them. He told me there had been three terrorist bombings on Herzl Street. "What can we do to stop that?" he asked with a tone of resignation. "After all, Tulkarem [a West Bank Palestinian city] is only ten minutes away by car." Only the security fence currently under construction between pre-1967 Israel and the West Bank seemed to offer any hope of protection against these attacks.

When we returned to Ruchama's apartment, the local Israeli television news was reporting on the anniversary commemoration of Hannah Senesh's death. During World War II, Hannah Senesh, a young kibbutznik, volunteered for a mission in Nazi-occupied Europe. Parachuting into Yugoslavia in 1944, she made her way alone to her native Hungary in order to warn Jews of their impending fate, and there was captured and killed. All Israeli students learn about this young heroine who is remembered for her bravery, her diary, and her poems.

SUNDAY, NOVEMBER 8, 2003

After saying goodbye to Ruchama and Shani in the early morning, I caught a cab for Ashkelon. The taxi left Netanya along its beautiful scenic beachfront bordering the Mediterranean. There appeared to be construction along the bluffs overlooking the beach, but Ruchama had explained that this was old construction that had been halted in mid-stream. When the Palestinian violence started, tourism and investment dried up, stopping ongoing construction even in such choice locations.

It had rained continuously throughout the night. The ground was still wet and dark clouds over the Mediterranean warned of still further showers. As we headed south of Tel Aviv, the gentle rolling hills gave way to low sandy dunes covered with sparse vegetation. A beautiful Jacob's ladder broke through the clouds as we approached Ashdod, but the clouds darkened again and the rain began to fall once more. While rain is always welcome in such a parched land, it is not always welcomed by the soldiers. I saw soldiers waiting at bus stops for rides to their duty stations. Some stops had protection from the rain, but many did not, and at those stops, the soldiers could do nothing to avoid a soaking.

South of Ashdod, the traffic became sparse. The highway signs listed three further destinations, only the first of which would be safe for Israelis or Americans:

ASHKELON – 15 KM (SOUTH)
GAZA CITY – 25 KM (SOUTH)
HEBRON – 25 KM (EAST)

As we entered Ashkelon, a long and beautiful rainbow appeared over a new and very attractive complex of apartment buildings and shops. Apparently, we were driving through a trendy new Ashkelon neighborhood.

The cab dropped me off at the main Ashkelon bus station about ninety minutes before the scheduled army bus to Zikim. I waited in this small, crowded, open-air station, crowned by the presence of a McDonald's, which was closed. Without the soldiers, the bus station would have been nearly deserted.

The military bus we boarded for the Zikim base was occupied

by a single unit of female trainee soldiers, along with their sergeant. As soon as the bus started, orders rang out from the sergeant:

- "You are on a military bus now, so there are certain rules to follow."
  Response from all: "Yes, *Mefakedet*."
- "In case of an emergency, crouch below the level of the bus window."
  Response from all: "Yes, *Mefakedet*."
- "No cell phones, radios, or CD players."
  Response from all: "Yes, *Mefakedet*."
- "No rowdy behavior or noise."
  Response from all: "Yes, *Mefakedet*."
- "Have a good trip."
  Response from all: "Have a good trip, *Mefakedet*."

The volunteers trickled onto the base during the course of the morning. We sat outside our bunks around our table and entertained each other with stories about our weekend experiences. Some of the volunteers had gone to Jerusalem and the Dead Sea, others had gone shopping at an Arab flea market and at a diamond market, and others had toured the canyon at Machtesh Ramon. Everyone was refreshed and high-spirited after a weekend of rest, ready for the workweek.

After a lunch of schnitzel (breaded chicken cutlets) with the logistics company, we headed out for our work assignments. Mike and I spent the afternoon working with Avitan in the warehouse complex. Avitan was one of the least-liked sergeants in the logistics company. He was short in stature and extremely aggressive. We quickly noticed that he treated soldiers roughly, raising his voice and barking out orders, in contrast to the other sergeants, like Bobby, who simply talked to the soldiers when giving direction. Avitan seemed to suspect that all soldiers were malingerers who had to be pushed, so he was constantly "on their case."

Avitan treated the volunteers only slightly better, regarding us as additional laborers who were more likely to obey his barked-out orders. The volunteers quickly christened him with the nickname "Little Napoleon" because of his short stature and his need to be giving orders all the time. The soldiers were not so charitable in the nicknames they assigned to him.

The project Avitan gave us to was to move two sheds filled with heavy boxes and barrels about fifty yards away because the area where they stood was being fenced in for a new purpose. The boxes and barrels bore various signs indicating that their contents were dangerous. While I knew the universal meaning of the skull and cross bones displayed on many of these containers, I did not understand the Hebrew words stamped on them in red, so I copied them down. During a work break, I checked my dictionary and learned they stood for things like: "Toxic chemicals – handle with care," "Danger: Carcinogenic," and "Poisonous." I ignored these warnings, as did the soldiers who worked with us, all without any protective gear.

Despite our dislike for the man, we were impressed with Avitan's inventiveness in solving the various logistical challenges this project posed, since we had no truck or tools. All we had were our bare hands and two small two-wheeled handcarts. After emptying the contents of the sheds, at Avitan's direction we stripped each shed down to a bare shell. Then we lined up the two handcarts and, with the assistance of nearby soldiers, lifted and balanced one shed at a time onto the two carts. With each shed teetering on the carts, we all pushed/pulled it through the sandy soil to its new destination, anchored it, and filled it back up with boxes and barrels. In the whole process, we used boards, poles, rocks, and rope we found scattered on the ground. We had previously viewed these items as just so much junk laying around, but now realized that these were "tools" used by the logistics company. By the end of the afternoon, we completed our task and Avitan was satisfied with the results.

Heading back to the bunks, Karine warned us that the weather was about to turn colder and rainy, and that we should arrange to get army jackets issued to all of the volunteers. Accompanied by Etty, who signed for them, Mike and I brought ten jackets back to the volunteers' bunks from the warehouse.

At the end of the afternoon, we observed lines of newly arrived trainees waiting in front of the armory for issuance of their m-16s. They had just arrived, and we could now see the difference in appearance (sloppy) and manner between these very new soldiers and the more experienced trainees on the base. After dinner, we heard the crackle of rifle fire as the trainees practiced at the shooting range. This was the rhythm of the base. Soldiers graduated on Thursday and new ones arrived to take their place on Sunday. We soon appreciated that the drill sergeants had the hardest job, staying on top of their trainees for their full training period. Etty told us that the trainees were busy from the time they woke up until "lights out" with very little free time. That meant a lot of hard work for the drill sergeants.

For our after-dinner evening activity, Etty gave us a talk about the origin of the Ladino language. (Etty knew a lot about Ladino because her Greek grandmother spoke that language; she herself spoke Spanish and Portuguese.) Ladino is a combination of medieval Spanish and Hebrew, with some Turkish, Greek, and Arabic added. It was spoken in the Middle Ages by Jews expelled from Spain during the Spanish Inquisition and their descendants who settled in countries bordering on the Mediterranean. Ladino is to the Sephardi Jews (Jews of Spanish descent, from the Hebrew *Sepharad*) what Yiddish is to the Ashkenazi Jews (Jews originating in Central Europe). The difference is that Ladino has completely died out as a spoken language, while Yiddish has not.

MONDAY, NOVEMBER 9, 2003
The predicted winter storm had moved in overnight. Before going to bed late last night, I was treated to a thunder and lightning display that was particularly awe-inspiring in this desert area. I could understand why biblical people were put in fear of God

by such natural phenomenon – after all, what else could explain such power?

It rained and thundered for most of the night, and the wind howled through the sand dunes behind our bunks. By morning, the temperature had dropped and the howling of the wind had only partly abated. The only saving grace was that the rain had stopped.

The company of trainee soldiers in the tents next to us did not start with *Chamesh Shniah* until 5:30, so my "wake-up call" was delayed. I suppose they were given an extra half-hour of sleep because of the colder weather. As I got out of bed, I saw how their sergeants warmed them up. They had the soldiers running in place while clapping. Showering and washing up was more of a challenge than usual. While our small bunks had been kept warm by the warmth of our bodies, walking to the bathroom exposed us to a cold wind. And showering was tricky because, although we had hot water, the bathrooms were unheated and cold. Nevertheless, like the trainee soldiers, we washed, dressed, and headed for breakfast in our hooded green army jackets. These jackets, called *dubon* ("teddy bear" in Hebrew), were particularly warm, albeit heavy. Once zipped up, you felt like you had closed yourself into a sleeping bag. With the hood on, it was extremely cozy.

After breakfast the rains returned, so flag-raising was canceled. The wind continued to howl as Etty gave us the morning news. The proposed release of 400 Palestinian prisoners had fallen through. Although the Israelis agreed to the exchange, at the last minute the Hezbollah terrorists insisted that the released prisoners include those who had "blood on their hands." This was something that Prime Minister Sharon, as well as the bulk of the Israeli population, consistently refused to accept, and so there was no deal.

We went to our work assignments bundled up in our *dubon*. By mid-morning, our coats and army shirts were off, and we were down to our tee-shirts under the warm sun. Although the wind continued to blow, the combination of strenuous warehouse work and the warmth of the desert sun heated us up.

We took a break shortly before lunch in order to meet with General Aharon Davidi, the founder and civilian head of Sar-el. He enjoyed speaking to Sar-el groups around the country, and had spoken to my group of volunteers at Batzop the previous year.

This time, General Davidi spoke about the danger to the Western world of Islamic extremism and the tactics used by the extremists. As an illustration of these tactics, he told us the following story: In the seventh century, Mohammad led an insurrection within the city of Mecca in an attempt to take over that city. Mohammad and his followers were unsuccessful and were expelled from the city. Subsequently, Mohammad entered into a ten-year *hudna* (or armistice agreement) with Mecca. After one year, he broke the *hudna* to attack and conquer the unprepared city. Ever since, Muslim extremists have used that example to enter into agreements temporarily and then break them when it was to their advantage. In fact, when Arafat entered into the Oslo Accords with Israel in 1993, he confronted a hostile crowd of Palestinians angry at him for negotiating with the Israelis. He silenced the crowd with these words: "Remember Mohammad's *hudna* with the city of Mecca." They all understood the reference – and that Arafat's entry into the Oslo Accords was a ruse. General Davidi's point was that the West does not understand that this is a tactic used by Muslim extremists.

General Davidi also spoke about Osama Bin Laden's plan to spread Muslim extremism worldwide. He complimented President George Bush's response to the September 11 attacks on the U.S. and his actions in invading Afghanistan and Iraq. He only had one disagreement with U.S. policy in Iraq – that American goals for a democratic Iraq were too optimistic: "Americans view Iraq the same way they view the other countries they've conquered and occupied – Germany and Japan. After conquering these lands

the U.S. successfully restored each as a country, established democratic self-governing institutions, and withdrew its forces. But
treating Iraq like the U.S. treated Germany and Japan is a mistake,
because it ignores the fact that Iraq is inherently different – it is
not a single nation."

His point was that present-day Iraq was a geographical creation of French and British colonial powers of a previous century
and its population did not exhibit a commonality of history, religion, or culture sufficient to form a single, unified state. General
Davidi believed that Iraq was inherently ungovernable except by
a dictator like Saddam Hussein. In this respect, he likened Iraq to
Tito's Yugoslavia, which fell apart once the iron hand of its dictator
disappeared. He maintained that Iraq, like Yugoslavia, should be
allowed to split into the three separate groups it really represents
(Kurds, Sunnis and Shiites). In his view, the U.S. effort to establish
a democratic Iraq, although well-intentioned, would fail. General
Davidi's remarks gave us much to think about and were the topic
of much discussion around the lunch table immediately following our session with him.*

We stopped work early this afternoon so that we could take a bus
into Ashdod with Karine. Ashdod was Karine's hometown, and she
was very proud of it. Because Ashdod sits on the coastal land route
between Egypt and the rest of the Middle East, it has been the route
taken by many conquering armies over thousands of years.

Karine brought us to an historic outdoor memorial on
the outskirts of Ashdod called Ad Halom, which means "Until
Here" – and explained how the place got its name. In Israel's War

---

* General Davidi's suggestion that Iraq be split into the three countries it really represents was a new concept to me, but seemed very logical. Upon my
return to the U.S., I learned that this concept was being raised by certain foreign policy makers in Washington. The major stumbling block to this concept
was American's ally in the region, Turkey. With a large ethnic Kurdish population in its eastern half, Turkey feared that an independent Kurdish nation in
northern Iraq would spur Kurdish separatists in Turkey.

of Independence, the final crucial campaign occurred when the Egyptian Army sent a powerful invasion force, spear-headed by a tank column, up the ancient coastal invasion route to Ashdod. The Egyptians had been successful in overrunning a number of Israeli defense outposts and settlements until they reached Ashdod. If the Israelis had been unable to stop the Egyptians at Ashdod, the road to Tel Aviv would have been open and the war for the new state could have been lost.

The Israelis, with no weapons capable of stopping tanks, came up with a clever plan. The Egyptian tank column had to cross an old Arab-built bridge over the Lachish River to proceed through Ashdod. The Israelis made a crude bomb with dynamite, which they exploded when the lead column of tanks was already on the bridge, tumbling the bridge and the tanks into the river. Then, as the Egyptians hesitated, Israeli forces attacked the length of the column with the kind of close fighting in which tanks are useless. A panic took hold of the invasion force and they fled, abandoning their tanks and equipment. The people of Ashdod are understandably proud of this accomplishment in beating back the Egyptian invasion force and saving the country. We could see that pride in Karine's eyes as she recounted the story, which every child in Ashdod is taught in the fourth grade. Karine emphasized that the Israelis had nothing to match the weapons and manpower of the Egyptian invasion force. Yet they knew they had to stop that invasion and used their heads when all else failed.

TUESDAY, NOVEMBER 10, 2003

This was the first morning that I woke up to my alarm clock rather than the shouts of *Chamesh Shniah* from the trainee company next door. Was I getting so used to that sound that my mind was subconsciously screening it out? That had already happened with regard to the popping noises of M-16s coming from the firing range on the western side of the base. Unless someone actually commented on the gunfire from target practice, I no longer even noticed it.

After washing up, I watched a squad of neighboring soldiers exercising under the direction of their sergeant. She yelled out "push-ups," counting down until she got to "two." Then like a broken record she counted "two, two, two, two" until her soldiers were fatigued. I continued to be impressed with the female Israeli sergeants. Even though many of them were a head shorter than the recruits in their charge, they commanded absolute obedience from their soldiers.

We walked to breakfast bundled up in our warm army jackets. The wind was blowing cold off the Mediterranean. The wind continued to whip up the nearby sea, accompanied by a constant low roar throughout the day that I assumed was the sound of breaking waves. Although Etty had promised that the weather would warm up, it was at least as cold as yesterday (in the fifties) and the wind made it feel even colder. At breakfast, for the first time we saw something heated to eat – some kind of oatmeal. It was hot and sweet and tasted of cinnamon.

Before flag-raising, Etty gave us the news. With the last few days' storm, winter had arrived. The heavy rains had flooded roads throughout Israel. The benefit, though, was that the level of the Sea of Galilee (Israel's sole source of fresh water) had risen.

For morning work, Mike and I returned to the warehouse complex to work with Ilya. He had given me a present the previous week of an Israeli army watch protector, so now I was pleased to reciprocate by giving him a Swiss army knife. By day's end, I also gave him my work gloves to protect his hands. He had the long delicate hands of a musician, but they were marked with cuts and scars from the heavy warehouse work he did everyday. Today was Ilya's last day before he went on a 30-day leave, which corresponded to the length of his mother's visit. He was understandably very excited about it.

Ilya had his shoulder bandaged up from an injury he received while carrying a heavy object the day before, so we tried to do as much as possible to lighten his load. We moved tables, chairs, large water containers, tents, and many other items. Trucks dropped off supplies and picked up supplies while we worked. By lunchtime, our backs were telling us that we'd put in a full morning of hard work. We needed Advil and a short post-lunch nap to recover.

The work continued after lunch. We gradually cleaned up and organized two large warehouse rooms. We boxed, packed, stored, folded, and reorganized. At our mid-afternoon break, we were so tired that two of the three of us (Mike and Keren) simply laid flat on their backs on two wooden pallets on the floor and fell instantly asleep. A soldier came by, looked at the two still bodies and asked: "What happened to them?" "The work was so hard, they dropped dead," I replied. He looked startled until my face broke into a grin. He understood my joke – my first joke in Hebrew – shook his head, and walked past us.

By the end of the afternoon, we had completed both warehouse rooms, and swept them out clean. It had been such a chore to sweep them out that we asked Ilya, jokingly, whether it was true that the last time the rooms were swept was under the British. "No," he replied with a smile, "under the Turks." Bobby came by to inspect the rooms. He said in a light-hearted tone to Ilya: "It's too clean." Bobby was clearly impressed and shook our hands in thanks for a job well done.

We had worked later than usual to finish the job, so we were off to dinner shortly thereafter. Along the way, we observed trainee units of soldiers marching crisply across the grounds, showing their growing *esprit de corps*. This reminded us again of the rhythm of this base. Trainees arrived as ragged lines of high school graduates and gradually matured into soldiers who were proud of their units, showing their pride in how they marched and in shouting louder than the next unit.

Our evening speaker was the rabbi for the Zikim base. Rabbi Shaul was also a captain in the Israeli army. He brought us to the small but beautiful synagogue. The sanctuary seated about one hundred people and was by far the nicest room on the base. He put his M-16 down in front of the ark containing the Torah. One of the volunteers asked him how he felt about having to carry a rifle. "Wonderful," he quickly replied. "The Bible allows every person to defend himself." He explained that as rabbi for the base, he acted as a counselor for the soldiers as well as their religious leader. As the religious leader, he conducted services three times a day, with the first service at 5:45 A.M. He also thanked the volunteers for coming to the base, repeating what we had heard from others previously – that it motivated the soldiers on the base to see us working side-by-side with them. Then he spoke about the special relationship that all Jews have with Israel, emphasizing that Israel is a special and holy place.

WEDNESDAY, NOVEMBER 11, 2003

Today was our last full day of work for the week and our last day together as a group of ten volunteers. Sam, the first of our volunteers to go, was leaving after lunch. This was Sam's sixth Sar-el stint, having done his previous one during the Second Gulf War this past March. Five more volunteers (including me) would finish our Sar-el stint at the end of the workweek tomorrow, leaving four volunteers to stay on for their third week.

It was cold in the morning and so we bundled into our army jackets to head to breakfast. After flag-raising, we took group pictures and gave Etty a present from our group (a necklace). Then we headed to work, where shortly we were down to our tee-shirts as the sun broke through the cloud cover. The weather varies dramatically in the desert – cold at night and hot by 10:00 A.M.

Richard and I worked with Raz in the warehouse this morning. We did various odd jobs, including throwing away old pipes and capping water bottles with cloth coverings for storage. At one point, Bobby came over and said to Raz (pointing at me): "This one is better than any of the soldiers in the warehouse." I thanked him for the compliment.

During breaks in the work, we mentioned to Raz that the Palestinian violence seemed to have subsided over the past several weeks. He said that he knew the reason. The army had been very successful in arresting a number of Hamas and Hezbollah terrorists lately. Based on his experience in his combat unit in Ramallah, he believed that most Palestinians would accept a two-state solution, with Israel co-existing with a Palestinian state. However, Hamas and Hezbollah were sworn to the destruction of Israel and so any Palestinian who might propose acceptance of a two-state solution would be killed by these terrorist groups. Therefore, the majority of the Palestinians suffered in silence because their leadership (i.e., Arafat) supported the terrorists rather than trying to shut them down.

While we worked in the warehouse complex, a team of volunteers toiled away in the armory (weapons depot) and another team reinforced the tents. The latter task involved filling up sandbags and then tying them to the soldiers' big tents to hold them down in the event of windstorms. The volunteers also retied the ropes holding the tents to the tent pegs, to make certain they were tight. The key talent on this volunteer team was my bunkmate Rob. From his service in the New Zealand navy, he had acquired a knowledge of rope knots that was unsurpassed and came in very handy. We had heard that, during the windstorm the previous evening, one of the female company's tents had collapsed, throwing the occupants into a panic. That incident put Rob and his team of volunteers in even greater demand, in light of the additional winter storms the base was expecting.

Just before the lunch break, I had given Bobby a present of a Swiss army knife. He had thanked me and said one of his sons would be entering the army in December. For this occasion, he had planned to give him a present of a new knife – so now he planned to give him this Swiss army knife. I said I would be pleased if he treated my gift as a present to his son. (While working with Bobby in the afternoon, his cell phone rang. It was his son, who was calling to thank me for the present. I wished him good luck in his future army career.)

At the end of the workday, I gave my last Swiss army knife to Raz. He seemed very touched to receive a present from me and gave me a big hug. I wished him success when he returned to his combat unit. I knew that very shortly he would be back with his unit, patrolling the streets of Ramallah.

I returned to my bunk after sunset. A few minutes later, Raz appeared out of the darkness in front of my door. He was holding a Bible (in Hebrew) – and not just any Bible. It was a new Israeli Defense Force Bible of the type that every soldier receives when they graduate from basic training. With their hand on their Bible, each graduate swears to defend the State of Israel. On the inside cover of the Bible, Raz had penned a personal note to me: "Heart to heart, blood to blood, you can be a very good Israeli soldier."

Needless to say, I was delighted with his thoughtfulness. I told him that I had given him a small gift, but that he had given me a much bigger one that I would treasure forever. His face lit up into a big grin, we hugged, and he disappeared into the darkness.

After washing off the dirt of a full day's work and changing into civilian clothes, we headed out of the base for a different dinner experience. Shachar, one of the soldiers who worked with the volunteers in the armory, had mentioned that after hours he also worked in a restaurant in Ashdod and invited us to his restaurant for dinner tonight. We all accepted immediately. Anything would be better than the hard-boiled eggs and tomatoes that a Zikim dinner offered us.

As we left our bunks, our path was blocked by a long line of trainee soldiers from Company Eight next to us, headed by the base mascot dog, Colonel Be-seder. They were returning from a full day's march through the desert. Their faces were blackened with camouflage paint and they looked like they had crawled through a good part of the desert. We waved at many of them and they greeted us back. One told us that this had been their best day in training camp because it had been the most fun. We even saw some of the female companies returning – also in a good mood and with blackened faces. The soldiers in Company Eight were in a good mood for another reason: tomorrow they were graduating from basic training.

The restaurant we drove to in Ashdod was named La Sipood. It was fantastic. We started out with about ten different types of appetizers, such as fried eggplant and various salads. Then we moved to pita and humus, and then to delicious main courses of chicken, steak, and kabobs. We topped off the feast with mint tea, strong Israeli coffee, and Moroccan baklava. Shachar came by to tell us that the restaurant would only charge us for the main courses. Everything else was "on the house." It was the least they could do for the volunteers, he explained. Regardless of the amount of work that we completed, our most important impact was simply our presence on the base. He said it lifted the soldiers' morale to see us there, because they were under the impression from the international media that the entire world was against Israel. We strongly made the point to Shachar that there are many people back in our home countries who are very supportive of Israel and that the international media does not reflect those people's views. He responded with "I love you all!" in Hebrew. He was very emotional in expressing his feelings. His sister had been our waiter. He even brought his father over to introduce him to us.

As we sat around the table on our last night together, we all commented on "the most surprising thing" each of us learned at the base. "I was surprised by how poor the Israeli army is and how they have to make do with very old, but serviceable equipment," Richard remarked. "I was struck by how young these soldiers are," Elsie said. All of us seconded that impression.

After such a terrific meal, the ride back to the Zikim base was filled with boisterous laughter. Amidst the laughter, I explained to Etty that we realized that, with budget cutbacks in the army, there was little or no money for the side trips Sar-el had formerly offered. However, the volunteers were happy to fund their own entertainment, whether it was half-day sightseeing trips or visits to local restaurants. We came home as a very happy bunch, and much heavier no doubt.

As we walked from the main gate to our bunks we were surprised to hear the shouts of one of the female trainee companies exercising on the parade grounds. Even though it was already 10:00 P.M., their sergeants had them doing stretching exercises and sit-ups. They seemed to be in a happy mood too, because they were also graduating tomorrow.

THURSDAY, NOVEMBER 12, 2003

My alarm woke me at 4:30 A.M., thirty minutes before the *Chamesh Shniah* of our neighboring Company Eight would have done so. Richard, Mike and I bundled into our army jackets and trudged across the desert sand of the base towards the synagogue. The sun hadn't yet risen and the nearly full moon lit the way. Outside the synagogue, the trainee soldiers were already starting their morning exercises. We joined over forty soldiers, including the rabbi and the base commander, in the synagogue for the 5:45 Thursday morning *Shacharit* service. All brought their M-16s into the sanctuary, but put them down in order to put on *tefillin* and prayer shawls and to pray. Several female soldiers sat in a separate marked-off section of the sanctuary.

Most morning services on the base are short, but this one took a little longer than usual because it included reading a passage from the Torah. A soldier opened the ark in the front of the sanctuary. From the ark, he removed a beautiful upright cylindrical wooden Torah case, of Near Eastern style and almost completely covered in blue and gold velvet. Soldiers kissed the Torah case as it was brought to the *bimah* (pulpit) in the center of the sanctuary and placed standing up. The rabbi opened the two sides of the Torah case, identified the correct passage, and called up a soldier for the first *aliyah* blessing. Just as the rabbi peered at the text to begin chanting, we could see the sun beginning to rise through the window just to the right of the Torah. It was a memorable sight – the first rays of the sun striking the blue and gold of the velvet-draped Torah as the rabbi chanted.

The base was quiet this morning. After flag-raising, several companies of trainee soldiers stood in rows on the parade grounds to rehearse the graduation ceremony. As we walked to our work-stations, we saw a squad of trainee soldiers on the basketball court, practicing close combat use of their rifles. It struck me that, although the base had a fine outdoor fenced-in basketball court, I had never seen it used for basketball. Instead, I had seen squads of soldiers being trained in close combat drills on this court, or else doing calisthenics on it.

We all knew our morning work assignments. By now, the soldiers in the warehouse complex knew us well. They gave us the keys to whichever rooms we needed access to and let us work quite independently of them. They trusted us and knew that we were serious and hard workers.

After lunch, we were finished for the week. The environs of neighboring Company Eight rang out with happy laughter because they had just completed their basic training. The company soldiers packed up their knapsacks and emptied out their tents. For the first time, we saw them dressed in parade uniforms, rather than army fatigues. Many of them came over to the volunteers' bunks to shake hands, take pictures with us, and say good-bye before they lined up to march over to the parade grounds. One soldier named Or insisted that I pose in a picture with him and his buddies, probably because I was wearing a Sar-el tee-shirt. I reciprocated by getting a picture taken of the two of us. I had never seen a happier or more excited bunch of eighteen-year olds.

Finally, orders rang out from their sergeants. The soldiers (no longer mere trainees) of Company Eight ran to pick up their knapsacks and line up. They marched off to a cadence called out by their sergeants: Smoll, smoll, smoll, yemin, smoll... ("Left, left, left, right, left..."). Their boots hit the ground simultaneously, making a crisp sound. These soldiers were sharp, and they were proud of themselves. They slowly marched out of sight. A few minutes later, as we were leaving the base, the breeze carried strains of martial music to us. Their graduation had begun. As we drove off, we saw the crowds of family members ringing the parade grounds to watch their loved ones graduate. And so the rhythm of the base continued to make a permanent imprint on these soldiers' memories, as it had on ours.

CHAPTER 4

Observing the Middle East from a Distance

My return home to Raleigh hit me like a slap in the face. Catching up on my work consumed me for many weeks, even though I had only been away for two. Pleasant thoughts of time spent at Zikim quickly receded into the recesses of my memory. I resolved that I would schedule any future Sar-el stint only in the summer months when my clients' vacation plans make it somewhat easier to get away.

News from Israel continued to capture headlines. In the absence of a Palestinian government willing to restrain terrorism and to engage in meaningful negotiations, Prime Minister Ariel Sharon shocked the Israeli populace in late 2003 by announcing his support for a unilateral withdrawal from both the West Bank and the Gaza Strip. This was contrary to the hard-line platform upon which he had been elected. As a first step, he put the concept of a unilateral withdrawal from the Gaza Strip to a vote within his own rightist Likud Party. In early May, two-thirds of his party rejected the Gaza Strip withdrawal, putting a temporary halt to plans for a pull-out.

Despite Sharon's efforts to seek a withdrawal from the Gaza Strip, Palestinian terrorists continued to target Israeli civilians. The attack on May 2, 2004 was particularly heinous. Palestinian gunmen in the Gaza Strip forced a civilian car off the road, walked up to the vehicle and then shot to death all of its five occupants – an Israeli woman, eight months pregnant, and her four young daughters. Islamic Jihad claimed credit for these murders. The Palestinian Authority's official radio station praised the murderers as "heroic" and refused to condemn this grisly attack on unarmed Israeli civilians. Despite Arafat's statements to the western world condemning terrorism, his own radio station praised it to the Palestinian people.

Israeli soldiers, occupying the Gaza Strip to protect the 7,500 Israeli settlers there, continued to be killed by Palestinian militants. This fueled the sentiment of the majority of Israelis who supported a pull-out from the Gaza Strip. And terrorist attacks continued throughout Israel. Most notable was a homicide bombing in the southern port city of Ashdod, a short distance north of the Zikim base. The southern portion of Israel had previously been relatively immune from terrorism. The attack at Ashdod demonstrated that the Israeli border with the Gaza Strip, previously thought to be impervious to penetration, could in fact be penetrated.

Construction of the security fence separating Israel from the West Bank continued. Correspondingly, the pattern of terrorist bombings against Israeli civilians seemed to support Raz's assertion that the reason the Palestinians opposed construction of the fence was that it worked. Specifically, the fence made it harder for Palestinians to cross over into Israel to conduct terrorist attacks. More and more, those attacks were limited to those areas of Israel where the fence had not yet been completed. Unfortunately, Jerusalem was one of those areas.

In mid-May, Israeli intelligence got wind of a cache of weapons piled up on the Egyptian end of the Gaza Strip. The imminent smuggling of these weapons to the Palestinians, by way of underground tunnels between the Egyptian side of the border and the town of Rafeh in the southern Gaza Strip, concerned the Israelis greatly. This was because the weapons included heavy caliber arms capable of destroying Israeli tanks and shoulder-launched anti-aircraft missiles capable of shooting down Israeli civilian aircraft. In the absence of a Palestinian government willing to interdict this shipment of arms, Israel was forced to do it herself. Israeli forces occupied Rafeh to search for and destroy the tunnels. Militant terrorist groups attacked the Israeli soldiers to prevent their smuggling routes from being discovered and destroyed. The Palestinians highlighted their casualties to the world media, which criticized Israel for the incursion and ignored the fact that it had been necessitated by the Palestinians' refusal to crack down on the terrorists. A United Nations resolution condemning the Israeli move into Rafeh was passed. I was disappointed that the U.S. abstained from the vote rather than voting against the resolution.

II

By late June, progress was made on the issue of Israeli withdrawal from the Gaza Strip. The crucial factor seemed to be the greater participation of Egypt. *The Jerusalem Post* carried a report that, in furtherance of the U.S. Roadmap for Peace, Egypt demanded that Arafat relinquish control over the various Palestinian military forces to Palestinian Prime Minister Abu Qurei and not interfere with Abu Qurei's plan to bring those units together into one force.* Egypt also demanded that Arafat not interfere with Abu Qurei's efforts to negotiate a peace plan with Israel.

At first Arafat refused the Egyptians' demands. After further discussions, Arafat reportedly gave in to the Egyptians. In the meantime, the Egyptians and Israelis agreed in principle to the entry into the Gaza Strip of Egyptian "police trainers" in the near future. Their goal was to train a police force that would enable the Palestinian Authority to take control over the Gaza Strip upon the Israelis' withdrawal. This Egyptian involvement and pressure upon Arafat was as much a turnaround as had been Sharon's surprise endorsement of an Israeli withdrawal from the Gaza Strip and the West Bank.

---

* Arafat's refusal to accede to the same demand from the previous prime minister, Mahmoud Abbas, led to Abbas' resignation.

What had caused the Egyptians to change course so dramatically and become an active supporter of the Roadmap for Peace? The first factor was the Egyptians' realization that Sharon was serious about unilaterally withdrawing from the Gaza Strip. In the absence of a negotiated withdrawal, the Israelis' pullback would likely create a power vacuum that would be filled by Hamas, the strongest of the Palestinian terrorist groups. As a militant Muslim group, Hamas had a natural ally in the radical Egyptian Muslim fundamentalist groups. One such group, the Egyptian Islamic Jihad, had engineered the assassination of Egyptian President Anwar Sadat in 1981. The Egyptians therefore viewed their Muslim fundamentalist groups as a destabilizing force in their country; they also realized that a Hamas-controlled Gaza Strip would likely become a breeding ground and safe haven for the radical Egyptian fundamentalist groups. Faced with this potential threat, the Egyptians decided that their best option was to strengthen the Palestinian Authority's power and authority so that Hamas would not rule the Gaza Strip. They realized that this could not occur with Arafat in control, since he was widely viewed by his own people as a corrupt, and hence discredited, leader of the Palestinian Authority. In effect, the Egyptians joined the U.S. and Israel in deciding that Arafat was either an obstacle to peace, or simply irrelevant to the peace process.

The second factor behind the Egyptian turnaround related to an economic inducement offered by the U.S. In the mid-1990s, with U.S. backing, Israel offered Egypt a proposal for joint Israeli-Egyptian industrial areas. The proposal involved the creation of Qualified Industrial Zones (QIZs) within Egypt. In these QIZs, factories employing Egyptian labor would produce goods incorporating a small amount of Israeli "inputs," such as Israeli-produced equipment or components. The Egyptian goods could be imported into the U.S. on a duty-free basis. When Egypt declined the proposal, the Israelis offered the same deal to Jordan, which accepted it in 1997. By 2004, the ten QIZs within Jordan contained 55 plants employing 30,000–50,000 Jordanians in the manufacture of textiles. As a result, Jordan's exports to the U.S. were expected to increase from $17 million in 1997 to about $1 billion by the end of 2004.

In mid-2003, realizing they had earlier lost a golden opportunity, the Egyptians requested a re-opening of talks for a U.S.-Israeli-Egyptian agreement to create QIZs in Egypt. A very significant percentage of the Egyptian workforce was employed in the textile business, which was suffering from competition from China and other low-cost Asian countries. The Egyptian request for economic assistance was expected to, and in fact did, result in Egypt favoring the U.S.-sponsored negotiated peace plan.*

III

The Egyptian turnaround coincided with Sharon's decision not to be bound by the hard-liners in his own Likud party. In early June, he fired two of these hard-liners from his Cabinet, replaced them with supporters of his withdrawal plan, and put the plan to a Cabinet vote. The Cabinet voted narrowly to support the plan. As a result, several rightist religious members of the Knesset bolted from his coalition government, and Sharon lost the slim Knesset majority that had allowed him to govern.

The Israeli papers carried rumors that Sharon had put out feelers to Shimon Peres to invite the Labor Party to join him in a Unity coalition government to keep the withdrawal initiative alive. At first, Peres rebuffed Sharon's invitation, even though the Labor Party supported a withdrawal from the West Bank and the Gaza Strip. The Labor Party insisted, as its condition for salvaging Sharon's government, that he agree, not only to withdrawal from

---

* The agreement signed in December 2004 created an immediate benefit for the Egyptian labor force. According to the November 28, 2005 *Jerusalem Report*, Egyptian Trade Minister Rashid Mohamed Rashid announced that more than 350,000 Egyptians were employed in the three QIZs established under this trilateral economic agreement between the U.S., Egypt, and Israel.

the Gaza Strip, but also to the simultaneous withdrawal from the bulk of the West Bank.

Formulation of the details of the Gaza Strip withdrawal was assigned by Sharon to a special commission. Soon details of the commission's tentative plans began to leak out into the press. These included the timetable for a phased withdrawal and compensation levels for the Israeli Gaza residents who voluntarily agreed to leave, versus those who did not and therefore would not be eligible for compensation. These details provoked further protests by these residents and other Israelis opposed to the withdrawal.

Even though an Israeli withdrawal from the Gaza Strip seemed likely, Gaza-based Palestinian terrorist groups contin-ued to target Israeli civilians. I paid special attention to an at-tack on the Israeli town of Sderot because it is only a few miles southeast of the Zikim base and also very close to the Gaza Strip. Over the past two and a half years, Palestinians had fired about 300 Kassam rockets from the Gaza Strip into Israel. Since the Kassams are crude rockets lacking a precision guidance system, their use was designed more to spread terror than for any tacti-cal military purpose. In that respect, they were similar to the v1 and v2 rockets that the Germans rained on London during the Second World War and to the Scud missiles that Iraq fired into Israel at the outset of the First Gulf War.

About 70 of these 300 Kassam rockets had fallen on Sderot but (seemingly miraculously) none had caused any casualties. On June 28, Sderot's luck ran out. Four Kassam rockets slammed into the town. While three caused only minor injuries, the fourth ex-ploded in front of a nursery school. A forty-nine-year-old man, who had just dropped a child off at the school, was killed. And a four-year-old boy standing with his mother in front of the school was killed, his mother seriously wounded. The Palestinian ter-ror organization, Hamas, immediately claimed credit for these civilian murders. Israeli helicopters retaliated by attacking two bomb-making factories in the Gaza Strip, and Israeli army units set up a security zone in the northern sector of Gaza to prevent additional rocket attacks.

Several days later, a July 5 headline in *The Jerusalem Post* caught my eye: "IDF Foils Twin Suicide Bombings Headed for Rosh Ha-Ayin." The article reported that the Israeli army had thwarted Palestinian terrorists attempting to transport two suicide bomb belts around a portion of the completed security fence. The security fence had obviously impeded the terrorists' access to Rosh Ha-Ayin.

This article prompted me to consider whether the fence was the answer to Palestinian terrorism. That evening, over dinner at my home, I posed this question to a young Israeli woman named Moran, who was spending the year in Raleigh. She had recently completed her military service as an Israeli air force officer. Moran responded: "The fence helps, but is only a temporary solution and not the final answer. Israelis cannot just build a fence and then hide behind it. We also have to deal with the Palestinians in a way that allows them to have a hopeful future. Otherwise, the Palestinians' feeling of hopelessness will continue to foster more terrorists who will eventually figure out a way to get through the fence." Moran's thoughtful assessment reflected a level of maturity that I have come to expect in young Israelis who have completed their military service.

IV

Events in early July brought the issue of the security fence into the international limelight. In the first week of July, the Israeli Supreme Court issued its ruling on a challenge to the legality of the security fence, brought by neighboring Palestinians as well as certain Israelis through the Israeli court system. The Israeli Supreme Court balanced the fence's hardship to the local Palestinian population against the Israelis' security needs. As a result, the Court ruled that the positioning of an 18-mile segment of the security fence unreasonably burdened the neighboring

Palestinian population. Accordingly, it ordered that the segment be re-positioned so as to cause less hardship to the Palestinians. Within 24 hours, the Israeli military began the process of re-positioning the fence. Here was a demonstration that the democratic institutions in Israel – the only ones of their kind in the Middle East – were capable of resolving issues arising from the construction of the security fence.

Despite the decision of the Israeli Supreme Court, a few days later the International Court of Justice (ICJ) issued a ruling condemning the security fence as a whole and demanding that it be torn down. Rather than balancing the security needs of the Israelis to be free from terrorism against the hardship the fence caused the Palestinians, the ICJ simply focused on the Palestinians' concerns. It did not acknowledge that the fence was designed to protect Israelis from terrorist attacks and, in fact, had significantly reduced the number of terrorist bombings. Terrorist attacks originating in the northern West Bank had been reduced by 90 percent following completion of the northern portion of the security fence. Correspondingly, more terrorist attacks were emanating from the southern West Bank, where the security fence had not yet been completed.

The ruling of the ICJ seemed to say that saving the lives of Israelis was not a factor to be considered when addressing the hardship the fence imposed on the Palestinians. Aside from the bias this reflected, I could not understand what business it was of the ICJ to decide whether Israel could protect its citizens from terrorist attacks, especially when the Israeli Supreme Court had already ruled on the matter.

This unfairness spurred me to read the ICJ's lengthy decision. I noted Israel's position was that the security fence was necessitated by the Palestinians' acts of violence. Specifically, the fence was a legitimate step by the Israeli government to protect its citizens from terrorist attacks launched by the West Bank Palestinians. The United Nations Charter recognizes that every state has an inherent right to defend itself. The ICJ decision did not accept

Israel's argument that, like other nations, it has a right to practice self-defense against terrorist attacks. Instead, the ICJ declined to address Israel's self-defense argument, simply dismissing it as not "pertinent" to the case.

The dissent by the only American on the ICJ panel, Judge Thomas Buergenthal, sharply rebuked the ICJ for its one-sided analysis. Judge Buergenthal criticized the ICJ for concluding that the fence was illegal, while completely ignoring that the fence derived from Israel's efforts to defend its citizens against terrorism. "To reach that conclusion with regard to the wall as a whole without having before it or seeking to ascertain all relevant facts bearing directly on issues of Israel's legitimate right of self-defense, military necessity and security needs, given the repeated deadly terrorist attacks in and upon Israel proper coming from the Occupied Palestinian Territory to which Israel has been and continues to be subjected, cannot be justified as a matter of law," he wrote. "The nature of these cross-Green Line attacks and their impact on Israel and its population are never really seriously considered by the Court."

Thankfully, the U.S. government announced that it would veto any U.N. Security Council resolution seeking to impose sanctions on Israel on the basis of the ICJ decision. However, the U.N. General Assembly voted overwhelmingly (150 to 6, with 10 abstentions) to approve a resolution endorsing that opinion and demanding that Israel tear down the security fence. The U.N. resolution was strikingly silent in failing to condemn Palestinian terrorism against Israel.

Moran's admonition that the Palestinian terrorists would figure out ways to circumvent the security fence was, unfortunately, proven correct. On Sunday, July 11, a terrorist bomb exploded at a Tel Aviv bus stop, killing a nineteen-year-old female soldier and injuring thirty-two people. The Al Aksa Brigade, the armed branch of Yasir Arafat's Fatah organization, claimed responsibility for the murder. On the one hand, this showed that the security fence could not stop all terrorist attacks. On the other hand, this was the first such bombing within the Green Line (pre-1967 Israel borders) since the March suicide bombings in Ashdod that killed ten Israelis. Clearly, the fence had significantly diminished the number of bombings, but could not eliminate all of them.

V

As the time for my upcoming Sar-el stint approached, chaos broke out in the Gaza Strip. With the realization that Prime Minister Sharon was serious about pulling Israeli settlements out of the Gaza Strip, three Palestinian factions vied to fill the power vacuum created by the impending Israeli departure. The first were the terrorist groups, led by Hamas. The second was Arafat's Palestinian Authority, representing the old-line Palestinian leadership that had returned with Arafat from exile in Tunis at the time of the 1992 Oslo Accords.

The emergence of a third group, representing Palestinians who rejected the authority of the old-line Palestinian leadership, was most interesting. This third group condemned Arafat and his cronies as corrupt and discredited opportunists who had abused their positions of power to line their pockets with bribes, taxes, and aid intended to benefit the Palestinian people.* This group blamed the corrupt Palestinian Authority leadership, as much as the Israeli occupation, for the dire economic straits of the Palestinians. They called for the old-line Palestinian leadership to relinquish control to a reform faction with more popular support, led by Mohammad Dahlan.

This situation came to a head on July 17, as terrorist groups conducted a series of kidnappings of Palestinians in the Gaza Strip. Among the kidnapped was the Arafat-appointed Gaza police chief. While the kidnappers subsequently released those abducted, these actions demonstrated Arafat's dwindling authority. This was rein-

---

* In 2003, Arafat made *Forbes* Magazine's list of the world's richest people, placing sixth in the category of "kings, queens, and despots."

forced when militants trashed the headquarters of Arafat's security chief over the Gaza Strip, Arafat's cousin, Musa Arafat.

In response to the chaos and apparent lawlessness in the Gaza Strip, Prime Minister Qurei submitted his resignation to Arafat, as had his predecessor Mahmoud Abbas. This time, Arafat refused to accept Qurei's resignation. But it was clear that Qurei represented a reform faction disgusted with Arafat's refusal to enact political and military reforms to restore the credibility of the Palestinian Authority.

The discredit in which the Arafat leadership was held by a majority of Gaza Strip Palestinians was illustrated in a surprising turn of events. On July 23, a fifteen-year-old Palestinian boy in Beit Hanoun (in the Gaza Strip) was killed as his family struggled to push Palestinian militants away from their farm. The militants wanted to set up Kassam rocket launchers on the family's farm in order to launch rockets into Israel. Realizing that the location of the rocket launchers would likely provoke Israeli retaliation against them, the family first argued with and eventually physically resisted the militants. The militants' shooting of the teenage boy provoked Palestinian demonstrations in Beit Hanoun and other Gaza Strip towns. The demonstrations protested the powerlessness of Arafat's Palestinian Authority to stop the Kassam rocket launches, which inevitably led to Israeli retaliations. It would have been unthinkable a year earlier to see Palestinians demonstrating against Arafat for failing to stop terrorist attacks against Israel.*

---

* A month later, Israeli authorities pointed out that the fifteen-year-old boy's name was incorrectly placed on a list of victims the Palestinian Authority offered to the media as Palestinians killed by the Israeli army.

CHAPTER 5

Welcome to the Israeli Navy

July 30–August 19, 2004

FRIDAY, JULY 30, 2004

The El Al 737 flying from London to Tel Aviv was packed with Israelis, mostly returning from vacationing in Britain. I sat next to a young Israeli woman currently living in London named Michal. She was returning to Israel to make preparations for her wedding to an English surveyor named David. Although she and David planned to live in London, Michal wanted the wedding to take place in Israel at her parents' home in Rishon Le-Tzion. Her parents were Yemenite Jews who had immigrated to Israel where Michal was born.

The five-hour plane ride passed quickly in conversation with Michal, who described the unique circumstances under which she met her fiancé. She had lived in London for almost ten years, working as an instructor for people becoming travel agents and airline counter agents. At that point, Michal returned to Israel intending to find an Israeli husband and settle in her homeland. She had heard about the reputation of an Orthodox rabbi in B'nai Brak who was renowned for advising soon-to-be married couples whether they were right for each other. She went to the rabbi to ask for advice on where to find the person who would be right for her. To her surprise, the rabbi told her not to move back to Israel because her intended soul mate was not an Israeli. Instead, he was a British Jew named David, previously divorced, and she would find him by returning to Britain. The rabbi instructed Michal to move to a different neighborhood in London named Golders Green, which contained a traditional and closely-knit Jewish community. He even told her in which of the many synagogues in Golders Green she would find David, and how many children they would have (two boys and a girl). Michal returned to London, moved to Golders Green, and went to a social event at the specified synagogue. Walking in the door, she met her David (previously divorced) who was with another woman. However, as soon as Michal and David were introduced, they instantly knew that they were intended for each other. His answer to her question about children? He wanted two boys and a girl.

Michal also talked about the recent upsurge in antisemitic violence in France, which had led to an influx of French Jews moving to Israel. Earlier in the week, Prime Minister Sharon had personally welcomed a contingent of 200 French Jews as they had arrived in Israel to relocate. An estimated 3,000–4,000 French Jews were expected to make aliyah to Israel in 2004, largely as a result of antisemitic violence in France and the inability of the French authorities to stop that violence.

While commenting on the dire situation in France, Michal did admit that just a month earlier she had had her first personal experience of antisemitic violence. Vandals had set a synagogue on fire in Golders Green and had desecrated its Torah scroll. She explained that the reason I hadn't read about this event in the newspapers is that the British media had agreed with the local Jewish community not to report it, so as not to encourage copycat violence. Although all of London's synagogues routinely hired security previously for protection against vandalism, this latest act had prompted stepped-up security.

The plane landed on time at a crowded Ben-Gurion airport. While waiting for my luggage, I placed a call to Pamela Lazarus. Pamela was excited about her good news. I had previously asked her for a new and challenging base assignment and she had one for me. The main Israeli naval logistics base, Betzet Tira, had never been opened to Sar-el volunteers. Its base commander had agreed to accept a contingent of Sar-el volunteers on a one-time trial basis. I was as excited as she was, especially because I had a special connection to the place: my cousin Michael had been stationed at the navy base in Haifa harbor just north of Betzet Tira for over twenty years.

Within minutes of touching down at Ben-Gurion, I was in a cab headed for Tel Aviv. As we whisked past orange groves I could see the skyline of Tel Aviv approaching. By 5:30, I was knocking on the door of my cousins, Bracha and Menachem.

Bracha and Menachem warmly welcomed me to their new home. With both of their sons in America, they no longer needed their big house. A month earlier, they had sold their home in Rosh Ha-Ayin and moved to a high-rise apartment in Ramat Aviv, a trendy northern Tel Aviv neighborhood near the sea.

After a home-cooked meal, the three of us walked to the Mediterranean under a full moon. Along the grass-covered bluffs overlooking the sea, families had set out blankets for picnics. Many had brought charcoal grills to barbecue dinner and the aroma of sizzling meat smelled delicious. Numerous couples walked along the beach holding hands. Because of the intense August sun, many families chose to go swimming in the sea after sunset. We stopped for ice coffee and chocolates at a seaside café.

I commented to Menachem that the level of Palestinian terrorism seemed to have decreased in comparison to the times I had visited over the prior two years. He agreed, and was eager to answer my question as to the reasons for this positive development. As a career military man, he was quick to credit Israel's Defense Force with having significantly damaged the terrorist infrastructure. Acting on good military intelligence, the IDF had aggressively hunted down terrorist leaders in the West Bank and Gaza Strip. On almost a daily basis, the newspapers reported the arrest or killing of key terrorist leaders or the foiling of attempted suicide bombings against Israeli civilian targets. For this strong military action, Menachem credited Prime Minister Ariel Sharon.

Menachem also attributed some of the decrease in terrorism to the construction of the security fence. He was quick to point out, however, that without the aggressive actions of the IDF in "taking out" the terrorist leadership, the fence alone would not be as effective. Menachem was cautious about attributing the decrease in terrorism to the recent infighting between Yasir Arafat's old-line leadership and the Palestinian reformers led by Mohammad Dahlan. He had seen Arafat survive other challenging situations and was not optimistic that Arafat would voluntarily step aside. He did agree, however, that the dismal state of the Palestinian leadership was what was standing in the way of an independent Palestinian state. "I am comfortable giving them the West Bank and Gaza Strip to create their own country, but not until they have a strong leader who commits not to attack Israel," Menachem commented. "Until Arafat is gone, the Palestinians will not have such leadership."

I agreed with Menachem. Like many politically moderate Israelis, I had held great hopes for peace in 1999 with the election of Ehud Barak as Israel's prime minister. Barak's twin campaign promises had been to withdraw Israeli troops from southern Lebanon and to negotiate a peaceful solution with the Palestinians. Upon his election, he immediately carried through on the promised withdrawal from Lebanon and sent the Palestinians clear signals that he was willing to trade land for peace.

The discussions between Barak and Arafat were conducted at Camp David in July 2000 under President Clinton's prodding stewardship. Barak carried through on his election promise. He offered Arafat virtually everything he had previously demanded – an independent Palestinian state consisting of the Gaza Strip, 96 percent of the West Bank, and a land swap of a portion of pre-1967 Israel for the 4 percent of the West Bank that Israel would keep. He also offered Palestinians sovereignty over Arab East Jerusalem and shared administration of the sacred ground of Jerusalem's Temple Mount. All Barak asked for in return was that the new Palestinian state act peacefully towards its Israeli neighbor.

Arafat walked away from Barak's offer. He didn't even counter-offer. Two months after the Camp David summit, the second Intifada broke out, ostensibly in response to Ariel Sharon's walk (as a private citizen) around the Temple Mount. Later, one of Arafat's ministers admitted that the second Intifada had been planned in advance by Arafat and was not a spontaneous uprising. Arafat had sent a clear message to his people that they could accomplish more through violence than negotiations.

Arafat's refusal to negotiate when confronted with Barak's offer ended Barak's prime ministership. Many Israelis felt he had been overly generous in his search for peace. More importantly, it put the lie to Arafat's assertions to the West that all he sought was the creation of an independent Palestinian state. Arafat's rejection of this golden opportunity revealed that he had never really accepted a two-state solution – Israel and a new Palestinian state, existing side-by-side. His actions disclosed that his ultimate goal was a one-state solution – a Palestinian state that would be established upon the land of a destroyed Israel.

The ensuing four years of Intifada violence resulted in the deaths of many Israelis and Palestinians, but did not accomplish Arafat's goal of the destruction of Israel. And it brought economic misery to the Palestinian populace. By 2004, many Palestinians privately acknowledged that Arafat's rejection of Barak's offer had been a blunder of historical proportions.

By now, Barak's offer was no longer "on the table" in the eyes of a great majority of Israelis. Arafat's blunder and the death and destruction wrought by the Palestinian violence had pushed the Israeli electorate sharply to the right. Many Israeli moderates no longer regarded Prime Minister Sharon as an extreme right-wing hawk. Instead, Sharon's tough military responses to the violence seemed entirely appropriate in light of the need to protect the country against terrorism. And even the most dovish of Israelis acknowledged that Arafat had proven that he was not a partner with whom a peace could be negotiated.

We walked back to Menachem and Bracha's apartment along the shore. The sound of the waves splashing onto the beach was very relaxing. After watching Tom Cruise in the movie *Top Gun* (with Hebrew subtitles), we turned in for the night.

SUNDAY, AUGUST 1, 2004

Following a relaxing Saturday with my cousins, I was energized to start my Sar-el stint this morning. With Menachem leaving for work at 6:00 A.M., I had a chance to chat with Bracha before my 8:00 cab pick-up. We talked about her job as director of a boarding home for at-risk children and about the challenges the children face. Because they came from broken homes, they craved the chance to see what a "normal home" looked like. Families from the Tel Aviv area often volunteered to take a child in for Sabbath weekends. The children very much looked forward to these visits, but they had to take turns since there were not enough volunteers for all the children every weekend. They also had to take turns to be taken out by "their family" on a mid-week evening for shopping or a movie.

Although Bracha had a psychologist, psychiatrist, and a social worker on staff to help her with the children, as the home's director she acted as the on-site "mother" for all sixty children and teenagers. Even though she described herself as a tough disciplinarian, Bracha clearly had a warm heart for her children. The teenagers who had "graduated" from the home into the army still came back to her on weekends and she allowed them to stay at the home even though they were no longer residents there. "Where else can they go on weekends, with no home of their own?" she asked. "I would never turn them away!" As I listened to Bracha,

I kept thinking of the "Lonely Soldiers," the eighteen-year-olds without families whom I had met on my previous bases.

The Sar-el office in Jaffa was hectic on this Sunday morning because volunteers were arriving and waiting for their base assignments. I found Pamela Lazarus in the middle of a crowd of people as she tried to process their paperwork and answer their many questions, all the while answering her cell phone. It seemed like a madhouse, but Pamela was in her element. She was a master juggler who seemed to thrive on the craziness around her. Throughout the process, I watched her keep her cool as she attended to the flood of people demanding her attention.

Pamela finally called nine volunteers into her tiny office and told us we were going to work at a navy base near Haifa named Betzet Tira. As the first volunteers to be accepted by this base, she asked us to be on especially good behavior. She introduced us to our madricha, Tamar, a tall, bright-eyed, twenty-year-old woman with long brown hair and freckles. Tamar had already worked as a Sar-el madricha at ten bases and was one of the more experienced madrichas. She told us that her brother was a captain in the Israeli navy and that she hoped he could "pull some strings" – to have us tour the navy ships stationed in Haifa's harbor.

Tamar's instructions to us on the bus ride north to Haifa were easy to follow because her English was American English. Even though her parents, from New York and New Jersey, had made aliyah to Israel before she was born, they spoke English at home, so English was her first language. Before we arrived at the base, Tamar explained that "Betzet" is an acronym whose three letters stand for three Hebrew words: *Basees Tziud Tovalah*, which literally means "Base for Moving Equipment." It was the main base for supplying the Israeli navy's equipment needs.

Betzet Tira was picturesquely nestled at the base of the Carmel Mountain range, halfway between the sea and the mountains. Surrounding us were groves of banana trees. With the exception of the warehouses, the buildings on the base were simple one-story structures. As at Batzop, the living quarters consisted of trailers placed on concrete blocks, each one divided into several rooms.

While the base itself did not appear dissimilar from the army bases that all nine of us had experienced previously, the attitude and facilities on this base were very different. This was apparent upon our arrival. We were welcomed with a reception of bourekas, fruit, and cold drinks and each of us was given an Israeli navy cap with the name of the base embroidered in gold. Our rooms were air-conditioned (a blessing in the August heat!) and neatly laid out on our beds were a blanket, two sheets, two towels, and army fatigues. It appeared that the base had gone out of its way to welcome us. Our room even contained a small carpet. The only item missing was a pillow, which we learned to do without.

The first person we met on the base was Gilad, a senior naval officer with a short salt-and-pepper beard and a quick sense of humor. He explained that he was the commander of one of the two bases that made up the Betzet logistics complex. His base was Betzet Kishon (the original Betzet base), located on the far northern side of Haifa harbor. The base we would be living on was Betzet Tira, a newer base built in 1984, about ten miles south of Haifa. Gilad gave us a quick tour of the various warehouses for the naval equipment adjacent to our living quarters. The most impressive was an automated warehouse over 50-feet high, in which parts were ordered by computer and procured by an elevator-type device that grabbed the appropriate box from a high shelf.

Lunch in the mess hall was impressive. The tables were set (including napkins) and we were served soup and schnitzel. It was delicious and served to impress upon us that we would be treated better than we had been on army bases, even though we were told that all future meals would be self-serve.

We gathered in the *moadon* (recreation room) after lunch, to be addressed by Gilad about our work assignments. The volunteers on Betzet Tira would be assigned to the warehouses, the kitchen, and to gardening duties (which included painting). "But two of you will be assigned to come to my base (Betzet Kishon) every morning for heavy duty work," he added, pointing at me and Brian, a thirty-year-old body-builder from Chicago. "You will be very tired when you return at the end of the day from Betzet Kishon," he said ominously, but with a twinkle in his eye. He made a motion as if to crack a whip.

I thanked him for the assignment and rose to take the bait: "That's what they told me at my prior bases, but I still had to go running after work in order to get some exercise." A chorus of "Whoas!" rose from the group of volunteers, as they enjoyed the repartée. Gilad's response was quick: "You will be so tired at the end of the day that my soldiers will have to carry you back." He seemed pleased with the playful banter, but I knew Gilad would make sure that Brian and I would have some heavy lifting tomorrow.

The rest of the afternoon was taken up with exchanging our fatigues for the right sizes and providing Tamar with our shoe sizes so that boots could be sent from a nearby base. Meanwhile, I struck up a conversation with Marion, a petite blonde grandmother from Connecticut and one of the two female volunteers in our group. This was her thirteenth Sar-el stint. I asked her why she volunteered so many times. She chuckled, responding that she gets bored with the frequent Florida vacations she takes with her husband. Marion hoped to be healthy enough to take her granddaughter, now two years old, to Israel for her bat mitzvah.

Since we could not start work today, Tamar arranged for a *sherut* (a 10-seat taxi van) to take us all to see Haifa. We drove out of the base into the adjacent suburban town of Tira. Haifa is Israel's third largest city and its largest port. It is also distinguished by the fact that it is the largest city in Israel where Jews and Arabs coexist in peaceful relations, living in mixed neighborhoods as opposed to the segregated neighborhoods existing in Jerusalem. On the way, we passed the Maxim restaurant along the seaside, which had suffered a Palestinian terrorist bombing a year and a half earlier. As testament to the history of peaceful relations between Haifa's Arabs and Jews, it had been one of the few acts of terrorism in Haifa.

The *sherut* wove its way up the winding highway until it emerged on the rim at the top of the Carmel Mountains, overlooking the great curved harbor of Haifa. From there we had a magnificent view of the entire harbor complex. Over a dozen ships, mostly oil tankers, were anchored well out in the middle of the harbor. Tamar pointed out the Betzet Kishon base at the far (northern) edge of the harbor complex. She also pointed out the battleship-gray ships of the Israeli navy, anchored within the safety of a great breakwater barrier.

We walked along the promenade, which was 2,000 feet above the harbor basin, passing couples sitting on the public benches to capture the cool breeze at that altitude while they watched the sun set. From the high point of the promenade, terraced gardens wound down to the gold-domed Ba'hai Temple that graced Haifa's harbor. As darkness closed in on the harbor and we turned to walk back to the *sherut*, one of the anchored ships bellowed its foghorn as if to say goodnight.

MONDAY, AUGUST 2, 2004

Tamar gave us the news prior to flag-raising: Just thirty minutes earlier a Kassam rocket, fired by Palestinian terrorists in the Gaza Strip, had slammed into a home in the southern Israeli town of Sderot. Luckily, the house was unoccupied at the time and so there were no casualties. The strike of the burial workers' union throughout Israel was continuing. And the nineteenth day of a strike of the Haifa dockworkers continued to paralyze the port. (Apparently, at least some of the ships we saw crowded into the harbor last night were waiting for the end of the dockworkers' strike.) The temperature would be hot today, approximately 33° C (91° F).

Flag-raising on the base was similar to that of my prior army bases. The only difference was that the flag of the Israeli navy was raised along with the Israeli flag and that a high-pitched bo-sun's whistle accompanied the raising of the flags. Our British volunteers noted with satisfaction that the Israeli navy had adopted this British naval tradition.

Our driver from the Betzet Tira base to the Betzet Kishon base was a slim, dark-haired, young female soldier named Sivan. Her job was to shuttle people and things between the two bases. Sivan was from nearby Atlit and her parents were of Israeli and Moroccan origin. She liked loud music and liked to drive very fast because her shuttle back and forth was very boring; today she said she would drive twenty times between the two bases. She raced Brian and me up to Haifa and drove us through the commercial port facility, passing large numbers of police, apparently lined up to keep the striking dockworkers at bay. Sivan was friendly and liked to talk. She warned us that the base commander (Gilad) at Betzet Kishon thought that she drove too fast and would ask us if she did. We promised to tell Gilad that she was a fine driver.

Sivan dropped us off at Gilad's office, where the first words out of his mouth were: "Does Sivan drive too fast?" We lied and said, "No, she's a fine driver." Then Gilad drove us through his base, which was much larger than the Betzet Tira base and consisted of long rows of old warehouses. He dropped us off at one such warehouse, to work under the supervision of a young sergeant named David.

For the morning, Brian and I were assigned to load big sheets of aluminum (about 4′ × 20′) onto wooden pallets. We worked as a team with David. When we got to the sheets that were a half-inch in thickness, David told us that each sheet weighed 120 kg. (over 250 lbs.); he handled these sheets with his forklift.

Walking to the mess hall for the lunch break, we turned a corner and confronted five large naval guns, each perched on top of a separate wooden structure. The guns looked like the type that destroyers typically carry as their main weapon, firing 76 mm. shells. Each gun was the size of a small room. Apparently, the guns had been taken off some of the older Israeli missile boats to make way for newer guns or missile-launchers.

Over lunch, I got better acquainted with my work partner,

Brian. He was a ruggedly handsome native Chicagoan with bright orange hair, broad shoulders, and a martial arts background. Brian had been a volunteer at the Julis base near Ashdod immediately before coming to Betzet Tira. (Julis is the Israeli army base that specializes in tank maintenance and repair.)

Brian's Sar-el stint was unusual in that, after working on two bases, he did not plan to return to the U.S. Instead, he intended to move to a kibbutz to enroll in a five-month work/study program – half-day in an *ulpan* (Hebrew language course) and half-day working on the kibbutz. All this was a prelude to his making aliyah to Israel. As a Chicago commodities broker, he had made and then lost a lot of money. He was single and ready for a change in his life. Although he was not religious, he felt a deep attachment to Israel as a Jew and was drawn to the country. Therefore, he was contemplating settling in Israel and finding an Israeli wife with whom to start a new life.

Our afternoon work consisted of cleaning up the area outside of the warehouses under David's command. My guess was that this assignment was David's way of testing whether we were willing to "get our hands dirty." We passed the test. We filled numerous large trash containers with old wooden boards, rusted pipes, used wire, and debris of every kind. By the time Gilad drove through our area to inspect our work, "our street" of warehouses was orderly and spotless.

Soaked in perspiration from the afternoon sun, we were glad to see Sivan's car pull up at the end of the workday. She raced us through the streets of Haifa back to the Betzet Tira base. Although I was dog-tired, I went for a run around the base so that Gilad's prediction would not be true.

This evening at dinner we met four more newly arrived volunteers: a couple from Teaneck, Howard and Terry, and two English women, Sylvia and Helen. After dinner, Tamar organized a meeting so that we could introduce ourselves to the now fully constituted group of thirteen volunteers. She told us that she would take us all to the Haifa beach after dinner tomorrow. Additionally, she warned us that our base would be without water from 9 A.M. to 9 P.M. tomorrow due to water main repairs, so there would be no showers after work tomorrow.

Our first nine volunteers were tired. For many of us it was our first full day of manual labor since our last Sar-el stint. The soles of our feet especially hurt because of the long hours on our feet. We all went to bed unusually early.

TUESDAY, AUGUST 3, 2004

I noticed certain niceties on a naval base that would be unthinkable on the two army bases on which I had previously worked. First, the bathrooms were nicer and cleaner (although, like in the army, they occasionally ran out of toilet paper, so you learned to bring your own). The mess hall had napkins at most meals. And there was actually an air-conditioned fitness room on the base with aerobic equipment and weights. This was the only Sar-el base I had ever heard of with a fitness center.

Tamar's news update just before flag-raising was very brief: The national burial workers' strike was continuing, so according to Tamar, "There will be no dying in Israel today." And Prime Minister Sharon had succeeded in cobbling together his governing coalition in the Knesset. He had persuaded the liberal Shinui party to join his coalition together with an Orthodox religious party.

After flag-raising, Tamar ushered the volunteers into the office of Shy Davidi (no relation to Aharon Davidi, the founder of Sar-el), the commander of all naval logistics and in charge of both Betzet bases. He had been in charge of the Betzet bases for only eight months, and in that capacity reported to the head of the Israeli navy. It was Shy Davidi who had agreed to allow Sar-el volunteers onto the two Betzet bases.

Shy gave us a short slide presentation about the Israeli navy. He described the types of potential terrorist attacks that the Israeli navy was designed to combat. The first were seaside attacks from boats originating from Lebanon. It is only a five to six-mile trip for a boat to travel from the Lebanese coast to Israel. There had been several such attacks from Lebanon. He described one such attack on the Israeli coast where a force of Palestinians had landed and killed many civilians near the northern Israeli town of Nahariya.

Similar threats came from the Gaza Strip. Ashkelon, Israel's southernmost Mediterranean port, is only seven miles north of the Gaza Strip, a distance that would take only ten to fifteen minutes to travel by boat. Shy talked about Palestinian terrorists on jet skis, who were particularly difficult to detect because their low profile was hidden by the waves. He showed a video of the destruction of a jet ski terrorist attacker off the northern coast of Israel near Rosh Hanikra in 1993.

There was also a risk from merchant ships, which could drop off small fast attack boats as they passed the Israeli coast. In 1985, one such passing merchant ship launched attack boats containing twenty-seven Palestinian terrorists planning to land on the Tel Aviv beaches on Israel's Independence Day and slaughter the crowds of anticipated holiday beachgoers. The Israeli navy apprehended all twenty-seven terrorists before they reached their target.

Merchant ships could also drop off weapons to Palestinian fishing boats as they passed the coast off the Gaza Strip. According to Shy, this was a particularly difficult threat to combat. Every day, many ships from the Suez Canal pass that coast as they emerge north into the Mediterranean Sea. These ships pass through the Palestinian fishing fleet of over 500 small boats. The infamous merchant ship, *Karine A*, which was captured in 2002 in the Persian Gulf, was headed for such a drop-off point with a cargo of Iranian-supplied weapons for the Palestinian terrorists.

Shy had been involved in the logistics supporting the capture of the *Karine A*. After the capture, Arafat had assured President Bush that he had no connection to the ship, but was embarrassed when the ship's commander revealed that he was operating at Arafat's direction. Shy told us that advance intelligence about the intended drop-off by the *Karine A* had allowed the Israeli navy to track and capture it.

Since the seizure was planned to occur on the "high seas" in the Persian Gulf, the Israelis did not want to attract attention by interdicting the *Karine A* with one of its major ships (i.e., a missile boat). And since they wanted to capture the *Karine A* without any naval gunfire, which might blow up the explosives-laden ship, they planned to seize it by surprise. Shy described how the Israelis sent a cargo ship containing fast rubber boats and commandos into the Persian Gulf to meet the *Karine A*. The *Karine A* was quickly boarded by these commandos. The attack took the crew completely by surprise and there was little resistance.

Israel has successfully blocked all sea-borne terrorist attacks over the past ten years. To combat these threats, the Israeli navy relied on radar stations positioned along the coast, fast patrol boats, and land-based surveillance aircraft. The radar stations are operated exclusively by female soldiers in the Israeli navy because, according to Shy, women proved to be more patient and observant than men in watching the radar screens over extended periods of time.

Sometimes the terrorists tried to blow up their boats alongside an Israeli patrol boat. (This was similar to the Al-Qaeda tactic that almost sank the American destroyer, the u.s.s. *Cole*, off the coast of Yemen in 2000.) To combat this threat, Israeli patrol boats no longer allowed other boats to get alongside them.

The final threat that Shy mentioned was that of magnetic mines, which the terrorists try to lay in the water approaches to Israel's ports. The Israeli navy needed an all-wooden boat to act as a mine detector. In an ironic twist, the Israeli navy seized Yasir Arafat's luxury yacht (all wooden) in 1994 and converted it into Israeli's only minesweeper to combat this threat. The ship was renamed the *Temanun* (meaning "octopus" in Hebrew).

Shy commented that, after 9/11, the U.S. realized that its navy of big ships was ill equipped to combat the terrorist threat. Instead of big ships, the U.S. needed much smaller boats for anti-terrorism efforts. Consequently, Israel was sharing with the U.S. its experience and tactics in using smaller boats to search for and apprehend terrorists coming from the sea.

We were impressed with the sophisticated capability of Israel's navy, especially because it was a relatively small branch of the Israeli military. To give us some perspective on how small it really was, Shy told us that all 6,000 members of the Israeli navy could fit on one U.S. aircraft carrier. He wished us luck and thanked us again for volunteering to work on his bases.

After Shy's presentation, all of the volunteers went to their work assignments. Sivan had waited patiently for an hour to pick up Brian and me and drive us to the Betzet Kishon base. She had taken to Brian in a flirty sort of way, so the conversation on the car ride was lively. To make up for lost time, she raced up the coast to Haifa swaying to the music on her radio, which alternated between American rock "oldies" (such as Aretha Franklin's "Respect") and fast Israeli music.

I noticed that as Sivan drove her military stick-shift car, she occasionally reached into the center console, pulled out a medal, and kissed it. I asked to see it and saw that on the reverse side of the medal was printed the Hebrew prayer for the safety of travelers, *Tefilot Ha-Derech*. "Why do you kiss the medal?" I asked. "Because it gives me good luck," she replied. "Do you need good luck?" I asked. "Yes," she said, "I have gotten several speeding tickets and I broke my arm two months ago in a car accident, so I've slowed down." If this was "slowing down," we clearly had to rely on the prayer!

Our assignment for the day consisted of working under David's direction in a warehouse full of metal pipes of all different lengths, widths, and weights. In order to inventory and mark the pipes, we moved, weighed, and counted them all day. The Israeli soldiers we worked with went out of their way to make us comfortable and encouraged us to drink water during breaks.

I was teamed up with a twenty-year-old Israeli reservist named Naftali for most of the day. He was a strapping young man from Nahariya with a bit of a wild side. I commented to Brian when we started the day that he looked like the Israeli equivalent of

John Travolta in the movie *Saturday Night Fever*. He was tall (6′2″), dark-haired, and handsome, and he knew it. The only English words he knew were the lines of various American rock songs. As his radio blared, he sang along loudly and swayed to the music while he worked. His hair was moussed just so and he wore sunglasses on his head all day. To better exhibit his muscular physique to occasional female soldiers passing by our warehouse, he worked only in a sleeveless undershirt, or completely stripped to the waist. Indicative of his irreverence to navy rules, he parked his car across the road from our warehouse at the top of a high platform, as if to show it off to the world. All of the other soldiers parked their cars in a parking lot far away from their workplaces.

Reinforcing the John Travolta image, at 4:00 P.M. Naftali decided we had worked enough. As we closed up, David's boss, Meir, came by. He and Naftali broke into a heated argument. Meir wanted us to work until 5:00. Naftali argued and pleaded with Meir that we had worked enough and that he had to leave early to get home to Nahariya. After a lot of loud shouting back and forth, Meir left, unpersuaded. Unlike John Travolta, who quit his paint store job when his boss in *Saturday Night Fever* wouldn't let him leave work early, Naftali could not quit the navy – so Naftali and I went back to work.

At 4:30, Sivan came by to drive Brian and me back to the Betzet Tira base. Since Naftali and I weren't finished, we asked her to wait. While she waited Naftali flirted with Sivan and then asked if she wanted to see his car. "Of course," she said, and he tossed her the keys. Ever the free spirit, Sivan promptly disappeared with his Honda Civic.

Sivan returned thirty minutes later, with a chastened look on her face. She had loaned Naftali's car to her girlfriend, Na'amah, and the two of them drove around the base for a "joy ride." They were caught by one of the base officers, who also noted that Na'amah did not have a license to drive. Sivan was afraid that the officer would advise Gilad of the infraction tomorrow morning and Gilad would impose some form of punishment.

Driving us back to Betzet Tira that evening, Sivan suddenly turned around to Brian sitting in the back seat (we would have preferred that she watched the road) and asked: "Are you married?" "No," he replied. "Do you have a girlfriend back in America?" she asked. "No," said Brian. "I'm thinking of moving to Israel and I'd like to find a nice Israeli girl to be my wife." With a twinkle in her eye, Sivan quickly responded: "I can help you find such a girl." We couldn't tell whether she was referring to herself.

After dinner, Tamar arranged for an evening at Haifa's Hof Ha-Carmel beach. We split up along the beach promenade, bordered by sidewalk cafés. I walked with Tamar for a couple of miles along the promenade, past an amphitheater hosting a rock concert and skirting a large circle containing well over a hundred Israeli folk dancers. The promenade was packed with young people, socializing or walking in couples. Wherever we walked, we could hear the rhythmic beat from the rock concert reverberating throughout the beach area.

Security checks along the beachfront promenade were conducted by yellow tee-shirted private security guards. In passing through one such checkpoint near the concert, the guard waved me through but stopped Tamar. When she pulled out her army identification card, which had always sufficed to allow her to pass through security, the guard still did not allow her to pass until he went through her bag. Tamar was annoyed, but it made some sense. Given that Palestinian terrorists had been known to wear Israeli army uniforms to infiltrate their targets, the security guard had been appropriately cautious. Since she was "on duty," accompanying the Sar-el volunteers, she was in uniform and carried her M-16 rifle. Private security handled the beach, and so Tamar was the only uniformed and armed soldier on the promenade. As such, she looked out of place.

Tamar told me that she liked her job as a Sar-el madricha very much. She and Etty (my madricha the previous year at Zikim) were good friends, having gone through Sar-el training together and having earned the top two awards in their training class. The hardest part of the job for the Sar-el madrichas, according to Tamar, was getting emotionally attached to each group of volunteers and then saying goodbye to them after three weeks.

On the *sherut* ride back to the base, Howard and Terry, the volunteers from Teaneck, talked about their son's experience last summer as an intern for a member of the Israeli Knesset. What most impressed their son were the vociferous, almost vicious, arguments on the floor of the Knesset between opposing members in front of the television cameras. Later, in the privacy of the Knesset cafeteria, the same opposing members would eat with each other as the best of friends. It was in the Knesset cafeteria that political compromises, which seemed impossible based on the public debate, were worked out. Otherwise, the government would be paralyzed.

WEDNESDAY, AUGUST 4, 2004

Tamar's news was typical of what one can often expect of a day in Israel: The IDF discovered another arms smuggling tunnel leading from Egypt to a house in the Gaza Strip town of Rafeh and destroyed the tunnel. The Palestinians shot at the IDF soldiers destroying this tunnel, but luckily no Israelis were hurt. The burial workers' strike was still ongoing. And this morning, 250 new immigrants to Israel from the U.S. landed at Ben-Gurion Airport and were welcomed personally by Israel's President Moshe Katsav. This group of new immigrants included neighbors of Howard and Terry from their Orthodox Jewish community in Teaneck.

This morning, we received our distinctive blue and white Sar-el patches which we slipped over our epaulettes. Now the volunteers, with our epaulette patches and blue Israeli navy caps, looked very distinctive at flag-raising.

After flag-raising, Sivan sped Brian and me from Betzet Tira north to Betzet Kishon in Haifa. Sivan zipped in and out of lanes, passing cars at high speeds, never touching her blinker, but frequently kissing her good luck charm. Once we got into the harbor facility, she drove through the curved back roads of the facility, never slowing down, as if she were a NASCAR driver. With the radio blasting, she was in her element.

David, the sergeant in charge of our warehouse at Betzet Kishon, was a twenty-five-year-old from a Moroccan Jewish family. He was the only person in our warehouse who spoke English and he went out of his way to make us feel at home. David lived in Haifa with his parents and offered to put Brian up for a weekend and show him Haifa. I hoped Brian would take David up on his offer, so he could see more of what Israeli life was like outside of military bases. The soldiers called David by his nickname "Dudu," but we just called him David.

Brian and I worked all day in the warehouse weighing, counting, and making an inventory of metal pipes. We worked in two teams – Brian and a thirty-seven-year-old reservist named Nissim, and me and Naftali. Naftali was in a serious mood when Brian and I arrived, already hard at work. As the day wore on, his "fun" side took over. He took numerous work breaks, during one of which he walked me to the office of the base commander just to chat with the female soldiers there. He had numerous loud disagreements with David's boss, Meir, who seemed to enjoy giving Naftali a tough time. Throughout the workday in the warehouse, he swayed, danced, and sang to the music on the radio. Why did the navy tolerate Naftali? Because at six feet two inches and strong as an ox, Naftali could move heavy pipes like no one else. Teamed together with Naftali, we completed twice as much work as Brian and Nissim. Between breaks, Naftali was efficient and fast, and consequently the navy tolerated his idiosyncrasies.

The warehouses were not air-conditioned and the temperature became hotter inside than outside. Consequently, frequent breaks were necessary. This was especially the case when we reached the higher shelves. On top of a 20-foot ladder, the heat was difficult to bear for long periods and the pipes were heavy. The heaviest pipe we weighed today was 390 kg. (or about 850 lbs.). We needed a forklift to raise it up onto the scales.

Sivan, the free spirit, visited our warehouse for a chunk of the afternoon, since she was without her military car. She teased Naftali constantly. She told him that, stripped naked to the waist, it appeared that he was developing a beer gut. (This was far from the truth.) However, I noticed that within minutes of her remark, he donned both his undershirt and his army shirt despite the heat. He returned the favor, warning her she was gaining weight in her behind (also far from the truth; standing on the pipe weighing scale, she barely broke 100 lbs.). During a break, I asked Naftali if he had a girlfriend. He replied with a grin: "Not now, but I'm taking Sivan out on Thursday night."

We found out that Sivan was not disciplined for her "joy ride" the previous day because Gilad was never told about it. However, for some other reason, she was not allowed to drive us back to our home base at the end of the workday. Instead, a young soldier named Yossi drove Brian, me, and Sivan in the military car back to Betzet Tira. Sivan sat in the front passenger seat, something very foreign to her. Yossi was a careful, normal driver who stayed within speed limits. This drove Sivan crazy. Throughout the ride back, Brian and I sat in the back seat amused with the amount of verbal abuse she heaped upon Yossi for being a slow driver. She yelled at him to cut in and out of traffic, pointing out gaps he could dart into. When he refused, citing the speed limit, she hurled insults at him. At several points, she hit him over the head to vent her frustration at the slow ride.

Brian, Jordan (a twenty-five-year old volunteer also from Chicago), and I tried out the fitness facility for the first time just before dinner. It was a beautiful facility, staffed daily by a soldier named Dahlia who was a fitness expert. It was great to work out and then shower away the sweat of both work and exercise.

After dinner, Tamar announced that she would lead Israeli folk dancing for the volunteers outside the mess hall later in the evening. We invited the soldiers on the base to join us, if they were not on guard duty, and several accepted our offer. At the last minute though, a series of surprise drills were announced and so all base soldiers were fully occupied with their responsibilities.

Since it was after dark, the soldier in charge of the mess hall turned on the outdoor lights for us. We disconnected an ancient Coke vending machine outside the mess hall in order to plug in Tamar's CD player. Tamar taught the volunteers three Israeli folk dances, which we all mastered. Occasionally, a soldier stopped by to buy a Coke and we obligingly stopped our dancing temporarily to plug in the soda vending machine. We all had a good time.

The soldiers on the base continued to show their appreciation to the volunteers in many ways, both big and small. At dinner Gal, the sergeant who had been in charge of setting up our quarters so nicely, stopped by to inquire if everything was in order. We asked whether we could have a table in our outdoor compound area so that the volunteers could have a place to congregate. Within two hours, a picnic table was moved from another part of the base to our compound. And as we sat around that picnic table to talk after our session of Israeli folk dancing, several soldiers stopped by to thank us for volunteering on the base. At Zikim, we had to "liberate" a table for the volunteers – here all we had to do was ask for one. It felt wonderful to be appreciated!

THURSDAY, AUGUST 5, 2004

The news today from Tamar was mixed: Last night, an IDF helicopter blasted a Kassam missile launcher in the Gaza Strip just before it was fired. Minister of Defense Shaul Mofaz visited Sderot to give the townspeople moral support for the bombardment they have endured. Finally, the Israeli government had to find $2 billion in budget cuts and so announced that it was lowering government salaries to accomplish this. (Would this ever be a viable method of balancing a budget in the U.S.?)

After morning flag-raising, the overall Betzet commander, Shy Davidi, came over to the volunteers and said: "I live in Hadera with my family. Would a volunteer like to join my family for

Sabbath dinner?" No one jumped at this offer, but since I was going to be in Hadera on Friday morning, I said I would like to stop by his house for a Friday afternoon visit. He gave me his cell phone number.

Our schedule today was altered by an unusual event: the first Sar-el *keness* in over three years was scheduled to be held in Jerusalem this afternoon. Normally, once a year Sar-el gathered together all the volunteers currently working in Israel in order to thank them. This gathering, called a *keness*, had not been held for the past three years for budgetary reasons. The volunteers were told to stop working at lunchtime in order to prepare for the Jerusalem trip.

Since it wasn't worthwhile to travel to Betzet Kishon for only a half-day's work, Brian and I stayed at Betzet Tira. A team of us volunteered to set up bricks around three ancient olive trees between the mess hall and the volunteers' compound. The bricks were long and heavy (about 60–80 lbs. each) and it required two people to carry each one. It took a lot of digging to fit the bricks in a square perimeter around each of the olive trees.

Sergeant Gal, who officiated at flag-raising, led our team of workers, which included two Israeli soldiers. He took the lead in digging and carrying the bricks, setting a good example for his soldiers. At the completion of our task, his uniform was soaked through with sweat, so I complimented him for working harder than his soldiers. He said that, in the Israeli military, officers are expected to lead in this manner.

After work, Tamar gave us new Sar-el tee-shirts and caps. She asked us to wear the tee-shirts for our Jerusalem trip, but we all agreed to wear our navy caps rather than the Sar-el ones. The navy caps would set apart our group of volunteers at the *keness* because we were the only Sar-el volunteers at an Israeli naval base.

On the bus ride to Jerusalem, I sat with the additional madricha assigned to accompany us to the *keness*. Her name was Miri, a bright twenty-year-old, who had come to Israel with her parents from Kishinev (Moldova) when she was five years old. I was constantly impressed with the intelligence of the women selected as Sar-el madrichas. In addition to Hebrew and Russian, she spoke English and Spanish. Miri was even more experienced than Tamar as a Sar-el madricha; she had only two months left in the army, after which she and a friend planned to travel through South America.

Miri talked about the difficulties of having a combat soldier as her boyfriend. While it was considered "cool" to be going with a combat soldier, she hardly ever saw him. He would get a weekend off every three weeks. If she was on duty that particular weekend, they would be unable to connect. Her words reinforced what Raz had told me last year about the difficult life of combat soldiers.

The bus driver was a very friendly man who lived far north of Tel Aviv in Nahariya. After the *keness*, he was going to drop off the volunteers at the Jerusalem and Tel Aviv bus stations and then drive home. Once he learned that Miri and I were also headed north from Tel Aviv following the *keness*, he offered to take us north and drop us off in Netanya (Miri's hometown); from there, it would be a short cab ride for me to reach Hadera. We gladly accepted.

As the bus headed into central Israel, it began to climb the high hills approaching Jerusalem, my favorite city. The bus driver constantly shifted gears to handle the steep up and down driving. Actually, many of the hills were more like mountains, and the views overlooking some of the deep valleys were gorgeous.

Our first stop in Jerusalem was Ammunition Hill, southwest of the French Hill district near Mount Scopus. I had been there previously, having visited with my Sar-el group from Batzop, but most of the volunteers had not. Tamar had insisted on this site for our end-of-week tour preceding the keness. Once there, I realized why. Ammunition Hill is adjacent to Tamar's high school, which she attended as a resident of the nearby French Hill district of Jerusalem. As a member and eventually leader of the Israeli scouts in French Hill, she had led many scout and school groups through this site and so was intimately familiar with it.

Tamar explained that in the Six-Day War, Ammunition Hill was the lynchpin to Jordan's defenses in Jerusalem, so Israel had to capture this fortified stronghold. She walked us into the trenches leading up from the base of the hill. Because of her knowledge of the site, she stopped at several spots in the trenches to point out where a particular soldier (identified by name – they are heroes in Israel) gave up his life to protect his comrades. She showed us how the Jordanian soldiers from the crest of the hill and from various strategically placed bunkers on the sides of the hill had an open field of fire over the area the Israelis had to cross. At one point, she read an excerpt written by the only medic who was not killed in the battle regarding how difficult and bloody the battle had been. By the time they completed the conquest of the hill, they had suffered a terrible toll – 90 percent of the men had been killed or wounded. But they had been intent on rectifying what had happened in the 1948 War of Independence – when the Israeli army had been unable to defend its enclave in the Old City of Jerusalem and had been compelled to surrender it to Jordan.

As Tamar took us through the battlefield, school children wandered silently among the trenches, stopping at various marked spots to read the explanations on plaques. Every Israeli school child is required to tour this site to appreciate the sacrifice and bravery exhibited by the Israeli soldiers in taking this hill.

Both as a proud Jerusalemite and a proud Israeli, it was very important to Tamar that we saw Ammunition Hill. She told me she had been to this site over a hundred times, and had viewed the short movie we watched there at least ten times. Yet, she confided in me, this site always affected her and Miri in a powerful way. Every time they viewed the film, tears came to their eyes and a chill went down their spine, as the movie took the audience through the touch-and-go battle and the soldiers' sacrifices to re-conquer the Old City of Jerusalem in 1967. Although I had seen the site before, this time I was seeing it through Israeli eyes, those of our young madrichas.

As we drove from Ammunition Hill in the late afternoon, we passed the walls of the Old City. The sun reflected off the golden top of the Dome of the Rock. We drove past the King David Hotel and then Tamar pointed out a spot around the corner from the Inbal Hotel where a suicide bomber had blown up a bus last February.

Our bus dropped us off in front of the Jerusalem Theater for the *keness*. The theater plaza was crowded with various Sar-el volunteer groups. It took a while for our group to wend its way through the crowds of people, because so many madrichas stopped to hug and kiss Tamar and Miri. This *keness* was one of the few times that the madrichas got a chance to see each other. Consequently, they used the occasion to socialize a bit.

At the entrance to the theater, security guards stopped Tamar and Miri. Terrorists have been known to disguise themselves in Israeli army uniforms. Therefore, regular Israeli soldiers like Tamar and Miri were forbidden to bring their loaded rifles into the building, which was guarded by special Israeli security police. The police directed Tamar and Miri to leave their ammunition clips in a designated place, and they proceeded (with their rifles) to lead us into the building.

The lobby was jammed with people. Veteran Sar-el volunteers looked for other volunteers they had befriended on their prior stints. I was delighted to run into Etty, my madricha the previous year at Zikim. Many of the youth groups in the lobby were singing or chanting cheers, and the noise was deafening. The French teen-age groups were especially spirited in their singing and cheering. It appeared that about half of the people in the lobby were in their early twenties or late teens. Miri explained that in the summer months, Sar-el sees more young volunteers. In the non-summer months, older ones predominate.

As we entered the auditorium from the lobby, the noise from the cheering got louder. What spirit these young people showed! The Israeli army choir opened the session with fast-paced songs, which roused the crowd further. One of the songs, "Lach Yerushalayim" is a favorite of mine. Another one was "Jerusalem of Gold," written by the famous Israeli songwriter, Naomi Shemer, who had just passed away. "Jerusalem of Gold" had become the unofficial national anthem after the re-capture of eastern Jerusalem and the Old City in the 1967 Six-Day War. By the time the choir was finished, the crowd of about a thousand people was on its feet, singing and swaying to the music.

When the choir finished, we watched a short video depicting the different branches of the Israeli military in action (e.g., army, air force, tanks, navy). Members of the audience cheered for whichever branch operated the base at which they were stationed. We, of course, cheered as loudly as we could when the navy was depicted, as the thirteen of us constituted the only Sar-el group on a navy base. After the video, about twenty soldiers carrying flags representing various Israeli army units marched from the back of the auditorium onto the stage to martial music. They stood at attention as we all sang "Hatikvah."

Then General Aharon Davidi took the stage and thanked the Sar-el volunteers for their contribution to the Israeli military and to the country as a whole. He graciously gave his short speech three times – in English, French, and Russian – representative of the majority of the nationalities in the hall. The crowd loudly applauded for General Davidi. We felt great admiration for this founder of Sar-el who, at seventy-eight, still worked hard to lead this organization.

The session closed with various awards being given to outstanding Sar-el volunteers and graduating madrichas. The latter included Miri. Each award recipient was handed a plaque by General Davidi and a bouquet of flowers by another madricha.

At the end of the awards ceremony, a madricha named Paulina who was one of the award recipients was called back up to the stage. All of the madrichas receiving awards had been given passes to permit their parents to attend. But Paulina had come to Israel from Russia three years earlier without her parents and was serving in the IDF in Israel's "Lonely Soldier" program. To make up for the absence of her parents, the official at the microphone handed her a cell phone to speak with her father. Embarrassed in front of the crowd, she put the phone to her ear, spoke a few words to her father, and said: "He can't hear me – it's a bad connection." The official said: "Then why not turn around?" Paulina turned around and onto the stage walked her father. He had never been to Israel before, and the IDF had secretly arranged for him to travel to Israel to attend the *keness* and watch his daughter receive her award. She grabbed her father, started crying, and hugged him for a long time, unwilling to let go. There wasn't a dry eye in the audience as she finally led him off the stage, tightly clutching his hand with both of hers.

FRIDAY, AUGUST 6, 2004

I reached the home of my Hadera friends, Tova and Meir Meiner, well after midnight and slept late into the morning on a comfortable, full-size mattress. This morning Tova promised to show me the computer room that our Raleigh Jewish community had funded at one of the after-school facilities in Hadera.

Tova and Meir were Israelis who had lived in Cary, North Carolina for a few years, where my wife and I had met and befriended them. Tova was a social worker with the Hadera Foundation, a social service agency dealing with the welfare and education needs of new immigrants. It was natural, therefore, to use her knowledge of the welfare needs in Israel when our local Jewish community was looking for a worthy project to fund. Now we wanted to find a second project to support, which was one of the reasons I came to Hadera.

I knew a bit about the community from Tova's descriptions of it. Hadera is a town of about 80,000 people, along the northern coast of Israel between Tel Aviv and Haifa. It was unusual in that it contained a disproportionately large number of new Jewish immigrants (about 30,000), mostly from Ethiopia and the Caucasus Mountains region of the former Soviet Union (the latter group are known as "Kavkaz Mountain Jews," or in Israel, simply as "Kavkaz)."

With 100,000 Ethiopian immigrants in Israel, the Israeli government wanted to avoid the creation of a permanent poor black underclass. The risk of an underclass was a real possibility given that the Ethiopians came from a primitive farming society with no previous exposure to the modern world. To avoid this possibility, the government made special efforts to integrate Ethiopians into Israeli society by educating their youth. Nevertheless, many Ethiopian immigrants were still unemployed and unemployable, having language problems (many spoke only ancient Amharic) and lacking employable skills.

One means the city of Hadera used to improve the economic situation of the Ethiopians was the creation of five after-school facilities called "maxims," primarily for Ethiopian immigrant children; Kavkaz children were also invited to join. At these maxims, immigrant children received reinforcement of their school studies in the form of tutors who went over their homework. The price for parents to send their child to a maxim was minimal: 50 shekels (about $11) annually.

The Maxim Ganeh Alon was located in the Ganeh Alon neighborhood of Hadera. There we met Carol Shoval, the "overseas coordinator" or fundraiser for the Hadera Foundation, who was waiting for us by the open door of the computer room we had funded. She introduced us to Adugnia Takelle, an Ethiopian immigrant and the director of Maxim Ganeh Alon.

As we entered the air-conditioned room, I closed the door to the outside and asked why they had kept the door open with the air-conditioning on. Carol explained that, to Adugnia, it was very important to keep the door open when expecting a visitor. In Ethiopian society, an open door is a symbol of welcome and Adugnia wanted to welcome Tova and me.

Adugnia's background was unusual in that he had come to Israel much earlier than the 1990 wave of Ethiopian immigration. In 1980, at the age of fourteen, Adugnia and two older boys fled the war and famine in Ethiopia to try to reach Israel. They left on foot, heading south into the Sudan. The trip took them six months because they had to travel at night and hide from attack during the day. In the Sudan, through the Israeli Embassy, they were able to obtain transportation to Israel. Eventually, Adugnia brought his entire family to Israel, married, and had four children.

Ethiopian immigrants, Adugnia explained, care for their own people whenever they can. Once Adugnia was educated, he returned to his immigrant community to become a community leader, so that he could look after other immigrants. As director of the Maxim Ganeh Alon, he knew every one of the 140 children who spent their after-school hours there. Since the Ethiopian parents did not know how to relate to schools and teachers, Adugnia filled an intermediary role for them. He periodically checked in with the children's teachers and then communicated to parents if their child was having problems in school.

Carol proudly reported that the first of Hadera's five maxims (Maxim Ganeh Alon was the newest) was already producing remarkable results. Four of its children had just graduated high school and had done so well academically that they had been permitted to go straight to university and serve their army duty after their higher education. The option to go straight from high school to university is reserved in Israel for a few outstanding students, so Carol had a right to be proud. In fact, two of the four students were enrolled in the Technion in Haifa, Israel's equivalent of M.I.T.

She showed us what access to computers had done for the parents of children at this maxim. To allow the kids to introduce their parents to computers (most of the parents had never seen one), they installed computer genealogy software that required input of a person's family tree. Family genealogy is a subject that is of great importance to Ethiopian Jews. Using this software program, children sat together with their fathers at the computers, with the fathers providing the needed information and the children typing in that information. It was a good way to introduce the older

Ethiopians to computers and inspire the children in their studies. Carol recalled a father/son team in which the son put his hand over that of his father's, guiding it on the mouse to move the cursor on the screen. Within a few weeks, the father was comfortable being on the computer by himself.

I would have liked to spend more time at the maxim, but it was Friday afternoon and I had also promised to visit Shy Davidi at his home. Shy lived nearby in Hadera and was kind enough to pick me up at the maxim. As we drove to his home, I told him about my morning visit and my search for a second project for our community to fund.

The Israeli military also provided assistance in various ways to Israel's poor, Shy told me, but it was forbidden from giving money – only the country's welfare agency was permitted to do that – so the military gave its time instead. Shy allowed those twelfth-graders from poor families in the area who studied warehouse inventory management at school to spend two days a week in his warehouses as an internship. In this way, the students gained practical experience to better enable them to obtain jobs after graduation from high school.

Shy described the difficulties of some of the soldiers who grow up in broken immigrant families. He had one soldier of Kavkaz background whose father beat his wife and children. The family finally kicked the father out of the apartment for his abuse. The soldier did not see him again for five years, until he heard that his father was dying of cancer. Since he both loved and feared his father, the soldier was conflicted over whether to go see him. He brought this problem to Shy, who counseled that a visit to the father would be a good step toward reconciliation. Because the soldier still feared his father, Shy agreed to accompany him for this visit. The reconciliation did take place between father and son, although his mother still refused to allow her husband back into the house. It was not uncommon for officers to act as counselors to their soldiers concerning personal problems.

When we arrived at his house, Shy introduced me to his wife, Miriam, and two of his four children. Metalle, a pretty, dark-haired fifteen-year-old, was a very high achiever in the sciences and math and likely to follow in her father's footsteps into engineering. (Shy proudly told me that she had already been accepted into the program that allows academically gifted students to go directly to university from high school and serve their military duty after university as an officer.) And Daniel, his twelve-year-old son, took me out to the backyard to show me his collection of brightly colored parakeets. Housed in a series of five large outdoor cages, these parakeets were of several distinctive types, one of which lived in the wild in Israel. Daniel cared for thirty to forty parakeets. When their numbers occasionally increased, he would give a few away to friends.

Sitting with Shy and his wife in their living room, I learned more about Shy's background. His father had been a Mossad agent (Israeli secret service). In the early 1950s, he had been assigned to save Morocco's Jewish community by secretly smuggling them out of Morocco to Gibraltar and then to Israel. He met Shy's mother, a Moroccan Jew, in the camp in Gibraltar where the Moroccans were taken. After they were married, Shy's parents were assigned to many places, including sub-Saharan Africa and France. Shy himself was born in France and brought to Israel as a young boy. Consequently, in addition to being fluent in Hebrew and English, he also was fluent in French and Spanish.

A biochemical engineer by training, Shy was in his early forties. After serving on both a missile boat and a submarine, he chose to focus on the field of inventory management. He was very proud of the new inventory management system he had instituted in the navy, since it had automated and computerized the system of ordering, storing, and delivering parts. The Israeli army was in the process of adopting Shy's new system, and a delegation from the U.S. military was scheduled to visit Betzet Tira in the fall to see if they would recommend it in the U.S.

Starting to relax with each other, we talked a bit about the volunteers at the base. Shy explained why he originally had insisted on only volunteers between the ages of thirty and fifty. He thought that volunteers under thirty might not be serious about their work and spend too much time socializing with his soldiers, and he feared that volunteers over fifty would not be able to handle the physical nature of the work. Pamela was able to persuade him that some of the over-fifty volunteers could handle heavy work. Shy admitted to me that he had been wrong about the capabilities of the older volunteers. He specifically mentioned Ed, our oldest volunteer at seventy-two, whom he complimented as "a bear of a man."

As we sat talking in his living room, neighbors and friends dropped in for a brief Friday afternoon visit. Apparently, it is typical in Israeli society for people to spontaneously drop by without advance notice and everyone is welcome. The informality and spontaneity of the visiting process was new to me. One man, in the Israeli SEAL diving force, arrived with his son to drop off pita bread, just baked by his wife. Another neighbor arrived with her twenty-year-old daughter, Natale (also in the navy). Based on my wallet-sized photo of my family, Shy insisted that Natale was an identical twin to my daughter, Rachel. I respectfully disagreed.

Shy invited me join his family and friends for the evening, but I declined because I had promised to join my cousin Ruchama for Friday night dinner. Just then Ruchama called to find out where to come to pick me up. I put Shy on the phone and in the course of their conversation Shy discovered that he knew Ruchama's brother Michael quite well from the navy.

Ruchama, Shani, and Michael soon came over to visit in what was by then Shy's very crowded living room. Shy and Michael quickly got into a deep discussion about Shy's inventory management system, which Michael agreed was far superior to their old system or the one used by the army. We finally left close to 6:30 P.M. in order to get to Ruchama's apartment before the Sabbath started. Although Michael was not religious, he was uncomfortable being on the road once sunset signaled the arrival of the

Sabbath because there were many religious Jews in his neighborhood who frowned on driving on the Sabbath.

SUNDAY, AUGUST 8, 2004

I spent most of Saturday on the beach with my cousins, but Sunday
morning meant a return to Betzet Tira. Michael offered to drive
me back to the base, along with Diana, another Sar-el volunteer
who had spent the weekend in Netanya.

On our drive north, I learned that Diana was born in Iraq
and that she and her brothers were smuggled into Israel from
Iraq in 1951. Later, when she was eight, her family moved to the
U.S., where she now lives. As a young child, she spoke only Arabic
and Hebrew, but now she remembered neither. I was surprised
to learn of her Iraqi background because of her blonde hair, blue
eyes, and fair complexion.

Upon her first return to Israel in 2003, Diana learned from
a passport control official at Ben-Gurion Airport that she was in
fact an Israeli citizen. Consequently, she held both U.S. and Israeli
citizenship and was proud of both. Diana felt a deep sense of gratitude to Israel as the country that rescued her and her family from
the persecution of Iraq's Jewish community. But Diana's reason for
serving in Sar-el went much deeper than simply paying back her
debt of gratitude. She had come to feel a deep connection to the
country and valued her Israeli citizenship as part of her identity,
even though she makes her home in New York.

Halfway to Betzet Tira, Michael suddenly pulled over to the
side of the highway in front of what looked like a small convenience store. He jumped out of the car and moments later returned
with a newspaper under his arm. He explained that this was a
store exclusively for soldiers traveling to their duty stations. The
store served snacks and gave out newspapers, all for free. Local
restaurants and other establishments donated everything given
out by the store, to thank the soldiers for serving their country.
The store was completely staffed by Israeli volunteers. Michael
said that the volunteer staff for this particular store included the

grandmother of a Knesset member. There are five such "soldiers stores" in Israel.

Diana and I were among the first volunteers returning from the weekend. Diana and Ken (a volunteer from Florida) shortly went to their jobs painting fences, gates, and guardhouses on the base. Since I lacked transportation to Betzet Kishon, I volunteered to help Gal fill the bricked-in square enclosures around the three olive trees with small white stones we shoveled from the back of a truck.

While we worked on the olive tree enclosures, Azam came to inspect our work. Azam was a short, elderly Druze villager who volunteered as the base gardener. He tended to the beautiful shrubs and flowers as if he were tending his own backyard. Azam volunteered to spend his retirement years gardening on this base to thank the country for protecting him and his fellow Druze villagers. The Druze are a small Muslim sect that historically had been persecuted by Muslims in other countries, but lived peacefully in Israel as Israeli citizens. On our first day on the base, Azam observed that all of the volunteers were given a blue Sar-el cap. He asked Tamar for one too, since he was also a volunteer. I saw him later proudly wearing it, but just to meals, because he did not want to get it dirty on the job.

After completing the olive tree enclosures, Gal invited me into his air-conditioned office for a drink of water in a cool environment. I mentioned to him how surprising it was that Diana was from Iraq, given her appearance. Gal said that his father was also from Iraq and that he had come to Israel when the Iraqis began to persecute their Jewish population. Later, Gal's father was sent back to Iraq as an Israeli agent, to help smuggle other Iraqi Jews out of the country. Could Gal's father have been one of the people who enabled Diana to escape? I mentioned this possibility to Gal, who simply shrugged his shoulders and said with typical Israeli brevity, "It's possible." Gal was Diana's favorite soldier on the base and I wondered if it was because of their shared Iraqi heritage.

It was after ten and still no transportation had arrived to take me to Betzet Kishon, so I started walking towards the base commander's office to inquire. Along the way, I ran into David, the sergeant in charge of my warehouse at Betzet Kishon. He offered me a ride and I accepted. "But first," he said, "you must come to help us celebrate the giving of the *darga* to my friends at Betzet Tira." We walked into a small office in one of the warehouses where a table was set with pastries and sodas. It was a celebration for four female soldiers who were receiving an additional *darga* (stripe). Stripes are awarded for every year a soldier served during their mandatory conscription period, provided they were in good standing. David was invited because, until last week, he had been in charge of this warehouse.

Each of the four soldiers was called up individually to stand between an officer and a sergeant, and the latter explained why the soldier deserved her new stripe. Then the officer and sergeant pinned the stripe on each sleeve of the recipient and good-naturedly smacked her on her back. (Now I knew where the Sar-el tradition came from of smacking each volunteer on the back when they received their blue-and-white epaulette patches.) Then, as a surprise, the officer awarded David a plaque to acknowledge his years of service at the same warehouse. David looked pleased with his present. Ironically, on the same day he also received a gift from his new superiors at the Betzet Kishon base to welcome him – a shiny red tool kit.

After the *darga* celebration, Brian and I squeezed into David's vintage 1972 Volkswagen Beetle. It was bright orange and had "No Fear" painted in black English letters on both sides; it was un-air-conditioned and had cost him only 1,000 shekels (a little over $200) a year ago. In Israel, this was just a junky 32-year-old car. In the U.S., it would have been a much-in-demand antique.

David set off on the highway north towards Haifa, intent on proving to me that his orange Beetle could drive faster than many newer cars. As he proved his point, he slid a disc into his CD player and "Eye of the Tiger" from the *Rocky* movies blasted out our wide-open windows. It was fun driving in David's Beetle until we reached Haifa. The dockworkers' strike had ended this morning and the resulting traffic as we approached the city slowed to a crawl.

Work today fell into the same routine we had established during the prior week. We weighed, counted, marked, and stored metal pipes. We transported the heavier pipes to the scale on David's forklift. By now I had learned the Hebrew word for forklift (*malgezah*), which David referred to jokingly as "my car." There was a big sign outside the warehouse that read: *Zeherut Malgezot Nosot*, which means "Beware of Moving Forklifts."

The temperature outside was in the low nineties, and very muggy. As usual, Naftali was on a high ladder, counting and pulling pipes. Stripped to the waist and perspiring heavily from the strain of the physical labor at high temperatures, Naftali was the epitome of sweaty masculinity as Sivan walked in. As usual, Sivan came by to flirt with Naftali. As a twenty-five-year-old reservist, Naftali acted like Sivan was too young for his attention, telling her, laughing, "Go away little girl, you're only nineteen!" But like a bee attracted to honey, Sivan persisted in pestering Naftali until Meir chased her out. I wondered how their date went last Thursday night, but didn't ask.

At the end of the workday, a different soldier (not Sivan) drove us back to Betzet Tira. Sitting in the back seat, I was reminded of the fact that Israelis seem to ignore all rules of the road when they drive. This is why more Israelis are killed in traffic accidents than by terrorists. In the middle of Haifa, our driver decided to park in one of the two southbound lanes of heavy traffic so he could stop to buy cigarettes, leaving his car to create a traffic jam of angry honking cars behind us. Apparently, this is common on Israeli city streets.

MONDAY, AUGUST 9, 2004

The news this morning dealt with politics and the military – two

173

topics that are of the utmost of importance to Israelis. Tamar reported that negotiations were ongoing as Prime Minister Sharon's Likud Party reached out to the Labor Party and Shas (a religious party), seeking to reach agreement on the terms for a new coalition government. Yesterday, Military Chief of Staff Moshe Ayalon held a security conference that included the heads of all of the security and military forces. The directors of Mossad and Shin Bet, who did not fall within his chain of command, criticized Ayalon's use of the army against the Palestinians in ways they described as overly harsh. And finally, the Israeli delegation to the Olympics would leave for Athens today. The Olympics, which starts in five days, is always a sensitive subject for Israelis because of the terrorist massacre of the Israeli team at the 1972 Olympics in Munich.

At flag-raising, Gal announced that Magen David Adom (the Israeli Red Cross) would be collecting donations of blood this morning. Brian and I formed the beginning of what became a long line of soldiers volunteering to give blood. The only complication for us was that the consent form was in Hebrew. A medical technician named Avi carefully translated the form for me before I could sign it. A very pretty base nurse went over the same form with Brian, and it took them twice as long and involved lots of laughter. Both Avi and I both surmised it was because Brian was a good-looking young man looking to find a nice Israeli girl to settle down with in Israel and every girl on the base knew it.

While the medical technician collected blood from each of us, he asked us what type of work the navy was giving to the Sar-el volunteers. After we responded, he asked us to consider volunteering for the Magen David Adom ambulance service. He explained that, after an initial week of training, Magen David Adom volunteers ride in the ambulances with physicians and medical technicians to medical emergencies. He had found that trained volunteers were very useful in such emergencies and that they seemed to find their volunteer experiences rewarding. He did say, however, that the bulk of the volunteers who came to Magen

David Adom without medical training tended to be college and post-college students.

Sivan was in a good mood this morning. She drove up in Gilad's Renault sedan with her friend Na'amah in the front seat. This car was much more powerful than the military car she normally drove between the Betzet Tira and Betzet Kishon bases. With the radio blasting, she took off like a rocket towards Haifa. We quickly fastened our seatbelts.

The port facility was bustling with trucks this morning, since the longshoremen strike was over. Entering the military portion of the harbor, Sivan and Na'amah waved and called out to various soldiers they knew. They seemed to know practically everyone.

We walked over to our warehouse and found Naftali and Nissim already busy at work. Naftali was stripped to the waist, but today all he was wearing was his bathing suit. The radio was loud and played an eclectic set of music, ranging from Pink Floyd to "Have Yourself a Merry Little Christmas." The latter evoked raised eyebrows from all of us – Merry Christmas in Israel, and in the heat of August?

Naftali was in high spirits, dancing to the music and occasionally breaking into high-pitched laughter. When we finished a section of pipes, he would stop, do a bit of a jig, and loudly exclaim: "It is goood!" With Naftali in his bathing suit, Sivan soon stopped by to make some cracks about how terrible he would look at the beach and he reciprocated in kind. The wisecracking continued to the point of Sivan giving him a few shots on the arm, but Naftali was serious about the work because his goal was to finish the inventory of pipes today (which we did). It had been a daunting task when we started, but it had only taken us six days of work.

During a work break, David apologized for Naftali's antics. He explained that Naftali was a reservist, called up for his four weeks of reserve duty per year, who worked building fiberglass bodies of small aircraft in his regular job. He said that Naftali had a childish attitude toward life, and nothing he or Meir said could change that.

David also acknowledged that discipline was tighter at the Betzet Tira base than at the Betzet Kishon base where we worked. He gave two reasons for this: First, there were more officers at Betzet Tira, and the presence of these officers led to a more tightly run base. Second, the Betzet Kishon base was very old and was slated for closure at some future date, with its inventories transferred to an expanded Betzet Tira. Knowing this, its soldiers were less careful about the appearance of the place.

As we worked, Brian told me about the work he performed as a volunteer at the Julis base immediately prior to his assignment to our group. At Julis, he worked on tank maintenance. This entailed disconnecting the turret of the tank and removing its main gun barrel and its machine guns. These items were all inspected, oiled, and then re-mounted. He also replaced the ammunition storage bins in the tanks and assisted with other maintenance. The work was very greasy and, in the summertime, very hot because it was in the south of Israel near Ashdod. Whatever the inconveniences were, Brian didn't seem to mind; he felt good about having contributed to the needs of the Israeli military.

Since Tamar gave us a night off from any activities, all of the volunteers (except me) decided to walk into the town of Tirat Carmel to find dinner. I stayed to have dinner in the mess hall with the soldiers and then catch up on my travel journal. Sitting outside my bunk, facing the Carmel Mountain range as the sun set behind me, I appreciated the beauty of this base. After darkness fell, the silence was occasionally punctuated by a *targeel* (drill), in which helmeted and armed soldiers would run across the base on predetermined routes to address hypothetical emergencies. The soldiers took these drills very seriously, as illustrated by the urgency with which they moved as soon as one was announced.

Later in the evening, I stopped by the guardhouse to the main gate to chat with the soldiers on guard duty. They seemed to want to talk to combat the tedium of guard duty. I asked them what they planned to do after their military service. As is typical of young Israelis at that stage of their lives, all of them planned to travel abroad. The most common destination was South America, because it was cheap, with Thailand and the U.S. coming in second and third places. After two or three years of military service and a year of travel, some enroll at the universities. At that stage, they generally seemed more serious than American college students, because of their experiences and because they are three or four years older.

TUESDAY, AUGUST 10, 2004

Tamar reported this morning that shots had been fired at a bus and several cars in the Shomron area of the West Bank, but no one was hurt. I later learned that, in the search for the gunmen, three roadside bombs were discovered and deactivated. The weather today would be 33° c (91° f).

Work today with the pipes was all outside. Naftali played the warehouse music loud so that we could hear it outside. The Israeli rock station played mostly American "oldies," ranging from Beatles to ABBA music from the show *Mama Mia*. But when Naftali's favorite American song came on ("Pump It Up"), he wanted to make certain that people appreciated his music, so he turned it up to maximum volume. The entire base vibrated to "Pump It Up."

We cut our workday short for a late afternoon field trip to the old town of Zichron Ya'akov, one of the first Zionist settlements from the 1880s. Heading south and east, our bus passed numerous *moshavim* (collective farming communities). Row upon row of banana trees gave way to vineyards as our bus began to climb up into the mountains overlooking the sea.

A young soldier named Anat gave us a walking tour of the town of Zichron Ya'akov. Founded in 1882 during the First Aliyah (the wave of immigration that took place between 1881 and 1903), the agricultural community at Zichron Ya'acov was established by Romanian Jews. At first, it faltered, but an appeal to the French

Baron Edmond de Rothschild brought desperately needed financial support. Eventually, its vineyards provided the answer to their financial needs – the wineries at Zichron Ya'akov became a principal industry for the settlers and their wines developed an excellent reputation. In appreciation for Baron Rothschild's support, the community founders named the town after the Baron's father, James (whose Hebrew name was Ya'akov). Baron Rothschild is buried in the nearby gardens.

At Zichron Ya'akov's cemetery, we came to a monument honoring Aaron Aaronsohn, the eldest son of one of the town's founding families. Aaronsohn was an internationally known agronomist who discovered a special type of weather-resistant wheat that is still grown in Israel today. Anat also pointed out several small, unmarked graves. A cholera outbreak in the struggling community in 1900 took the lives of many small infants, who were buried in these unmarked graves.

As we left the graveyard, Anat told us the story of Aaron Aaronsohn's role in helping the British wrest Palestine from the Ottoman Turks during World War I. Together with his sister Sarah, and friend, Shalom Feinberg, they formed a clandestine group called NILI to relay information about Turkish troop movements to the British in Cairo. They transmitted this information by messenger across the Sinai desert, by carrier pigeon, and by means of small boats connecting to a British destroyer waiting offshore.

The Turks and their allies, the Germans, eventually became aware of NILI's activities. In 1917, one of NILI's carrier pigeons was caught by the Germans. Shalom Feinberg disappeared on one of his messenger trips across the Sinai desert and was presumed dead.* Two other NILI members were caught and hung by the Turks.

---

* Fifty years later, Israeli troops conquered the Sinai Desert from Egypt in the Six-Day War. South of Rafeh, they discovered the grave of Shalom Feinberg, marked by date trees growing from the dates he always kept in his pocket for sustenance. Apparently, he had died on one of his secret courier trips for the British.

Sarah Aaronsohn realized that it was only a matter of time before she was caught. Both she and her father were arrested by the Turks. After several days of torture at the hands of the Turks, she committed suicide to avoid being forced to disclose the names of her co-conspirators. Her death ended the activities of NILI just a few short months before British forces, led by the famous Lawrence of Arabia, swept the Turks out of the land. Sarah's younger sister, who lived into the 1970s, converted the Aaronsohn home into a museum to honor Sarah's memory. Aaron Aaronsohn died in a plane crash on his way to the Paris Peace Conference in 1919.

Anat walked us through the quaint streets of Zichron Ya'akov, which have been restored to what they looked like in the 1880s. The air in the mountains was dry and cool, providing a welcome change from the heat and humidity of the Betzet Tira base near the sea. She led us to the community's original synagogue, built in 1886 with funds supplied by Baron Rothschild. Inscribed on the back wall of the sanctuary were the names of the sixty original members of the congregation. The old caretaker of the synagogue gave us a short talk about its origin. Despite the fact that they were prohibited from constructing a new synagogue in Ottoman-ruled Palestine, the community secretly brought in people from nearby Haifa who had knowledge of building construction. All in one night, like an American barn-raising, they raised the roof of the synagogue. Under Turkish law, it was forbidden to destroy a place of worship that was covered – so when the Turks discovered it the next morning they allowed it to remain and be completed.

I felt a connection to the quaintness of Zichron Ya'akov. I imagined that the town's restored main street from the 1880s resembled the main street of my agricultural hometown, Vineland, New Jersey in the same period. Just as Zichron Ya'akov had been founded as a Jewish agricultural settlement with the help of Baron Rothschild, his German contemporary, the philanthropist Baron Maurice de Hirsch, had established a Jewish agricultural community on the outskirts of Vineland in the same decade. The early settlers of both agricultural communities came from the same Eastern European background and, as novice farmers, probably suffered similar setbacks in learning their new trade.

This evening, after our walking tour of Zichron Ya'akov, we sat around the picnic table talking with Tamar in the volunteers' compound. Somehow we got onto the subject of the M-16 rifle that she always carried. It was an old M-16 rifle. Tamar explained that the Israelis buy used M-16 rifles that the American army wished to replace. The American army charges Israel a dollar per weapon.

Tamar pointed out that the magazines for the M-16s are designed to carry 30 bullets, but Israeli soldiers are allowed to insert only 29. In the U.S. army, emptied magazines are normally thrown away after their first use. The Israelis obtained these emptied magazines from the U.S. army and re-used them. Placing 30 bullets in these magazines puts tremendous pressure on the spring mechanism. By loading each magazine with only 29 bullets, the Israelis tried to extend the life of each magazine. The Israeli army is stretched for money and this was one of the many ways it tries to re-use old parts to save on resources.

Our group of volunteers had jelled very nicely and we all got along with each other. Part of the reason was that we were all veterans of other bases and knew that it was important to be patient with and considerate of each other. It also helped that we were a small group and had all started together at the same time. We settled down to a routine on the base. After dinner, whether or not we had an evening activity, we often walked into the nearby town to pick up snacks. Then we sat around our picnic table to talk about that day's work and get to know each other better.

At seventy-two, Ed, a volunteer from New York, was the senior member of our group. He proudly carried with him his old Israeli driver's license issued in 1951. At that time he had moved from the U.S. to Israel and helped to found a kibbutz near the Gaza

Strip. He probably would have remained on the kibbutz but for the fact that he was drafted for service in the U.S. Army during the Korean War. He came back to the States to serve his country, got married, and settled down to have a family. After his retirement, his heart drew him back to Israel. He had come to volunteer every year over the past seven years. After his stint at Betzet Tira, he planned to stop at "his kibbutz" to visit old friends, where he would be welcomed as one of the founding members.

In some sense, I felt a commonality with Ed. Since my first (unsuccessful) attempt to visit Israel at age seventeen, other demands, such as completing school, starting my career, and raising a family, had kept me from spending time in Israel. Like Ed, I realized that my Sar-el stints fulfilled my need to participate in the life of Israel. Now that I had been able to connect with Israel many years later, I felt very comfortable with that connection and needed to maintain and strengthen it through my relationships with Israeli friends and relatives.

WEDNESDAY, AUGUST 11, 2004

Because we had a special trip scheduled this morning, we dressed in our "civvies" and could not attend flag-raising. It felt a bit strange to be on the base and not go to flag-raising.

Tamar's news, delivered around our picnic table, was unusually extensive today. She reported that twenty minutes earlier a Kassam rocket had hit Sderot. Luckily, no one was hurt. Last night, Israeli tanks entered Khan Yunis in the Gaza, Strip, searching houses for wanted terrorists. An Israeli woman was arrested yesterday for feeding information to a major figure in the Al Aqsa Martyrs Brigade. It is very unusual for a Jewish Israeli to provide assistance to a Palestinian terrorist organization. And in Jerusalem, swastikas were painted on walls condemning Mayor Uri Lupolianski, the first Orthodox Jewish mayor of the city. Apparently, the ultra-Orthodox were unhappy with him, declaring him too secular. Finally, in New York City a Pakistani citizen had been arrested for taking pictures of skyscrapers and, upon his arrest, pictures of other sensitive structures were found in his possession.

After Tamar's briefing, the volunteers were bused to the naval base in Haifa harbor for our most interesting tour yet. Tamar's brother, Michael, met us at the base entrance. Tall and lanky with curly, light brown hair, he looked a lot like his sister. He took us to the Officers Club at the base and gave us a short presentation on the naval vessels we were about to see. For security reasons, we were directed to take no pictures of what we saw at the base.

Michael had already served four and a half years in the navy and was a first lieutenant. During that time, he had captained an Israeli Super Dvora patrol boat. Therefore, he showed us a patrol boat first.

The Super Dvora was an extremely fast 66-foot patrol boat, capable of reaching speeds up to 48 knots (or 55 mph). It was designed to interdict terrorists trying to reach Israel by water. These boats are so fast that, before attaining high speeds, the crew must be strapped down to avoid falling off whenever the boat turned. The Israelis are about to introduce a newer patrol boat, capable of speeds up to 56 knots (64 mph). With a crew of ten plus the captain, these patrol boats can stay out to sea up to three days before returning to port. Each boat has a 25 mm. forward gun and a 20 mm. aft gun, in addition to two 30-caliber machine guns. The forward gun, called a typhoon gun, is radar-controlled and operated remotely from a video screen inside the main cabin with a joystick very similar to that used in video games. This gun is able to maintain its fix on a target, even in rough seas, and is very accurate at long distances. It struck me that the Super Dvora was the modern-day equivalent of the PT boats used during World War II and popularized by the story of President John F. Kennedy's PT-109.

The next vessel we visited was one of Israel's three submarines, called the "Dolphin" submarines. These German-supplied diesel-powered submarines had been built to Israeli specifications, with

Israeli construction managers living at the German construction port to ensure these specifications were followed. Operated by a 40-man crew, these submarines were capable of cruising for up to two weeks. As the "eyes of the navy," submarines serve as an intelligence-gathering tool for Israel. Women are not allowed to serve in the submarine crews (or on the fast patrol boats) because of the close quarters involved. The Israeli submarines periodically engage in "war games" with other countries' submarines. In fact, the next day a German submarine was scheduled to arrive at Haifa to engage in such exercises with an Israeli submarine.

The final vessel we viewed, and the only one we were allowed to board, was the Sa'ar 4.5 missile boat. This is the largest vessel in the Israeli navy and eleven of them are stationed at Haifa naval base. These boats carry missiles with a range of 75 miles. Also, most of them have a 76 mm. main aft gun. About 180 feet long and carrying a crew of fifty to sixty (which can include female officers), these ships are intended to attack an enemy in time of war. They can stay out on patrol for up to two weeks and normally go out to sea two to three days each week.

The missile boat we toured, called the *Yaffo*, had just returned from patrol an hour earlier. In fact, the sailors were still asleep in the sleeping quarters that we were not permitted to see. We were allowed to walk through the captain's bridge, along the deck, and into the ship's "brain," its Combat Information Center, which was a room about 10 feet by 15 feet in which twenty people work during operations. It was hard to imagine that many people could fit in such a small space since the room seemed crowded just with our small group of thirteen volunteers. Walking through the ship, we were impressed with how much was crammed onto the deck and within the ship in terms of weapons and equipment. Michael informed us that Israel was about to put into use a newer and larger missile boat, the Sa'ar 5.0, designed to carry a helicopter. The helicopter would be capable of directing missiles to a target after they were fired from the ship.

The captain of this ship was only thirty years old and he was a major. The officers we spoke with were also surprisingly young (twenty-two or twenty-three years old). Officers commanding Israeli navy boats are typically much younger than their counterparts in the U.S. Navy.

What especially struck us about the men who had told us about the three types of vessels we had seen was their evident pride in Israel's navy. The entry standards that Michael and all officers in the navy have to satisfy are very rigorous and many candidates are screened out. Those who make the grade are extremely intelligent, can make decisions in pressured situations, are good leaders, and are very physically fit. It was obvious that, whatever screening and training process was used, the end result was an officer corps with extremely high morale.

At the end of our tour, Michael told us a story about one of his recent missions. He had been directed to take his patrol boat to the coast of the Gaza Strip in order to fire on reputed terrorists. He was not allowed to fire, however, until given clearance by people on land who could verify both the presence of the terrorists and the unlikelihood that innocent civilians would also be hurt. Because both requirements could not be met, he was not allowed to fire. His point was that the Israeli military has shown tremendous restraint in trying to avoid Palestinian civilian casualties.

Inspired by this tour, we returned home to our base for lunch and an afternoon of work. Since I was unsure whether Tamar would assign me to David's pipe warehouse at Betzet Kishon for the following week, I decided to give him my present now – a pocketknife set – to thank him for the friendship he had shown Brian and me during our time on that base. The next day, to reciprocate, he gave me his navy pen and pencil set. The exchange of these small gifts of appreciation was very meaningful to both of us.

After dinner, most of the volunteers headed into downtown Haifa. The downtown area nightlife, which in Israel starts after eight, was a fun experience. Some of the volunteers attended an outdoor concert of traditional Israeli folk music. Howard and

Terry went to an outdoor entertainment area, featuring rap music and bungee jumping. I spent most of the evening with six of my colleagues and Tamar at a Sushi restaurant on one of Haifa's main streets.

Returning to our base in a *sherut*, the driver engaged us in friendly conversation. Once he heard that we were Sar-el volunteers and what we do, he invited any of us to join him and his family for Friday night Sabbath dinner. He even offered to take us anywhere we wanted for the rest of our stay in Israel, to show us how beautiful his country is. As we left his *sherut*, he asked us to promise to return to Israel. It was not a hard promise for us to make.

THURSDAY, AUGUST 12, 2004

Tamar reported that a bomb blast had occurred last night at a military checkpoint where the highway from Ramallah enters northern Jerusalem. Apparently, a suicide bomber changed his mind about dying with his victims. Instead, he took off his bomb belt and planted it near the Israeli border guards, three of whom were seriously injured in the blast.

She also reported that today was the commencement of the trial of a soldier who was caught on film abusing a Palestinian at a security checkpoint. It is absolutely correct for Israel to prosecute Israeli soldiers if they abuse Palestinians, despite the fact that Arafat praises his terrorists for murdering Israelis (whether soldiers or civilians). Israel is a democratic nation and a democracy must respect individuals' civil rights.

Our workday was broken up by an after-lunch presentation by General Aharon Davidi, the founder of Sar-el. As the civilian head of Sar-el for its entire lifetime, he travels throughout the country to speak with volunteer groups on each base. I sat with General Davidi during lunch before his presentation. I was struck by how much he had slowed down since I had seen him at the Zikim base. At seventy-eight, he was having trouble hearing despite the use of a hearing aid and commented that he might finally listen to his wife's entreaties to retire.

Since our group was an entirely veteran team, General Davidi dispensed with his standard presentation, which I had heard last year at Zikim. Instead, he provided us with an overview of Sar-el. He reported that, in 2003, 4,790 volunteers came to Israel through Sar-el from outside Israel. In addition to these overseas volunteers, Sar-el also benefited from Israeli volunteers, a fact I had not previously known.

The volunteers from abroad, he explained, separate into four distinct groups – those from North America, France, the former Soviet Republics, and the rest of the world. Up to twelve years ago the U.S. supplied about 2,000 volunteers per year. This gradually declined to 400 U.S. volunteers five years ago. Through greater recruitment efforts, buttressed by the hiring of Pamela Lazarus as program director, these numbers had risen to about 1,300 per year. This was an improvement, but was still proportionately less (per population) than the numbers coming from France (1,200 a year).

The Americans included a significant number of Christians (up to 30 percent of the American volunteers) who were strongly pro-Israel. For example, a Christian group from California annually brought about forty people each year to work at the Julis base on tank maintenance. General Davidi commented that the Christians who participated in Sar-el were "perfect volunteers" because they worked very hard and were very highly motivated.

The French office of Sar-el had been much more successful in recruiting volunteers for the program. Sar-el was very well known in France and the French volunteers were often young (sixteen to twenty-two years old). We saw the fervor these young people had exhibited at the Sar-el *keness* in Jerusalem. General Davidi noted that a greater percentage of French Jews participated in Sar-el than did American Jews. He felt this was due to the fact that a greater percentage of French Jews had maintained ties with their relatives in Israel, in terms of attending each other's life cycle events. He suggested that, in order to maintain their connection to Israel, American Jews should renew ties with their relatives in Israel and make new friendships with Israelis. That is exactly what many in our group tried to do on our weekends off the base.

General Davidi commented that most of the Sar-el volunteers from the Former Soviet Union (FSU) had weak ties to Jewish tradition, due to the anti-religion indoctrination they had experienced during years of communist rule. The FSU volunteers came for a different reason. Often they were parents of children who had immigrated to Israel and, after high school, had entered the military. The parents came to Israel through Sar-el to see their children. About 800–900 FSU volunteers, including Jews from Belarus, Kazakhstan, Latvia, Russia, Ukraine, and Uzbekistan, participated in Sar-el every year. Sar-el heavily subsidized their airfare, and this made Sar-el attractive.

The Israeli volunteers in Sar-el comprised three groups: The first were retired people who worked about four and a half hours once a week. Many were parents of fallen soldiers. For these parents, service in Sar-el was their way of continuing and honoring their children's service to Israel. Several hundred such parents currently serve in Sar-el, some having done so for more than thirty years.

The second group of Israelis who served in Sar-el were soldiers who were handicapped due to injuries incurred in the line of duty. Some had lost their self-assurance because of their handicap and some were confined to wheelchairs. One of General Davidi's former paratroopers, who was disabled during his service, told him that he loved going to work every day as a volunteer. It gave him back his standing not only in society but also in his family. His service made him feel whole and provided him with a sense of self-worth.

The third group of Israeli volunteers consisted of mentally retarded youngsters, most of them with Downs' Syndrome. Because of their condition, they could not serve in the Israeli military. Although they were not physically strong, once Sar-el put them in uniform they became excellent workers and as a group were very happy to work.

General Davidi loved to tell stories about his volunteers, so he closed with one such story. One year he visited the Julis base to speak to a group of French volunteers there. The volunteers, mostly teenagers, congregated around him to listen to his words. He noticed one volunteer who did not get off her tank to hear his presentation and instead continued working. When he asked her to join the group she declined, saying she would prefer to continue working on the tank and listen to him from afar. He took note of this seventeen-year old girl named Pascal. Shortly afterwards, he heard that she had been involved in a terrible accident back in France. She fell off a train platform in front of an oncoming train and nearly died. The doctors were compelled to amputate both of her legs above the knee. He visited Pascal in a hospital in France, and even though she looked pale and weak, she promised that she would be returning the following year with artificial legs as a Sar-el volunteer. In fact, Pascal did return as a volunteer, but without artificial legs and confined to a wheelchair. To help her overcome her inability to obtain artificial limbs, due to the extent of her amputation, Davidi sent her to specialists in Germany and Sweden where the limbs were ultimately developed for her. Pascal eventually moved to Israel, joined a kibbutz in the Golan Heights, and studied at the Technion Institute in Haifa. She recently married a Frenchman and returned with him to France, but Davidi was sure he'd see Pascal in Israel again because of her love of the land.

We said goodbye to General Davidi, towards whom we felt great admiration and respect, with a little sadness. The man was an institution in Israel and certainly in Sar-el, and given his age we did not know whether we would see him again.

While our tour of the navy ships at the Haifa naval base was certainly the "sexiest" of our off-base trips, the tour we had this evening was the more meaningful. Shy Davidi and Gilad joined us to visit Israel's national memorial in Tel Aviv for those who had fallen in the service of the Israeli intelligence community. The tour was given by one of the veterans of that community – Shy's father, Ehud Davidi, a twenty-eight-year veteran of Mossad.

Ehud Davidi was a slight man in his mid-sixties with sparse silver hair. He told us about the various roles of the Israeli intelligence branches. Obviously, its primary responsibility is to be the "eyes" of the Israeli military, in terms of giving advance notice of Arab countries' and terrorists' plans against Israel. Israeli intelligence had enjoyed many successes in this regard, most recently its ability to predict and thwart a very high percentage (over 95 percent) of Palestinian terrorist bombings.

He acknowledged that, historically, there had also been some significant failures by the Israeli intelligence services. The most spectacular one was the failure to foresee the surprise Egyptian-Syrian attack that initiated the 1973 Yom Kippur War. While Israel ultimately prevailed in that war, it paid a high price in terms of casualties. After the war, Israel went through a period of self-examination and discovered that it had possessed many clues that could have led it to predict the Egyptian-Syrian attack; however its intelligence services had not put the pieces together. (In this respect, I was reminded of the 9/11 Commission in the U.S., which reached the same conclusion regarding the information American intelligence services possessed before the attacks.)

In addition to its responsibility to act as the "eyes" of the Israeli military, the intelligence services bear a responsibility like no other in the world. They hold themselves responsible for the safety of Jews and Jewish communities around the world. For instance, in 1976, Arab terrorists hijacked a French plane carrying eighty-one Jews headed for Israel and flew them to Entebbe Airport in Uganda. The intelligence services planned a rescue mission while diplomatic channels were used to try to obtain the release of the passengers from the Ugandan dictator, Idi Amin. When diplomatic efforts failed, the intelligence services coordinated the successful Entebbe raid, which freed all of the hostages and returned them to Israel. The sole casualty was the leader of the rescue mission, Yoni Netanyahu, brother of former Prime Minister Benjamin Netanyahu.

Ehud also talked about the protection and rescue of Jews in North Africa. In the early 1960s, the Algerian independence movement against the French colonial power posed serious threats to the Algerian Jewish community. In advance of the war that eventually broke out in Algeria, the Israeli intelligence services smuggled young Algerian Jewish men to Israel to be trained as agents and then returned them to Algeria to protect the community there. When a gang from the Algerian independence movement attacked a group of Jewish worshippers leaving an Algerian synagogue, these Israeli-trained agents surrounded and killed the attackers. Then these agents sent a letter to the home addresses of all of the leaders of the Algerian independence movement (these names were supposed to be secret). The letter said that the Israelis knew where the leaders lived and that there would be retribution for any more attacks against the Algerian Jewish community. No further attacks occurred during the ensuing war of independence.

As his final story, Ehud Davidi told us about his personal participation in the rescue of North Africa's large Jewish population. In the 1950s and 60s, with the various independence movements springing up against the colonial occupiers of North African countries, Israel realized that the North African Jewish community was in jeopardy. This was especially the case because many of the independence movements were fueled by Pan-Arabism and anti-Israel sentiment. Therefore, Israel trained one hundred Mossad agents to deal with this threat. The agents were schooled in Arabic language and culture; they studied the countries in the region, and were even taught the Koran and how to pray in a Muslim mosque.

Ehud Davidi was one of these hundred agents. He was assigned to the rescue of the ancient Moroccan Jewish community, which dated back to Roman times. The newly independent Moroccan government had begun to issue a series of oppressive laws against Jews. Ehud organized an operation to smuggle them across the Mediterranean to Gibraltar and from there to Israel. In addition to using private ships, he acquired a small boat called the *Ergoz* to speed up the process. He and his Mossad partner and friend, Chaim, alternated as captain of the boat. After twelve successful trips in the *Ergoz*, they were told to conduct one more before the winter storms in the area closed their escape route. Their commander ordered Ehud to Paris and directed Chaim to chance a thirteenth trip. Ehud and Chaim argued with the commander to switch assignments because Ehud had a girlfriend in Gibraltar and Chaim had a girlfriend in Paris. Their boss refused to change his mind. Chaim captained the last trip of the *Ergoz*. Unfortunately, the winter storms came earlier than expected and the *Ergoz* was lost at sea with all its passengers – Chaim and forty-two Moroccan immigrants.

The tragedy of this failed rescue mission raised an uproar both in Israel and around the world. The uproar focused on the antisemitic laws passed by the new Moroccan government, which had forced Moroccan Jews to use this dangerous route of escape. That government relented and began to grudgingly issue collective passports allowing groups of Jews to emigrate from Morocco. Then Mossad's forgery unit went into action. It immediately forged a large number of these collective passports, allowing Morocco's entire Jewish community to escape to Israel. One of our volunteers (Marion) remembered that, on a trip to Israel in 1962, the hold of the boat she took from Italy to Israel was crammed with Moroccan Jews who were part of this rescue effort.

After telling us about his personal experiences, Ehud walked us through the outdoor maze of stone walls of this memorial. On each set of walls were engraved the names of intelligence agents who had been killed in the line of duty. The names were grouped around periods of time, usually associated with Israel's wars. From gratings in the floor, lights were directed upwards at the sets of engraved names to highlight them even in the nighttime darkness. We walked through the outdoor memorial in an eerie silence. At each set of names, Ehud would stop to quietly talk about a few of the individuals listed, what they had done, and how they had died; he had served with many of them. There were 630 names listed. They included the Israeli spy, Elie Cohen, made famous in the book *Our Man in Damascus*, who was caught and hanged by the Syrians shortly before the Six-Day War. They also included Yoni Netanyahu, who led the successful Entebbe raid. And, with a mixture of fondness and sadness, Ehud also pointed out the name of his friend Chaim, who had perished when the *Ergoz* was lost.

At one set of walls, Ehud stopped at the names of two brothers named Kaplan, who both served in the intelligence service. He mentioned that when telling their story during a previous tour, a man took him aside and said: "Thank you for telling the story about how my brothers died."

We thanked Ehud at the end of the tour. We were very moved by the stories of the men and women who had died in the service of their country. Between 50,000 and 200,000 people attend the memorial every year, most of them Israeli school children. The bus ride back to the base was a somber one.

FRIDAY, AUGUST 13, 2004

When I was growing up in Vineland, New Jersey, we often got together for family holidays with my father's cousin, Shlomo Hornfeld and his family. Shlomo's sister Yehudit had settled in Israel; I knew about her family, but had never met them. In advance of my visit I wrote to Yehudit's daughter Dvora, and Dvora's son Nir wrote back, inviting me for a weekend at their home in Pardes Chana.

Last night, a short taxi ride from the base brought me to my cousins' house. It was late, so my cousin Nir showed me to a bedroom where I quickly fell asleep.

I slept late this morning (until 8:30) and then got up to meet my cousins. Nir, a tall, red-haired, thirty-two-year-old, served as my host. His mother, Dvora, was a very gentle and self-effacing woman; his father, David, operated a machine shop for repairing specialty metal parts. Nir himself bore a striking resemblance to my cousin Shlomo.

Pardes Chana, a town of about 30,000 people, reminded me of my rural New Jersey hometown, a largely farming community in transition to other industries. After breakfast, Nir and I picked some ripe purple plums from a tree in his backyard. There were also orange, grapefruit, tangerine, lemon, mango, and macadamia trees. For a good part of the year, Nir's family enjoyed the fruits of the earth grown right in their own backyard. We ate the plums on the front porch while catching up on family matters.

Later Nir took me on a tour of the Carmel area, which was mountainous and had extremely winding roads. The sides of the mountains were pockmarked with natural caves. At one point, we stopped at an ancient limestone quarry that Nir explained had been quarried by the Romans. We drove through the Druze village of Daliyat el Carmel and proceeded to the Muhraqah, a site holy to Druze, Jews, and Christians. The prophet Elijah is said to have lived in this area and the Druze constructed a monument to the prophet at the Muhraqah. Across from this statute is the Stella Maris monastery, operated by Carmelite monks. The monastery was built over a grotto in which Elijah is reputed to have lived.

The rooftop of the Stella Maris monastery, built on a high rocky outcropping, provided a stunning view of a landscape rich in Jewish history. In one direction lay the Jezreel Valley where, according to the Book of Judges, the Canaanite king of Hazor battled the Israelites led by Deborah and her general, Barak. The Israelites routed the army of Hazor in that battle by forming on a hill overlooking what was then a swampy plain. The chariots for which Hazor was feared were rendered useless in the swampy plain and could not ascend the hill. Stripped of their main assault weapon and floundering in the swampy soil, Hazor's forces were overwhelmed by the Israelites.

In another direction lay the biblical site where Gideon took only 300 men to launch a nighttime attack against the army of the

Midianites. Gideon's men surprised and frightened the Midianites by blowing trumpets and setting fires with their torches. The Israelites scared and confused the Midianites into attacking each other and then fleeing.

Also visible from the top of the monastery were the ruins of the ancient city of Megiddo, an important Canaanite city conquered by Joshua. According to the literature handed out by the Carmelite monks, Christian belief states that the final battle between good and evil will take place at Megiddo. From this height, we could also see Mount Gilboa, the site of the battle in which King Saul and his son Jonathan were slain by the Philistines. This biblical event is especially important to me because my son's Torah reading for his bar mitzvah was the story of the great friendship between David and Jonathan and David's despair upon hearing of the death of his friend.

The heights of the Stella Maris monastery are a very spiritual place. With the cool air and the magnificent panorama of biblical history below us, we stood quietly for a while in silent contemplation.

After a leisurely lunch, we drove to Nir's high school, between the towns of Binyamina and Zichron Ya'akov. We hiked to the top of a hill overlooking the high school. Nir pointed out an archeological dig that had first been opened when he attended the school. Now fully excavated, the site consisted of a Roman aqueduct that channeled water from a natural spring originating in a cave into a Roman bathhouse. The water was crystal clear and cold.

The land around us appeared to be rocky and forbidding, covered with sabra cactus. But despite its outward appearance, the land abounded with food. The orange-colored fruit of the sabra cactus are picked and marketed in Israel. Nir picked ripe purple figs from trees lining the stream exiting the aqueduct. We also walked over to what looked like orange trees, but which turned out to be pomegranate trees. Since their fruit was red and ripe, we picked a few of these as well. Then Nir picked up what looked like a long, dark-brown bean pod. It was carob and its sweet brittle husk is used to make chocolate in Israel.

On the way home, we passed the Binyamina train station. Nir explained its historical significance: When the British relinquished their mandate over Palestine, they either turned over their armaments to the Arabs or withdrew with them. In Binyamina, the British loaded up a trainload of weaponry to take with them. The Israelis blew up the train tracks on both sides of the train station, marooning the train and forcing the British to leave its load in the station. The Israelis seized these arms and successfully used them to fend off Arab attacks in the area during the War of Independence.

Back at the house, we sat down for a sumptuous Sabbath dinner. I met Nir's sister, Sigal, also a redhead, currently completing her law apprenticeship in Ramat Gan, and his brother, Ziv, who lived nearby with his wife, Ayelet, and their baby son, Noam. Ziv worked in the bomb disposal unit of the local police. After dinner, we watched the opening procession of the Olympic games in Athens, munching on grapes harvested from the family's backyard.

SATURDAY, AUGUST 14, 2004

Today was a day that could only be interesting to someone like me, with a farming background. After breakfast, David took me and Nir in his pick-up truck to view his weekend love – an antique tractor restoration site at nearby Kibbutz Ein Shemer. This kibbutz had a reputation in Israel as the place that can rebuild any type of tractor or diesel engine. Just as antique car enthusiasts gather on weekends in the U.S. to repair or rebuild antique cars, David joins about ten or fifteen other men on this kibbutz every Saturday to work on old tractors. The group relies on David to make new parts in his machine shop whenever needed.

At the kibbutz, David proudly led us to a very large workshop where many men were working on antique tractors. Old and rebuilt tractor parts were strewn around on worktables. Next to the workshop, he unlocked a very large two-story barn containing the product of the efforts of these men: seventeen restored antique tractors, the oldest of which was built in 1929. The barn was not ready for display, but the collection of large and small tractors, all in working order, was impressive.

Walking through the tree-lined lanes of the kibbutz, we came across a museum of old tools and farm implements from the early days of the kibbutz in the 1920s. The kibbutz also operated a small, restored train for tourists that ran on a track around the perimeter of the kibbutz. As part of the attraction for school children, it operated a long, tractor-pulled wagon for hay rides.

Ziv arrived at the kibbutz with Ayelet and Noam, knowing where they would naturally find David on a Saturday morning. They placed Noam with another child on a battery-operated toy tractor to introduce him at an early age to his grandfather's infatuation.

Leaving David at Kibbutz Ein Shemer, Nir and I drove through the modern and very expensive area of Caesaria (which features the only golf course in Israel). We stopped at the Ralli Museum, founded by an Israeli Jew of Greek origin named Harry Recanati. This is one of four museums around the world that he built to house his art collection. This museum was dedicated to the memory of the Jewish communities of Spain wiped out in 1492 by the Spanish Inquisition and to the Jewish community of Salonika, Greece, which was destroyed by the Germans in 1941. The exhibits included colorful paintings by South American and Spanish artists, as well as a number of sculptures by Salvador Dali.

The Ralli Museum also had a separate section devoted to the history of Caesaria, which was built by King Herod between 22 B.C.E. and 10 B.C.E. Herod, the Roman-backed governor of Judea, was a great builder. He was most famous for constructing the Second Temple in Jerusalem and the mountaintop retreat at

Masada, which was subsequently used as a fortress by the last of the resisters in the Great Jewish Revolt of 66–73 C.E.*

King Herod created the port city of Caesaria as his masterpiece, constructing an artificial harbor made of huge blocks of stone. It was one of the most significant cities in the eastern Mediterranean during the Roman period. At the end of the Great Jewish Revolt, 2,500 Jewish prisoners of war, forced to fight as gladiators, were killed in Caesaria's amphitheater. Following the Roman and Byzantine periods, Caesaria's importance declined as portions of Herod's artificial harbor gradually fell into the sea. Later on, Muslim Mamluk rulers wrested the city from the Crusaders, completely destroying its fortifications to prevent the Crusaders from returning. The museum highlighted the fact that Caesaria rested on layers of history, each documenting the changing fortunes of the land.

From Caesaria, we drove to nearby Binyamina to view the Shuni, an old Crusader fort that had been refurbished by the Turks as a way station for overnight travelers. In 1947, this empty fort became the operational headquarters of the Irgun, the underground Jewish fighting unit headed by future Prime Minister Menachem Begin. Next to the old Turkish fort was a memorial to the Irgun fighters who were captured and hanged by the British at the prison in Acre. On the grounds of the Shuni, Keren Kayemet (the Jewish National Fund) maintains a public park where picnickers come to spend the day. The grounds are called Jabotinsky Park in honor of Ze'ev Jabotinsky, a leading Zionist activist in British-held Palestine.

On the way back, Nir stopped to show me the house that his great-grandfather had built when he came from Romania to Pardes Chana in the 1920s. He proudly recalled that, in Romania,

---

* It was at Masada that 960 Jewish zealots held off an entire Roman army for almost a year and then finally committed mass suicide in 73 C.E. rather than be taken alive by the Romans. Israel now swears in many of its elite military units at the top of Masada with the oath: "Masada will not fall again."

his great-grandfather had been a lawyer and the first Jewish officer in the Romanian army. When he came to Pardes Chana, he bought ten dunams of land (about 2.5 acres) and built the first two-story house in the town. The house was currently owned by Amos, an old friend of David, who fortunately was home when we arrived. Amos was happy to let us onto his fenced-in property, past his two large Rhodesian ridgebacks, massive dogs bred to fight lions.

Amos shared David's passionate interest in restoring old diesel engines. He invited us to his backyard to view his collection of equipment, including about twenty-five rebuilt tractors. They were not as old or in as good condition as those restored by David's diesel engine restoration club at Kibbutz Ein Shemer, but I was impressed to see so many, arranged in two long rows. They bore names that were familiar to me – McCormack, Massey-Ferguson, Caterpillar, John Deere, and International.

Amos' collection included two small locomotives and a dump truck, all in an obvious state of disrepair. Between them was his *pièce de resistance* – a massive, amphibious, Russian-built armored personnel carrier captured from the Egyptians in the 1973 Yom Kippur War. I was clearly astounded by the size of the carrier. "That's nothing," Nir laughed. "A few years ago, I located a Russian-built T-62 tank, also captured from the Egyptians in the Yom Kippur War. I bought it for Amos from a junkyard in southern Israel." "Well, where is it?" I asked. "Amos' neighbors complained," Nir responded. "They were afraid he would drive the tank on the local roads at night, fire its cannon and hurt someone, so the local police forced him to get rid of it."

Late in the afternoon, when Ziv dropped by his parents' house, I asked him to tell me about his job in the police bomb squad unit. He was pleased to do more than tell me – he showed me. Taking me out to his police van, he lowered a metal ramp from the back of the van and directed a bomb disposal robot out of the van by remote control. The robot carried three cameras that broadcast pictures back to Ziv sitting in the van. It also possessed an arm that he could operate by remote control to grab an object. Finally, it had a high caliber rifle that he could direct to fire into a suspicious package. Ziv also showed me the heavy-duty bomb resistant outfit that he wears when dealing with potential bombs in areas that the robot cannot access. He commented that Athens had no bomb disposal unit, so the Israelis trained Greek bomb disposal personnel in preparation for the summer Olympic games.

Ziv had been a policeman in the bomb disposal unit for the past eight years. David and Dvora showed me a newspaper photograph of him removing his robot after it had detonated a bomb (and had been destroyed in the process). They were very proud of him for his work, but hoped he could limit his activities to use of the robot at a distance. Ziv acknowledged that was not always possible.

After dark, David, Dvora, Nir, and I headed to the ancient city of Caesaria. We walked along the inner part of Herod's artificial harbor, which had been converted to an outdoor restaurant. On the outer edge of one of the jetties, we watched young children playing amidst the Roman ruins. The place was packed with families out for a Saturday night stroll. Strewn at random were the tops of marble Roman columns, on which people sat when tired of walking. The salty sea air blowing in from the Mediterranean was invigorating. David showed us where he used to go fishing as a child on one of the outer jetties. The restaurants were so crowded that we could not find a place to eat, so we drove to a nearby strip mall for a late dinner.

SUNDAY, AUGUST 15, 2004

At the entrance to the Betzet Tira base the guards already knew me, so that a wave and a "Shalom" were all that I needed to get through the gate. My army identification card remained in my pocket. Sivan was already at the volunteers' compound, waiting with her car to take two volunteers to Betzet Kishon. Tamar asked me and Jordan to go back to Betzet Kishon for the week and we were happy to do so.

Being back at Betzet Kishon was a comfortable routine. The

work was hot and physical, but that was what I had asked for. The day passed quickly and, in what seemed a short time, Sivan was back at our warehouse to pick us up. The cook at Betzet Tira had returned from a week's vacation, so to celebrate he made pancakes (and, of course, eggs) for dinner.

After dinner, I found a copy of yesterday's *Jerusalem Post*. It reported that last Wednesday's bomb blast just north of Jerusalem, which had killed three Palestinians and seriously injured three Israeli border guards, had not reached its intended target. The Palestinian terrorists had purchased a baby carriage in which they planned to conceal the bomb and explode it in a busy Haifa marketplace. However, the large presence of security forces at the checkpoint north of Jerusalem caused the terrorists to detonate the bomb prematurely.

MONDAY, AUGUST 16, 2004

Tamar announced the news that the government approved a new budget yesterday, after much wrangling among the parties in Prime Minister Sharon's coalition. Also, in terms of anti-terrorism actions, the IDF rocketed a Palestinian warehouse that was being used as a bomb factory. Finally, a report was issued highlighting inadequate environmental protection enforcement with regard to Israeli manufacturing plants and calling for an overall greater sensitivity to environment protection. The weather would be cooler today – 30° C (86° F).

Work at Betzet Kishon was sweaty, but not unpleasant. I could imagine that in more temperate weather work at the base could be quite comfortable. Certainly, the view of Haifa above us, built upon the Carmel Mountain range, was a gorgeous backdrop for our work.

We stopped work a little early in order to leave the base for a special dinner at a restaurant along the nearby beach at Hof Ha-Carmel. Sylvia would be leaving for England tomorrow and we wanted to give her a nice send-off.

Early evening at Hof Ha-Carmel was beautiful. Even though

it was only a Monday evening, the promenade stretching up and down the seashore was crowded with people. Cafés lined the promenade and music emanated from them. Couples ranging from eighteen to eighty held hands as they walked along the promenade. Young children splashed around in a large, fresh water kiddies' pool. As we walked, one of our volunteers surveyed this idyllic scene and summed up our collective impression: "There's nowhere else like this."

Eating dinner at an outdoor restaurant, we watched the sun slowly set as a magnificent red ball into the Mediterranean. The restaurant piped out a variety of Israeli and American music, including, at one point, the song "Staying Alive" from the movie *Saturday Night Fever*. Brian and I looked at each other and said simultaneously: "John Travolta – Naftali!"

Shortly after sundown, Helen, another volunteer from England, joined us with two female Israeli soldiers from Betzet Tira, Deena and Hadar, whom she just happened to meet on the beach. Of course, she invited them to join us. I got into an interesting discussion with Deena regarding her view of the Israeli Arabs and of the Palestinians. Deena's father owned a children's clothing factory that employed both Israeli Jews and Israeli Arabs. He also sold his products to both groups and had a number of Israeli Arabs clients whom he considered good friends. However, ever since the Israeli Arabs rioted in support of the Palestinians in the current Intifada, Israeli Jews, including Deena's father, no longer felt they could trust their Arab friends.

Deena felt that as long as the Israeli Arabs believed that the Palestinians were being short-changed, the bonds of trust and friendship between Israeli Jews and Israeli Arabs would not be rebuilt. With regard to the Palestinians, the solution was to help raise their standard of living so they no longer have a hopeless and frustrating outlook. Until their economic situation improved, according to Deena, there could be no peace. Of course, Arafat would have to be removed because the corruption he sponsors sucked all the resources out of the Palestinians.

After dinner, we all split up to wander along the beachfront promenade. Several of us sat in the amphitheater to listen to a concert given by a singing and dancing group, all dressed in white. They sang songs of peace and their concert was broadcast live on Israeli radio.

Shortly after the concert ended, most of us headed back to the base. Brian and Jordan, our two youngest volunteers, remained on the beachfront with Deena and Hadar. When I returned to the base, Sivan was hanging out at the gate with the guards. "Where are Brian and Jordan?" she asked. When she heard they had stayed at the beach with Deena and Hadar, she was visibly upset. They were "her volunteers," because she had befriended them and had driven them to Betzet Kishon every day. She proceeded to buzz around the base in a very angry mood. Sivan was somewhat mollified when the foursome returned much later. Deena immediately went to her bunk, but Hadar wanted to sit and talk more with Brian and Jordan. Sivan stood about twenty feet away and glared at Hadar until the latter got the message and retired to her bunk. Then Sivan moved in and "let" Brian and Jordan teach her how to play poker on our picnic table.

TUESDAY, AUGUST 17, 2004

As usual, the news from Tamar was both political and military. There was going to be a vote today in the Likud Party (biggest party in the Knesset) over whether to allow the Labor Party (second biggest party) into the coalition government. Separately, the Histadrut (the labor union for all government employees) announced that the recently agreed-upon budget cuts were unacceptable because they would lead to the firings of thousands of government workers. Therefore, the Histadrut announced a general strike starting September 1. Lastly, the hunger strike of Palestinian prisoners was in its second day. The strikers were demanding cell phones in prison, as well as elimination of the glass walls in the visitors' area of the prison that prevented the physical passage of written messages. The Israeli Interior Minister vowed to resist these demands, given that they posed security risks by allowing jailed terrorists to direct more terrorism from prison.

Sivan was completely silent on the car ride to Betzet Kison. She emitted monosyllabic responses to my questions until I gave up my attempts to strike up a conversation with this normally talkative nineteen-year-old. She was still upset that two Israeli army girls had "moved in" on her volunteers, and she clearly missed Brian and Jordan, who had been assigned to other projects. For over two weeks, she had been driving me and either Brian or Jordan to Betzet Kishon, but this morning, she had only one volunteer – me. Sivan felt slighted.

My last workday at Betzet Kishon was a busy one. Like the volunteers at Betzet Tira, I helped to fill orders for materials from various Israeli navy bases, especially those at Ashdod and Eilat. The only difference was that the orders we filled at Betzet Kishon were for pipes.

At the end of the day, I said goodbye to David. He had started at his new job at the Betzet Kishon pipe warehouse the day before we came to work for him. He inherited a mess of a warehouse. I felt pretty good that the three volunteers who had worked there made a significant difference in organizing and taking inventory of the pipes in the warehouse for him. These efforts made it easier for David to start filling orders.

We took another educational tour late this afternoon, this time to Atlit, a restored former British detention camp. Immediately after World War II, when Holocaust survivors in "Displaced Persons" camps in Europe tried to enter Palestine, the British continued their policy of restricting Jewish immigration. In response, Israeli Jews and Diaspora Zionists organized a channel of clandestine immigration using old ships to run the British blockade and bring the survivors to Israel. Many of these Holocaust survivors were captured by the British and put in detention camps on Cyprus and in Israel. Atlit was one such detention camp in Israel.

The camp was surrounded by a double barbed wire fence, with guard towers at numerous spots along the fence. The buildings consisted of about eighty one-story buildings that looked very much like the long, low barracks I'd see in documentaries about Auschwitz. We walked into one of the original barracks. Even with the front and back doors open, the heat was overpowering. The British would conduct a roll call at the end of every day and then lock shut all the windows and doors. It must have been stifling in these barracks. I wondered how many people died from the heat.

The only other original building restored on the Atlit site was the disinfection-shower building. New arrivals to the camp were herded into the building, their hair was cut, and they were ordered to take off their clothes for disinfection showers. The British were completely insensitive to the fact that this was the same sequence the Germans had used in their death camps. For these Holocaust survivors, such orders signaled that they were about to be gassed. The British order to enter the showers often provoked a panic among the new arrivals.

Our guide told us a story about Atlit that took place shortly after the end of World War II. The camp was packed with Jewish survivors from the Holocaust. It also held a group of 40 Iraqi Jews who had crossed over from Syria into Palestine and were captured and detained by the British. The British planned to send these Iraqi Jews back to Syria where they faced certain death at the hands of the Syrian government. On October 9, 1945, Palmach troops led by Yitzhak Rabin broke into the camp and freed about 240 of its inmates. The escapees were hidden on two kibbutz settlements in the nearby Carmel Mountains. Their hiding places were soon discovered by the British, who surrounded them with a large military force. To forestall their re-capture, the Jewish population of Haifa and the surrounding areas streamed into the encircled area. Without firing a shot, the crowds forced the British to withdraw without recapturing a single escapee.

After touring Atlit, Tamar took us into the Carmel Mountains to the Druze village of Daliyat al Carmel, where my cousin Nir had taken me the previous weekend. Some of the volunteers purchased the beautiful multi-colored woven fabrics in the shops before we stopped at a Druze restaurant for dinner.

As the bus winded its way down the Carmel Mountains with its magnificent views, one of the volunteers asked Tamar whether hiking in the mountains was possible. "Yes," she responded – and this got Tamar started on one of her favorite subjects. Hiking is extremely popular in Israel, and is mandated in the public schools where hikes are frequent outdoor outings. As a former scout, Tamar told us that these hikes foster teamwork, independence, and self-confidence. For hiking enthusiasts, she told us, there is an annual 300-mile trans-Israel hike between Eilat and the northern tip of Israel.

Tamar enjoyed sharing her passion for the national sport until our bus pulled into the base. Fortunately, it was only a short hike to our bunks.

WEDNESDAY, AUGUST 18, 2004

We did not have to go to flag-raising this morning, since we were scheduled to leave at 9:00 A.M. for another trip off the base. However, because this was our last full day on the base, we all agreed to don our grease-stained and paint-spattered uniforms to attend flag-raising once more. Appropriately, our most experienced volunteer, Marion, was asked to raise the Israeli flag.

Our morning trip took us to the Clandestine Immigration and Israeli Navy Museum outside of Haifa. I did not understand at first why "clandestine immigration" and "the Israeli navy" were covered in one museum, but I soon found out that the two subjects were historically linked.

There is no historical precedent for a people to smuggle itself into its own ancestral homeland. Yet that is what Jews were forced to do, starting in the early 1930s with the rise of virulent antisemitism in Europe, during World War II, and in the postwar period. In an effort to appease the Arabs, the British sharply limited the number of Jews permitted to immigrate to Palestine. The British policy virtually cut off Jewish immigration to Palestine, which led to a Jewish response: the clandestine immigration known as "Aliyah Bet." From the 1930s to 1948, seventy old and rickety ships carried thousands of Jews from Europe seeking to breach the British blockade on immigration.

Our museum guide, Adi, related the stories of several of these vessels that aroused the conscience of the world. In 1941, the *Struma*, a freighter loaded with 767 Jews trying to escape the Nazis, left Romania bound for British-held Palestine. The old ship came through the Black Sea to Turkey where it broke down and was forced to dock in Istanbul. The Turks could not fix the ship's engines, but refused to admit the refugee Jews. Making an exception to their usual policy of barring Jewish immigration to British-held Palestine, the British opened negotiations with the Turks to save the children on board by providing them overland passage to Palestine. Instead, the Turks towed the ship out into the Black Sea, where it drifted helplessly. Eventually, it was torpedoed by a Soviet submarine and sank, with the loss of all but one of its passengers.

Another tragic wartime story concerned refugees on the *Patria*. In 1940, three small ships carrying Jewish refugees from Vienna, Gdansk, and Prague made it to Palestine, but were captured by the British. The British loaded the passengers from these three ships onto the *Patria*, a large French passenger liner that had been seized by the British. The British intended to send the *Patria* back to Nazi-occupied Europe – and likely death for all of its passengers. The night before the ship's departure, the Jewish resistance exploded a small bomb under the ship, intending to disable it from taking to sea. The resistance miscalculated; too much dynamite was used, and the explosion sank the ship, taking 267 lives.

The most famous of the ill-fated ships seeking to break the British blockade was the *Exodus 1947*, later made into a movie starring Paul Newman. The Exodus was one of eleven ships purchased and equipped by the American Jewish community to carry Holocaust survivors to Palestine after World War II. Originally designed to hold 450 passengers, in July 1947, 4,530 Holocaust survivors crammed aboard this ship bound from France to Palestine. Just short of its destination, the *Exodus* was intercepted by six British destroyers but refused to stop. The destroyers tear-gassed, machine-gunned, and eventually rammed the *Exodus* to stop her. Finally, with three dead and many wounded, the *Exodus* was forced to surrender. Normally, the British would have dispatched the refugees to internment camps in Cyprus, but this time they chose to make an example of them. They patched up the ship and sent it back to Marseilles, and from there, to "Displaced Persons" camps in Germany.

Adi walked us through the museum exhibits, making the connection between the clandestine immigration and the birth of Israel's navy while filling in the historical background: In November 1947, the United Nations approved a partition plan to terminate the British Mandate of Palestine. In its place, the U.N. plan directed that two states be created side-by-side, one Jewish and one Arab. The Jews of Palestine accepted the U.N. partition plan, but the Arabs immediately rejected it – and began to attack Jewish communities even before the British departed. The Grand Mufti of Jerusalem, the spiritual leader of the Palestinian Muslims, had spent the war years in Berlin recruiting Muslim soldiers on behalf of Hitler. He incited Palestinian Arabs to reject the U.N. plan and to attack Jews instead. Armies from five neighboring Arab countries immediately occupied what was to have been the independent Palestinian Arab state and invaded the small Jewish state as soon as it declared independence.

At this point, Israel had no navy. The IDF took five of the most seaworthy of the interned clandestine immigration ships docked in Haifa harbor. It enlisted anyone with sea experience (e.g., local fisherman) to serve as crews for these five ships. And since it had no weapons to arm these ships, it outfitted them with fake guns made of wood and heavy cardboard.

This was only a temporary makeshift navy. Israel's first real warship was an antiquated icebreaker that it purchased from the U.S. navy and renamed the *Eilat*. Prime Minister David Ben-Gurion directed that it be given the number 16, to fool the Arab nations into thinking that Israel had at least fifteen other warships. The icebreaker had no weapons, and the Israelis had no naval guns with which to arm it. Out of expediency, the Israelis equipped it with an old 65 mm. field artillery piece from World War I. This cannon was designed to be pulled by horses in support of infantry, and so came on a wheeled base. The cannon was so old that the crew named it "Napoleonchik," as if it had come from Napoleon's era. The wheels supporting the weapon caused it to roll backwards all over the deck whenever it was fired, posing a serious risk for the crew. Eventually the crew figured out how to keep it stationary when fired, but as a field artillery piece, it had a very limited range. Yet, from these makeshift beginnings, Israel created a navy equal to that possessed by Egypt within nine months of its declaration of statehood.

I learned more about the birth of the Israeli navy two weeks after returning to the U.S., when I called my cousin, Shlomo Hornfeld, in New York. He had once served in the Israeli navy, and I thought he might be interested in this story about how the Israelis managed to so quickly establish a navy in 1948. After listening patiently to my story, Shlomo chuckled and said: "Would you really like to know how we did it?" He then proceeded to relate a first-person account of the creation of the Israeli navy.

Shlomo, now in his early eighties, had served in the British navy during the Second World War, rising to the rank of chief petty officer. He had been stationed in various British naval ports in the eastern Mediterranean, specializing in the repair of ships' engines. After his discharge, he volunteered his services to the Haganah, the underground Jewish army, to work as a ship's engineer on the ships used for the clandestine immigration. Here is his account of the conversion of these vessels into the first five ships of the Israeli navy:

About three months before the May 14, 1948 Declaration of Statehood, the Haganah contacted about twenty of us ex-British navy men living in what was then British-held Palestine. We agreed to muster in as the first members of the Israeli navy and gathered near Herzliya. Shortly afterwards, we moved north to an evacuated British air force base on the outskirts of Haifa, which is the city where my family lived. We were shortly joined by others with experience on ships, so that we totaled about forty or fifty men.

Anchored in Haifa harbor were rows of small, broken-down refugee ships that the British had captured and impounded, sending their refugee passengers to detention camps in Cyprus or in Atlit. We received orders from two Haganah commanders (Kazak and Bertchik) to pick five of the most seaworthy of these ships and get them ready for sea duty. We knew we were going to refurbish these five ships into the first vessels of the Israeli navy.

One morning, shortly before dawn, we slipped aboard the five selected ships, crawling up their anchor cables from the seaward side, out of view from the nearby British naval base. Once aboard, I and several other ex-British navy men went to work on the engines and generators while the rest of our contingent repaired other parts of the ships.

On our first day of work, we had no food and avoided the water we found on board, fearing it was contaminated with disease from the refugees the ships had carried. That night, I went home and asked my mother to gather as much bread and as many tomatoes as she could, since this was the only food available at the time. Late into the night, my mother made mounds of tomato sandwiches. The next morning, I took a giant sack of sandwiches on board to feed the men working with me.

We worked continuously in secret for many weeks to repair these five ships, undetected by the British. We completed all five before the Declaration of Statehood. We named the first ship we finished refurbishing the "Hannah Senesh." We did so to honor the young Jewish heroine who parachuted into Nazi-occupied Europe to save Jews and was captured and executed by the Nazis in 1944.

Once refurbished, the five ships had no guns. Consequently, we fashioned fake guns from anything we could lay our hands on. For the Hannah Senesh, I remember positioning a thick metal pipe on her deck to look like a real cannon.

The first real fighting vessel in the Israeli navy was an old icebreaker we acquired from the U.S. navy shortly after the May 15, 1948 Declaration of Statehood. We renamed her the "Eilat." I repaired her engines after which she was armed and went to sea.

We returned to Betzet Tira in the late morning, where most of the soldiers were busy cleaning the base for a special inspection. Two years ago, Betzet Tira had won the award for the cleanest military base in Israel and a banner proudly hung in the mess hall commemorating that distinction. Last year, it lost this competition. Today, it was to undergo the first round of annual inspections.

At lunch, David stopped by to say goodbye to me. David expressed his appreciation for our friendship and, as a parting gift, surprised me with a present of three CDs of Israeli music that he had downloaded from the Internet. During the three weeks we worked together, David had frequently asked me whether I liked a particular song on the radio. Unbeknownst to me, he had been keeping a mental record of my answers in order to create this gift. He expressed his wish that listening to this Israeli music would bring back good memories of our time together. I wished him good luck on his career in the navy and we hugged before parting.

The inspectors were due on the base sometime in the afternoon, so after lunch I joined Ken and Diana in painting the area around the base commander's office. We finished just as the inspectors walked by at the commencement of their tour. Shy Davidi gave me a friendly wave as he walked past us with the inspectors. Hopefully, they were impressed, not only with our paint job but also with the mounds of trash the volunteers had removed from around the base, leaving it spotless. The entire base was galvanized to impress the inspectors, hoping for a first place designation.

After work was over, our three weeks of service were completed. Even though we were all tired, we resolved to go off base for our final night. Sivan called me to ask me to invite Brian and Jordan to join her and her friend Chana at the Haifa mall for an evening of bowling. But by the time I located Brian and Jordan, Hadar and her friend Carol had made plans to take them to the Hof Ha-Carmel beach. Sivan borrowed her father's huge (by Israeli standards) Mazda 626 car and showed up to find "her volunteers" taken again. This time, the very amply endowed Hadar was in civilian clothes, wearing a low cut outfit leaving little to the imagination. Sivan, to say the least, was not pleased when she came across this scene outside the volunteers' compound. Of course, she was also in civilian clothes, which were as tight and revealing as possible. Both Sivan and Hadar were very obviously interested in Brian.

Caught between these two, Brian and Jordan chose to go to the beach as originally planned with Hadar and Carol; Sivan and her friend Chana were stuck with taking me and Ed to the nearby mall. After a bite and some shopping, it came as no surprise when Sivan suggested we skip the bowling and head for the Hof Ha-Carmel beach. We agreed and shortly found a contingent of volunteers, including Brian, Jordan, Hadar, Carol and Tamar at the outdoor amphitheater. After listening to what we all agreed was a lousy local Israeli rock band and indulging in beer and pizza, we all walked along the promenade one last time together.

While we wandered along the promenade, Carol commented that she was glad that the volunteers had come to the base. We would be missed, she said, because we had "livened up" their otherwise boring existence there. She hoped that we would return.

Dropping me and Ed off at the base at the end of the evening, Sivan pressed an envelope into my hand that she asked me to open after she left. It contained two pictures of her, one of which was in her "dress Navy whites." Along with the pictures was a letter expressing how much she enjoyed our conversations over the past three weeks while driving back and forth to Betzet Kishon.

She invited me to return to Israel soon and promised to show me more of what the Haifa area had to offer. I was truly touched by her heartfelt letter. I had also enjoyed getting to know her and appreciated her irreverent and energetic personality. Sivan was one of the many soldiers on our base who went out of their way to make us feel welcome. I knew that I would miss her.

THURSDAY, AUGUST 19, 2004

It felt strange to go to breakfast today in civilian clothes, realizing we wouldn't be going to work afterwards. Nonetheless, Tamar gave us the news one last time: Yesterday, the Likud Party rejected the proposal of their own party leader (Prime Minister Sharon) to allow the Labor Party into his bare majority coalition government. In the Gaza Strip town of Nevet Ga'alim, a Jewish settler was injured when a Kassam rocket landed on his house. A suspect in the Madrid terrorist bombings was caught. In the Olympics, Israel's doubles tennis team was eliminated in the quarterfinals. One of Israel's last hopes for a medal was pinned on its entry in the judo competition, an athlete who had previously won the European judo championship. Earlier in the Olympics, an Iranian judo competitor had forfeited rather than compete against an Israeli, as part of the Arab countries' continued refusal to recognize the State of Israel.*

After the news, Shy Davidi met with us to thank us for volunteering and serving on his base. He had heard very positive feedback from his officers and soldiers about how hard we had worked. And he announced that the base had been declared the winner over all other naval bases after yesterday's inspection, graciously remarking that our hard work had contributed to this distinction. We were elated, as we all identified Betzet Tira as "our base," just like the soldiers did. He said that, as a result of what he had seen our group do, he intended to open his base to more Sar-el vol-

---

* Shortly after I returned to the U.S., Gal Friedman won Israel its first ever Olympic gold medal (in windsurfing) and the entire country celebrated.

unteers. And he asked us to take back to our home countries the message that Israelis very much appreciate people coming from abroad and especially those who come to support Israel.

Then we sat down with Shy to hear his long-promised story about the search for the wreck of the *Dakar*. I knew that he had played an important role in the search and looked forward to hearing his account.

The *Dakar* was an old World War II T-class submarine, commissioned by the British in 1943. It was originally called H.M.S. *Totem*, and a real Indian totem pole was placed in the sub for good luck. In addition to the *Totem*, Israel purchased another T-class submarine in 1965 and renamed the two vessels *Livyaton* (Whale) and *Dakar* (Swordfish). Both submarines were completely refurbished in Portsmouth, England. The Israeli crew of both vessels lived in Portsmouth for two years, along with their families, as the vessels underwent modernization and trial runs. In the course of modernizing the warships, the totem pole was removed from the *Dakar*, despite British warnings that it would bring bad luck.

Both submarines left Portsmouth in early 1968 and the crews' families flew ahead to Haifa to prepare for the naval celebration over the receipt of the first Israeli submarines. The captain of the Dakar was Ya'akov Ra'anan who had three sons, two of whom later served in the navy with Shy.

When the *Dakar* reached the sea off the Greek island of Crete, it radioed to Haifa and asked for permission to arrive a day ahead of the planned celebration. Permission was denied because the navy wanted the *Dakar* to arrive as part of the scheduled event. Captain Ra'anan radioed back his displeasure at the order, especially with a storm blowing in the eastern Mediterranean Sea. Since the *Dakar* was newly refurbished, it did not yet have permission to dive underwater. While a submerged submarine can ignore a storm at the surface, a submarine on the surface gets bounced around, making it very rough on its crew.

The *Dakar* was supposed to radio its position to Haifa every six hours, but contact with the submarine was lost. On January 26, 1968 an international search effort was commenced. On January 27, a transmission on the emergency frequency of the *Dakar* was received, but it was in gibberish. By January 30, the international search team gave up and by February 4 the Israeli navy concluded that the submarine had been lost with all of its crew.

To compound the misery of the crewmembers' families, the sister submarine of the *Dakar,* the *Livyaton,* arrived in Haifa a few days after the scheduled arrival date of the *Dakar.* The silhouettes of the two vessels were identical. Living on the Carmel Mountains overlooking the harbor, Haifa residents called the families of the *Dakar* crew to tell them, mistakenly, that the *Dakar* had arrived. With their hopes up, the families rushed to the Haifa navy base only to have those hopes dashed.

Israel did not give up searching for the *Dakar.* Many international partners who, at times, rendered assistance in this search could not understand why Israel would continue to search for the submarine for thirty-one years. Consequently, they suspected that something very secret and sensitive (i.e., nuclear capability) was on the vessel. But the answer was much simpler. In Judaism it is very important for the family of a deceased person to bury their dead, in order to make peace with their loss and move on with their lives. In the case of the *Dakar,* the grieving families had not been able to obtain closure on their loss.

The only clue discovered to help in the search for the *Dakar* was its emergency identification buoy. It was discovered in 1969 by a fisherman off the northern Sinai town of El Arish. The buoy was tested and found to contain traces of underwater sea plants that exist at a depth of between 100 and 350 meters.

With this clue, the Israeli navy started to search from the point of last contact of the *Dakar,* off the island of Crete, in ever widening concentric circles. The underwater search technology was somewhat limited in the 1970s and consisted of dragging sonar equipment along the bottom of the sea. The Israeli navy purchased sonar equipment capable of searching up to a depth of

1,000 meters, given the clue about the plants on the buoy living between 100 and 350 meters of water.

In addition to the laborious and slow concentric-search approach, there were two other theories as to where to look. The first was that Captain Ra'anan had headed northward into the more sheltered waters off the Greek islands of the Aegean Sea to escape the heavy waves. The second revolved around the fact that, on the day of the *Dakar's* disappearance, the Egyptian navy had been conducting an anti-submarine drill just off the northern coast of Egypt. Captain Ra'anan might have detoured southward towards Egypt to see if he could learn anything about Egypt's anti-submarine capabilities. The discovery of the *Dakar's* emergency buoy off the northern Egyptian coast supported this second theory.

The Israeli navy searched the areas pointed to by these theories. The search off the northern Egyptian coast was particularly sensitive. This was because the only Israeli ship mounted with underwater search gear was its wooden minesweeper. This was formerly Arafat's personal luxury yacht, which the Israelis had seized in 1993. Had the Israelis simply placed that ship off the coast of northern Egypt, there was a possibility that the Egyptian navy would re-seize the ship. In an example of local regional cooperation, a call from the Israeli prime minister to the Egyptian president obtained an Egyptian promise to leave the minesweeper alone and the search was conducted off the Egyptian coast without issue.

All of this effort proved fruitless until newer and more effective sonar equipment was developed which did not have to be dragged along the bottom of the sea. Shy was put in charge of the logistics of the underwater search in 1995. He hired a firm which, using this newer equipment, had previously located the wrecks of the *Titanic* and the German battleship *Bismarck*.

In 1999, the Israelis decided that the buoy might have misled them for thirty years. They decided to search the route of the *Dakar*, from the point of last contact directly towards Haifa, and to do so at a deeper depth. The U.S. provided assistance in the form of the NR-1, the smallest nuclear submarine in existence.

On May 24, 1999, this search effort finally located the *Dakar*. The buoy had been a misleading clue, not only in terms of location but also in terms of depth. The *Dakar* was located 3,000 meters underwater, off the island of Cyprus, on a direct route from point of last contact towards Haifa. Captain Ra'anan had not gone north into the Aegean Sea, nor had he headed south to check on the Egyptian anti-submarine drill. He apparently had continued on his direct route to Haifa, presumably at a slower speed.

In Shy's view, the submarine's fate was likely caused by a sudden mechanical failure that had allowed water to rush into the vessel, causing it to sink very rapidly. A similar mechanical failure had occurred in a trial run off the coast of Portsmouth, almost sinking the submarine, but the engineers thought they had rectified the problem. According to Shy, the descent of the vessel had been so rapid that there was no time for any of the crew to escape. At a depth of 400 meters, the pressure on the hull probably crushed the vessel, causing it to break into the two parts, which were found at the bottom of the sea.

At the conclusion of this somber but intriguing tale, we thanked Shy for allowing us to work on his base. Then we headed back to our bunks to finish packing and to return our bunks to the same clean condition in which we had found them three weeks earlier.

While waiting for the military bus to the airport, we sat around the volunteers' table with Tamar one last time. Because he didn't speak Hebrew, Brian asked her to call the clerk at a Tel Aviv hotel to confirm his stay for the next several days prior to moving to his kibbutz. Brian had come to Israel not knowing a word of Hebrew. However, over the course of our warehouse work, Brian had mastered Hebrew numbers. This had been necessary in order to call out the weight of each pipe that we placed on the scales. While on the phone, Tamar asked Brian for his cell phone number to relay to the hotel clerk. Brian recited it to her in Hebrew. Accustomed to translating Brian's words, Tamar automatically translated and began repeating the numbers in English over the phone. Midway through the phone number, she stopped. Her eyes lit up and her mouth dropped open in recognition that she was relaying English numbers to a Hebrew-speaking clerk. She broke out into laughter over her mistake, along with the rest of us.

The bus arrived on schedule, half-full with a group of French teenagers who had just concluded their Sar-el stints at a nearby base. We piled our luggage under the bus and boarded. As the bus slowly pulled out of the freshly painted gate, we all said our silent good-byes to the friends we had made on the base and to the best base we had ever experienced.

As the military driver headed south on the highway towards Tel Aviv, Tamar walked up to him and whispered something in his ear. The driver smiled and nodded in the affirmative. A five-foot long cloth sunscreen was stretched across the top front bus window. On it the driver had displayed a collection of over fifty pins from all of the IDF units that the driver had ever carried on his bus. Tamar proudly placed a Sar-el pin onto the driver's collection, in order to add our symbol to the panoply of the IDF. We all applauded this fitting end to our time together.

CHAPTER 6

On the Eve of the Pullout from Gaza

"How would you like to go back to the Betzet Tira base? Ken and Diana are there now." This short note from Pamela Lazarus caught my eye in the midst of a myriad of other e-mails. It immediately brought to my mind the picturesque view of the Carmel Mountains overlooking the base. And mention of Ken and Diana evoked fond memories of two volunteers who were usually spattered with blue and white paint from painting they had done on the base.

It is very unusual for a volunteer to know his or her base assignment in advance of arrival in Israel. I assume this is for reasons of security, as well as to offer the military the maximum flexibility with the labor force of volunteers. In my three Sar-el stints, I had developed a good relationship with Pamela and she knew I was a hardworking volunteer with a positive attitude. By now, she trusted me sufficiently to ask whether a base suited my preference.

"I'm happy to go to any base where you need me," I responded, intending to give Pamela as much latitude as possible. I did not

219

want to be the type of volunteer who complained about things like their base assignment – I know there were a few like that.

II

A lot had happened in Israel and in the world since my time at Betzet Tira the previous August. Yasir Arafat had died and was replaced with the first elected Palestinian leader, Mahmoud Abbas, also known as Abu Mazen. Although Abbas publicly renounced terrorism as a means to achieve Palestinian statehood, he did not appear to take any meaningful action to stop it. Prime Minister Sharon pushed through a hostile cabinet and Knesset his plan to withdraw all Jewish towns and settlements from the Gaza Strip and parts of the West Bank. The unilateral withdrawal from the Gaza Strip, which was expected to be physically resisted by tens of thousands of religious Israeli Jews, was scheduled to occur in August 2005.

In the meantime, despite Abbas' ineffectual calls for an end to the Palestinian violence against Israelis, the terrorism continued. On July 11, 2005, an Islamic Jihad suicide bomber blew himself up outside a crowded Netanya mall during the evening rush hour. The blast killed three people and wounded ninety. This was the mall where my cousins Ruchama and Michael had taken me on each of my previous trips to buy gifts for the soldiers. The only "silver lining" was that this was the first suicide bombing in Israel since February. While the terrorist violence continued, it did so with less frequency. The Palestinian leaders had declared a *hudna* on violence, but it was clearly not being honored by certain terrorist groups.

In the rest of the Middle East, the situation in Iraq continued to capture headlines. The positive news was that Iraq held its first popular election and 30 million Iraqis voted. The negative news was that the Sunni Muslim minority boycotted the elections and the situation deteriorated into a violent conflict between Sunnis and Shiites. The American military, which sought to turn control over to a new Iraqi government, was unable to quell this civil war.

As this situation continued with no end in sight, it seemed more and more likely that General Davidi's prediction was coming true; he had warned that it would be impossible to impose a democracy on three warring Iraqi factions (Sunnis, Shiites, Kurds) that did not want to be part of the same country.

III

The London terrorist bombings in early July shocked the Western world into realizing that militant Islamic extremism had become embedded in British society. As opposed to the nineteen 9/11 highjackers, who were mostly Saudis, the four men who committed bombings on three London underground trains and on a double-decker bus were British-born Muslims. While the casualties were horrendous (50 killed, over 700 wounded), the bigger shock to the British psyche was that the bombers were from their own country.

I had flown to London on business the day after Pamela's welcome e-mail. The next day, July 21, 2005, four more bombings were attempted on the London transit system. I was at work in a London suburb at the time. Through a stroke of luck, the terrorists wired the bomb detonators backwards so that the detonators went off without exploding the bombs. The British police swung into action. They published pictures of all four bombers, seeking the assistance of the public in apprehending these criminals. Until that point, I had not realized that London is the most "wired" city in the world in terms of having cameras placed to survey most public places. Therefore, the police had surveillance photos of all four bombers.

On the car ride to Gatwick airport for my flight home to North Carolina, the London driver was eager to talk about the bombers, using some choice expletives laced with his strong Irish accent. The discussion turned to Secretary of State Condoleeza Rice's visit to Lebanon the day before and the Israeli-Palestinian conflict. He blamed the Israelis for that conflict, condemning them for occupying the West Bank and Gaza Strip. "You Americans have a different view of the situation because your media is so biased," he said. "Your media covers up the fact that the Israeli army indiscriminately murders Palestinian women and children. That's what sets off the Palestinians."

Stunned by his ignorance, I tried to correct this misinformation as calmly as I could. I cited the fact that I had spent a great deal of time with Israeli soldiers and learned of the constraints they operate under in order to avoid civilian casualties. Stories about indiscriminate killing of Palestinians, I told him, were false propaganda spread by Palestinian public relations people.

Ignoring my response, the Irishman pressed on: "It's all the fault of the Israelis for occupying the West Bank and Gaza Strip. If Israel pulled out of the occupied areas, then the Palestinians would have no reason to direct violence towards Israel."

"What if Israel pulled out completely and the Palestinians continued their terrorist attacks against Israel?" I asked. "Palestinian terrorist organizations such as Islamic Jihad and Hamas have publicly committed to the complete destruction of Israel, not simply the creation of a Palestinian state. What if they're true to their stated intentions?"

"Well," he replied, "if that happened, then the sympathy of the international community would switch to Israel's side."

"What good would that sympathy do Israel?" I responded. "Israel is a tiny country that can't afford to make a mistake with its security."

The driver insisted: "The international community would commit to support Israel if the terrorists continued to attack. That would settle the matter."

This conversation was making me boil inside, but I tried to keep my emotions in check to give him a credible answer. I told him about an article I had just read commemorating the tenth anniversary of the massacre of 8,000 Muslim men and boys by the Serbian army at Srebrenica in Bosnia. This was the largest massacre in Europe's history since World War II. U.N. troops had invited Bosnian Muslim refugees to Srebrenica as a safe haven from the Bosnian/Serbian war; tens of thousands of Bosnian Muslims trusted this international guaranty and fled to Srebrenica. But when the Serbian army approached Srebrenica, the 600 Dutch u.n. troops in the town stood aside and refused to defend the Bosnians. The Serbs picked out 8,000 Muslim men and boys and slaughtered them. "Given this shameful example of u.n. 'protection,' why should Israel put its faith in the hands of international guaranties?" I challenged him.

The driver grunted an incomprehensible response and fell silent for the rest of the ride to the airport. This conversation brought home to me how the European media had turned European public opinion against Israel. By accepting and passing on to the public the lies generated by the Palestinian public relations machine, the European media had convinced "the man in the street" that Israel was the evil oppressor and that the Palestinians were the blameless underdogs. I was pessimistic that anything could be done to undo the effects of this biased reporting.

The only thing that I could do was show my support for Israel directly. When I got home, I immediately packed for my return to Betzet Tira.

CHAPTER 7

Return to Betzet Tira

July 28–August 18, 2005

THURSDAY, JULY 28, 2005

The El Al terminal at JFK airport was not crowded. I expected a tough time from the El Al agent questioning my line of waiting passengers, based on his interrogation of the young man just in front of me. The agent, a young Israeli probably freshly out of his military service, was more than thorough:

Q. What do you do?

A. I am a Talmud student in Los Angeles.

Q. So what is the *parsha* (Torah reading) for this week? Recite some of it.

A. I didn't memorize it, but I can tell you generally what it is about.

Q. But you can read Hebrew, can't you?

A. Yes.

Q. Here – read this line in Hebrew and tell me what it means.

The interrogation continued for another ten minutes until the agent had exhausted his curiosity.

My turn. The agent started:

Q. Why are you going to Israel?

A. I am a volunteer in Sar-el. I volunteer to work on military bases.

Q. How many times have you done this?

A. This will be my fourth time.

Q. Where have you served?

A. Ramle, Zikim, and Betzet Tira.

Q. Why do you volunteer?

A. It is a good way to show support for Israel.

The formality and stiffness left the agent's tone and he stopped his interrogation into my background. After the usual closing questions as to whether I had packed my bag or had accepted any packages, he waved me forward. As I bent over to pick up my carry-on bag to walk forward, the agent bent down and tapped me on my shoulder. Smiling for the first time, he said in a low tone: "It is a good thing what you do. Have a safe trip." The entire process had taken less than three minutes.

FRIDAY, JULY 29, 2005

Dinner was ready when I arrived from Ben-Gurion airport at the home of my cousins, Bracha and Menachem. During our light meal, I learned from Bracha that, as usual, she had a difficult week as the director of her Tel Aviv boarding house for at-risk children and teenagers. One of her sixty charges had announced she was pregnant. Another had tried to commit suicide by downing a bottle of pills. By the week's end, Bracha was worn out, but as I learned on previous visits, that didn't stop her from planning an active weekend.

After a short nap, we were ready to go. Bracha and Menachem's friends, Gadi and his wife Irit, picked us up at 10 P.M. and drove us to a nightclub named "Camelot" in nearby trendy Herzliya.

The club was sold out, crammed with about 200 patrons. Luckily, Menachem had reserved tickets for us.

While we waited for the show to start, I asked Gadi about the impending withdrawal from Gaza. "We are taking a big chance," he said. "Most Israelis support the withdrawal in the hope that the Palestinians will establish a state and stop their terrorism. A sizeable minority of Israelis, perhaps 40 percent, are against the withdrawal because they do not believe the Palestinians will be satisfied with their own state. They fear that the Palestinians will use a state as a stepping stone to attack and destroy Israel."

I asked him about the recent decline in Palestinian suicide bombings. "It's not for lack of their trying," he said. "There is a clear pattern. As parts of the security fence are completed, the suicide bombings dramatically decrease in those portions of Israel protected by the fence. Also, the Israeli military is very active in stopping most of the suicide bombers before the bombers set off on their missions. Through good intelligence, the military conducts raids to stop these people while they are still in the West Bank. But we know this is not a long-term solution and that is why we are willing to take a chance by withdrawing from Gaza. We hope that the Palestinians will have the good sense to care more about establishing their own state in the West Bank and Gaza than about destroying Israel. But, as Abba Eban used to say, 'The Palestinians never miss an opportunity to miss an opportunity.'"

The start of the show cut short our political discussion. The big attraction at the Camelot was a singing duo that performed only Simon and Garfunkel songs. One of the singers was Israeli; the second was an American named Larry, from Miami. Between each song, they kept up a running "shtick" of jokes and commentary about Simon and Garfunkel. The Israeli's jokes were in Hebrew; Larry's were in English. For two hours, the duo entertained the charged up crowd, proceeding through a repertoire that included "Feeling Groovy," which the Israeli called "Feeling *Sababa*" (Hebrew slang for "cool"). The crowd sang along, stomping, clapping, and swaying to the music. At one point, Bracha and Menachem jumped out of their chairs and began dancing, even though there was no dance floor and little room between the crowded tables.

The show was fantastic. It ended at about 1:00 A.M. and we drove to a nearby ice cream parlor. By 2:30, we headed back to Bracha and Menachem's apartment. Even at that hour, Herzliya's streets were still crowded with Friday night revelers.

SATURDAY, JULY 30, 2005

Today I had an opportunity to talk further with Gadi. Bracha and Menachem had invited Gadi and Irit, along with Irit's sister, Dalit, and her husband, Avi, for the traditional big Sabbath lunch.

When the company arrived, Bracha was ready with a multi-course meal, all prepared Bukharian-style. While we ate, Gadi and I discovered that we were both serious stamp collectors. I mentioned that the day before I had left for Israel, I had received an e-mail from Yad Vashem, Israel's Holocaust museum and research institute. The e-mail notified me that Yad Vashem's Hebrew edition of my father's book, recounting his experience as a member of a Jewish resistance unit during the Holocaust, had been specially recognized. On the sixtieth anniversary of the end of World War II, the Israeli government had chosen to issue a stamp to commemorate the contributions of the Jewish partisan fighters in helping to defeat Nazi Germany. The Israeli Postal Service used the photograph from the cover of my father's book, depicting his partisan unit, on a stamp. Gadi offered to find the stamp for me on the website of the Israeli Philatelic Service.

While we were on the subject of stamps, I mentioned that I had learned a lot about Israel's history through stamp collecting. I told Gadi that on my last trip, my cousin Nir had taken me to see the Shuni, the old Crusader/Turkish fort near Binyamina. Shortly after that, Israel had issued a series of stamps commemorating ancient sites, including one picturing the Shuni. The brochure from the Israeli Philatelic Service about this stamp helped me place the Shuni in the context of Israeli history.

This prompted Gadi to tell me a story about the Shuni that connected his family to an important event in Israeli history. First he asked me whether I knew what the Irgun was. "Yes," I replied. "It was a militant group that resisted the British occupation of Palestine before 1948. The Haganah was the main resistance group and the Irgun was one of the more radical versions."

"Correct," Gadi said, noting that Israelis also refer to the Irgun as "Etzel." He told me that the Shuni was the staging area from which the Etzel left for its most famous action. In 1947, the Etzel launched a surprise attack on the most heavily fortified British facility – the military prison at Acre. It was a multi-pronged operation that successfully broke into the prison and freed thirty to forty Jewish resistance fighters. Gadi maintained that this attack, which demonstrated the power of the Jewish resistance to British rule, contributed to the 1947 U.N. vote for the partition of Palestine into two states, one Arab and one Jewish.

I told Gadi that I was familiar with this famous attack, because it was highlighted in the movie *Exodus*. "The people who conducted the attack are heroes in Israel," he said, "and one of them was Irit and Dalit's father."

"Did your father ever tell you about this?" I asked Irit. "No," she replied. "He was a very modest man. We only learned about his role in this attack from historical documents and from Gadi's conversations with my father about it shortly before he died. But we are very proud of our father for the role he played in Israel's history."

During the rest of lunch, I studiously avoided broaching the topic of the Israeli withdrawal from the Gaza Strip. Gadi had warned me that Avi was a political rightist who was very much opposed to the withdrawal and that he and Gadi were on opposite ends of the political spectrum on this issue. I did not want to spark a fight over lunch.

SUNDAY, JULY 31, 2005
With a 5:45 A.M. wake-up knock from Menachem, I got up and

dressed quickly; by 6:45, he and I were walking on the Souk beach in northern Tel Aviv. After a brisk four-mile walk up to the Herzliya marina and back, Menachem forged into the Mediterranean with his swimming buddies for a 30-minute swim. As usual, they finished their morning regimen in the parking lot with pretzels and a shot of vodka. Then Menachem drove me to the Sar-el office in Jaffa.

On the Ayalon Highway I noticed that some cars had blue and white streamers attached to their windows or antennae. I asked Menachem if these streamers had any significance, other than the fact that they were the colors of the Israeli flag. "The rightists who oppose the withdrawal from Gaza have adopted the color orange," he replied. "For example, they wear orange tee-shirts to signify their political views. In response, those who favor the withdrawal have adopted the colors of Israel, blue and white, and are now displaying these streamers as a political statement." I noticed that in the Tel Aviv area that morning, there were many cars bearing the blue and white streamers. None bore the color orange.

The Sar-el office was crowded this Sunday morning with new volunteers showing up for their assignments. On the wall I noticed a picture of a graduating madricha class that included Tamar and Etty, madrichas from two of my previous Sar-el stints. I knew I would not see them, however, because they had completed their army service several months previously.

Pamela Lazarus gave me a big welcome hug. We exchanged presents. I gave her a copy of my father's book (in English) and she reciprocated with a copy of *A Psalm in Jenin* by Brett Goldberg. This book was written to refute the false rumors of an Israeli massacre of Palestinians in Jenin in 2002, widely circulated by the European press at that time.

Pamela explained that she was a bit nervous about the team of volunteers she was assigning to Betzet Tira. This would be the third time a team of volunteers would be assigned to this navy base. The first time was my volunteer stint last summer, which worked out well because we were all Sar-el veterans, hand-picked by Pamela. The second group had just finished their time at Betzet Tira and had also done a commendable job, which pleased the base commander. They also consisted of a mostly veteran team, including Ken, Diana, and Marion from the first team the previous summer.

The third group included a number of newcomers to Sar-el as well as veterans. Marion and Barbara, a volunteer from New York, would be holdovers from the second team. The rest of the third group would convene at the Sar-el office and travel on the bus to the base together.

I had arrived early at the Sar-el office, as had Paola – another volunteer assigned to Betzet Tira. Paola was a young woman in her late thirties with short, reddish-brown hair and a prominent Star of David on her necklace. While we waited for the rest of the volunteers to arrive, Paola told me a bit about herself. She was originally from Trieste, a seaport city in northeastern Italy. About ten years ago, she had moved to Brussels to start a career as tour guide.

Assuming from her Star of David that she was Jewish, I asked her: "Are there many Jews in Trieste?" "Oh, I'm not yet Jewish," replied Paola. "In Trieste, my family is Catholic. We were very close with a local Jewish family. That is how I was first exposed to Judaism. I became more interested and, since moving to Brussels, have started the process of converting to Judaism through a local Reform synagogue."

I asked her why she had volunteered for Sar-el. "I have fallen in love with Israel and everything Israeli – its people, wine, music, everything," she replied. "I spent the last few weeks working on a kibbutz in the extreme south of Israel. It was a small agricultural kibbutz founded by Americans a number of years ago. It was so hot there that we had to start working in the fields at 5:00 A.M. and stop by lunchtime. The work was hard, but I loved it!" Although this would be her first time volunteering to work

231

on an army base, she was looking forward to the experience and especially to interacting with the soldiers. Paola's Hebrew was already far better than mine.

Paola was a divorcée and was clearly on a journey searching for a new religion and for a new life, possibly in Israel. "I like it in Brussels," she continued, "but Israel draws me and I am tempted to move here. Perhaps if tourists returned to Israel in large numbers, I could become a tour guide here."

By 10:00 A.M. our small group of volunteers had gathered in the Sar-el office. We were introduced to Noa, one of our two madrichas, and loaded our luggage onto the bus. Forty-five minutes later, we pulled into the familiar back gate to Betzet Tira.

The first person we met as we tumbled off the bus was Marion. She gave me a big hug and introduced me to the only other holdover volunteer, Barbara. Then Sergeant Gal came over to greet us. With a warm and sincere smile, he hugged me and welcomed me back to the base. During lunch, Gal proudly pointed to a plaque in the mess hall. The plaque commemorated the award that Betzet Tira had won in 2004 for being not only the cleanest navy base in Israel, but the cleanest of all military bases in the country. The volunteers last year had significantly contributed to that honor and it made me feel great to hear about it.

The afternoon was taken up with unpacking our bags, obtaining correct-fitting uniforms, and taking a tour of the base conducted by Gal and Noa. The base had physically changed in a very major way since the prior summer. An old railway car, mounted on train tracks, had been deposited in the middle of the base. Gal explained that the base commander, Shy Davidi, intended to establish a computer resource center in the train car where his soldiers could learn basic computer skills. His goal was to enable them to be employable after their obligatory service in the military.

After dinner, Noa gathered the volunteers together to get to know each other. We realized we were a very international group. In addition to Paola, several of the volunteers were European. Angela was a medical secretary and artist from London. Paul was a thirty-year-old electrical engineering professor at a college in Stuttgart. Adrian from Holland was a single man in his mid-forties who was considering making aliyah to Israel. The rest of the volunteers were American. Marcelino, my roommate, was born in Puerto Rico and raised in Chicago. After retiring as a federal parole officer, he had started a second career as a high school counselor in Chicago. The other Americans, besides Marion and Barbara, were Judy, her eighteen-year-old daughter, Rachel, and Candace from San Diego.

In the middle of this introductory session, in walked the base commander Shy Davidi, accompanied by Sergeant Gal. Uncharacteristically, he was wearing a white tee-shirt instead of his naval officer's shirt and his normally shiny black boots were covered with white dust. He spotted me, shook my hand, and then sat in the middle of the room.

Shy explained that he had just returned from the outskirts of the Gaza Strip. In order to accomplish the withdrawal of its 7,500 Jewish residents, the military required a force of 40–50,000 troops and police. The navy contributed one thousand troops to this force and put Shy in command of this contingent. He had spent the day ensuring that his soldiers were given proper accommodations and provisions.

The military had been given two main tasks in the Gaza withdrawal, he explained. The first was to bar Israelis living outside the Gaza Strip from entering the Strip to block the withdrawal. Some of these Israelis had already moved in with their Gaza brethren to resist the evacuation. He also mentioned that thousands more were massing in Sderot, near the Gaza border. The military expected these protesters to attempt to march into the Gaza Strip in the next several days and so had positioned large numbers of troops and police to bar their way.

The second task given to the military was to remove the Jews from the Gaza Strip. Hopefully, Shy said, this would be accomplished by persuasion and not by force. Shy's soldiers, along with the other troops, had been given special psychological training in how to persuade the residents to voluntarily evacuate their homes. In the event this failed, they were given training in how to physically remove people who resisted.

Before saying goodnight, Shy thanked us for volunteering and pointed out that our labor would be especially appreciated in the next several weeks. In order to supply the thousand troops for the evacuation, the navy had had to send one out of every six of its personnel to Gaza. This meant that troops had been stripped from every naval base, including Betzet Tira. Our hands would help fill-in for those soldiers sent to Gaza in terms of performing the regular work on the base. Therefore, he pointed out, we were supporting the historic withdrawal about to occur.

After Shai had left, Noa practically gushed in commenting on what a great a base commander he was. Her biggest compliment was that he truly cared about the soldiers under his command. In fact, he asked the navy to send their problem soldiers to his base. These were soldiers with family and morale problems who wanted to drop out of the navy. Oftentimes, one or both parents were alcoholics or were in jail for drugs or, worse, domestic violence and child abuse. Shy and his officers counseled these soldiers, helped them finish their military service, and tried to give them employable skills.

MONDAY, AUGUST 1, 2005

Today was our first full workday on the base. Gal offered to send me and Marcelino to Betzet Kishon to work. We were willing, but when our transportation was delayed until mid-morning, we both decided there was plenty to keep us busy at Betzet Tira. Our big project for the day was to paint the *moadon* (recreation room). We removed the furniture, took off the wall hangings, and turned the inside of the *moadon* from dark blue to light yellow by mid-afternoon.

Later I joined Angela and Marion, who had been painting

the outside of a large warehouse all day in the hot sun. We made more progress, but didn't nearly finish by the time we stopped for the day. A quick workout in the delightfully air-conditioned fitness center revived the six volunteers who visited it that afternoon. We also met Huston, a thirty-year-old American from Florida, the last of our volunteers to arrive on base. With his dark complexion and curly black hair, Huston looked every bit like an Israeli. He bunked with Marcelino and me.

Shy stopped by the volunteers' tables at dinner to ask if we were satisfied with our accommodations and our work assignments. We had no complaints. After he left, Noa commented: "At other bases, the volunteers are lucky to see the base commander once in a three-week stint. Here, the commander constantly checks in with the volunteers. This is the only base I've experienced where the commander is so visibly concerned about the welfare of his volunteers."

After dinner, Shy reinforced Noa's remarks by stopping by the volunteers' compound to chat. While he was in the compound, the soldiers excitedly gathered around to engage him in conversation. Shy had a very informal, friendly manner with his soldiers and it was clear that they liked to talk with him. Just before he left the compound, I gave him a copy of the Hebrew edition of my father's book. Shy looked pleased to accept it, but first insisted that I inscribe it.

TUESDAY, AUGUST 2, 2005

At breakfast today, Marcelino and I sat with two Israelis – Tzila, a young female soldier and Moshe, a civilian kitchen worker in his fifties. Tzila spoke very little English, but Moshe quickly broke into a conversation in Spanish with Marcelino. Originally from Morocco, Moshe did not often have the pleasure of speaking in his nature tongue with someone on the base. At times, Tzila spoke to us in Hebrew, Moshe translated what she said into Spanish, and Marcelino translated it into English for me.

Tzila was a very large and talkative young woman with a strong personality. Immediately after breakfast, she explained, she had to attend a special three-day training program on how to peacefully evacuate the settlers in the Gaza Strip. She was one of the thousand soldiers that the navy had contributed to the August 15 evacuation.

We painted all day – the exteriors of the barracks, parts of the *moadon* and a big warehouse. It was hot work under a blazing August sun, but we took lots of water breaks. At the end of the day, the volunteers were invited to attend a special base party in the mess hall.

Two young soldiers, Rafi and Aharon, had just completed their three years of obligatory military service and were about to leave the navy. Rafi was a regular soldier, but Aharon was a special success story.

Aharon was one of the "problem" soldiers whom Shy Davidi had asked to be sent to his command. These at-risk soldiers were only required to serve for two years instead of the mandatory three years, due to problems in their family life. Like many of these soldiers, Aharon had been assigned to guard duty at Betzet Kishon, the sister naval supply base in the Haifa harbor complex. After eighteen months, he asked for a transfer to Betzet Tira. He offered to work in the kitchen and liked it so much that he volunteered to put in a full three years of service even though he did not have to.

The event was very moving. The entire base (except the guards on sentry duty) assembled in the mess hall. Rafi and Aharon's commanding officers each spoke, praising their charges as good soldiers and good people. Then Shy Davidi added his words of praise. He mentioned that it was in the navy that Aharon first learned how to use a computer. Aharon's first e-mail was a short note to Shy, thanking him for the opportunity to learn how to e-mail. Shy said that Aharon had shown responsibility and initiative in his duties, which would lead him to success in any field of endeavor he chose.

Then Aharon took the floor. He was a tall and heavy-set young soldier with a round baby-face. He spoke slowly and in a somewhat hesitating manner. He said that the navy had been the best thing that ever happened to him. The navy had given him structure and friends. He also added that he very much appreciated his commanding sergeant in the kitchen. Referring to his sergeant, Aharon said: "He has been my mother, my father, and my big brother all rolled into one person." At that point, Aharon was overcome with emotion and could not continue speaking. The crowd broke into applause, as he turned away to hide his tears and hug his buddies from the kitchen crew. Then, still choked up, he went over to hug and kiss Shy Davidi. Some of the young female soldiers became teary-eyed, because they knew what a long road it had been for Aharon to change from a problem soldier to one whom everyone on the base would celebrate. We all milled around, eating cold watermelon and congratulating Rafi and Aharon.

Gilad, the base commander at Betzet Kishon, came over to welcome me. His salt-and-pepper beard had turned a bit more salt than pepper in the year since I had last worked on his base in Haifa harbor. He told me that he and Dudu (the nickname of David, my commanding sergeant last year, whom we continued to call David) were looking forward to my starting to work at his base the next day. He also confirmed my question about his future plans. In two months, after twenty-five years in the navy, Gilad would retire. He had no immediate plans, other than to rest and travel with his wife.

Straight from the party for Rafi and Aharon, Shy and Gal pulled up in two vans and the volunteers piled in for a quick trip to the Druze village of Daliyat el Carmel. The cool dry mountain air was a welcome relief from the sweltering August humidity near the coast. They brought us to the main shopping street of the village, where for an hour the volunteers wandered the stores, buying the handmade, multi-colored Druze cloth and pastries, especially baklava. When we tired from our shopping outing, Gal and Shy brought us to a small Druze café for a dinner of local foods. We feasted on falafel and Druze pita bread, many of us sitting on pillows on the floor.

Since the volunteers were starved for news, I asked Shy for the latest news in Israel. He said that 40–50,000 Jewish religious zealots from Israel and the West Bank had massed in the southern Israel town of Sderot. This town had been hit repeatedly by Kassam missiles fired by the Palestinians in the nearby Gaza Strip. As a result, the townspeople were very much against the Israeli withdrawal from Gaza, which they saw as a prelude to more attacks on them. For this reason, Sderot was a very welcoming place for the protestors.

Shy expected that the protestors would try to march to the Gaza Strip the next day. The protestors' aim was to put so many people in the Strip that it would be impossible for the military to evacuate the settlers. To counter this, the military had placed a line of soldiers in the roads and nearby fields to block this march. Shy said he planned to be with his thousand navy soldiers for the next two days as they tried to keep the protestors out. It was clear that the military expected a battle. The entire country was focused on the roads leading from Sderot to Gaza. Shy mentioned that so many police had been sent to block the march that there were almost no other police left in the rest of the country.

I felt a bit guilty that Shy was spending so much time with our group of thirteen volunteers. I would have almost preferred that he had spent his evening with his family, given the weighty military responsibilities on his shoulders that kept him away from them for long hours and many days. Instead, he acted as our tour guide, patiently explaining the history of the Druze people and pointing out noteworthy spots on our drive.

Later, after our return to the base, one of the more religious sergeants who knew me from the previous summer asked me where Shy had taken us for dinner. I answered that we had dined at a Druze restaurant in Daliyat el Carmel. "Was it kosher?" he asked. I instantly realized that he was, in effect, checking up on Shy. Even though Shy was widely admired among his soldiers as the base commander, several of the very Orthodox sergeants, whom we dubbed "the religious police," still monitored him. If he misstepped, the "religious police" would complain to the religious authorities. Not willing to give this sergeant any ammunition, I replied: "Of course it was kosher!" Actually, I had no idea whether it was kosher, and none of the volunteers seemed to care.

Since last summer, an eight-foot, wire-mesh fence covered with heavy aluminum sheets had been erected to separate the men's and the women's barracks. This had been done at the insistence of the "religious police." Tonight, as I was sitting outside my bunk talking on the phone with my wife, several female soldiers led by Tzila started banging on the fence and eventually collapsed one corner of it. Like a troop of antelope, a line of young female soldiers leaped over what remained of the fence and headed toward the men's barracks and the *moadon*. Those female soldiers were aggressive!

WEDNESDAY, AUGUST 3

After about an hour of painting this morning, our driver finally appeared. Moran, a pretty green-eyed soldier, drove Marcelino and me north into Haifa. She was the navy driver between Betzet Kishon and Betzet Tira, replacing Sivan, last year's driver, who had been transferred to Eilat. Moran drove us through the commercial port of Haifa, and finally deposited us at the Betzet Kishon base in front of the office.

Gilad, the base commander of Betzet Kishon, was there to welcome us and assigned us to the same pipes warehouse where I had worked the previous year. Happily, David was still in charge of that warehouse and was anxiously awaiting our arrival. He gave me a big hug and I introduced him to Marcelino. He thanked me for the pictures of our work team, which I had sent him last year following my Sar-el stint. They were on display in his tiny office.

David was especially happy to see us because the only soldier assigned to his warehouse had been among the naval contingent sent to the Gaza Strip for the impending withdrawal. Without an extra set of hands, it would be very difficult for David to get everything done in the warehouse.

After a full day's work in the pipes warehouse and Moran's drive back to Betzet Tira, Shy Davidi gave us a late afternoon presentation about the Israeli navy and about his corner of it (logistics). While I had heard the presentation the previous year, Shy had updated it. For instance, I learned that the Israeli navy planned to supplement its existing force of three submarines by buying two more from Germany at a price of $500 million each. A force of five submarines would ensure that Israel always had at least one submarine on patrol at all times.

Later this evening, the volunteers trekked to Hof Ha-Carmel, the beach just south of Haifa. The three-mile walk through the town of Tirat Karmel gave me a chance to catch up with Marion, the dynamic Connecticut grandmother now on her fourteenth Sar-el stint. I asked what kept bringing her back. She explained that she focused her life on her three priorities – her family, her religious life, and Israel. Like me, she felt that Israel was the Jewish homeland, as well as protection for Jews worldwide. She was also very involved in her Conservative synagogue in Connecticut. Although she did not come from a very religious background, she had become interested over time in the study of Judaism. A big proponent of adult Jewish education and of women's full participation in religious services, Marion was proud of the fact that she had been the first woman to be counted in the *minyan*, the quorum of ten required for public prayer, at her synagogue.

The beachfront was teeming with people, especially young teenage girls, when we arrived. The big attraction was an Israeli rock star, Eyal Golan, who was putting on a live concert in the beachfront amphitheatre. We got to the amphitheatre shortly before the 9:00 show and squeezed into the area to find a small piece of grass to sit on. As soon as Eyal Golan started the concert, sitting was no longer an option. Dressed in a white tee-shirt and jeans, he was a young good-looking heartthrob and the girls in the audience hung on his every word and motion, especially a collection of groupies closest to the stage. He reminded me a bit of an Israeli Elvis Presley. With a background of colored strobe lights and smoke, the rhythmic beat of his band vibrated through the ground. Thousands of people started swaying and dancing to his music. The crowd obviously knew all of his lyrics, as they sang along with him. At one point, he stopped singing altogether, held his microphone towards the crowd, and let the crowd carry the melody while his band played on.

THURSDAY, AUGUST 4, 2005

Work fell into a comfortable routine for Marcelino and me in the pipes warehouse. Since so many soldiers and officers from Betzet Kishon had been sent to Gaza, David found himself to be the senior commander on the base for the day. The demands of other parts of the base drew him away from his immediate duties in the warehouse. Being familiar with the routine of the place, we worked quietly and independently without the need for his ongoing supervision.

Breaking the solitude was a young female soldier named Lee. She was a chain-smoking, cherub-faced nineteen-year-old with jet-black hair and striking blue eyes. She had immigrated to Israel with her mother and older sister from Uzbekistan. Lee was on and off sentry duty during the day and during her breaks came to the pipes warehouse to "shoot the breeze." She wanted to practice her English and to express whatever was on her mind. Mostly, she talked about her future plans for university education and about her boyfriend, a student at the Technion. We provided a willing ear, although we did not stop working while we listened. We appreciated her appearances because it made the time pass quickly.

Work for the volunteers ended at lunchtime and I headed for the home of my friends, Tova and Meir Meiner, in Hadera. As promised, Tova took me to the Maxim Ganeh Alon, the after-school facility located in a very poor Hadera neighborhood that I had visited last year. There we met with Adugnia Takelle, the Ethiopian director of the facility and three members of the Ethiopian neighborhood immigrant association. They showed me around the two projects that the Raleigh Jewish community had already funded in the facility, the computer room and the library, and described their ideas for future projects for which they were seeking funding. I gave them some advice on how best to describe them in the proposals they were preparing.

With my "business" completed, I rejoined Tova and Meir for a drive to Caesaria for dinner. Listening to the news in Hebrew on the car radio, they suddenly became agitated. "What's the matter?" I asked. "An Israeli religious zealot just boarded a bus in an Arab neighborhood in Shefaram and opened fire on the Arabs on the bus," Meir replied. "He killed the driver and three other Arabs, including two young women, before the other Arabs on the bus overpowered and killed him." The man was a member of the extremist Meir Kahane group and had deserted from the army a year ago. The news carried a live broadcast of the situation in Shefaram (about twelve miles east of Haifa). Hundreds of angry Arabs had surrounded the bus and were keeping the police from retrieving the bodies. Some of the border police sent to monitor the situation in Sderot were being diverted instead to this crisis. "Never a dull moment in Israel," Meir commented.

In Caesaria we ate at a restaurant on the ancient pier built by King Herod two thousand years ago. Then we stopped at a gas station to pick up the Meiners' son Shlomi and a female soldier accompanying him. Still in uniform, they had just come from Shlomi's unit in Gaza. They dumped their backpacks in the trunk and laid their M-16s on the floor as they squeezed into the back seat with me. Tova and Meir dropped the female soldier off at her home in Hadera before heading to their own house.

Shlomi's older brother met us as we drove up to their home.

Shlomi looked tired, but when his brother suggested they go out to see friends, he agreed in a mega-second. He jumped into the other family car with his rifle and drove off with his brother, leaving his backpack in our trunk. What energy these young soldiers have!

FRIDAY, AUGUST 5, 2005

This morning Tova dropped me off at my cousins' home in nearby Pardes Chana before 8:00 A.M. This allowed me to catch an early train with Nir into Tel Aviv. Nir had invited me to join him on his weekly trip to see his collector friends and do some sightseeing. The train was crowded with soldiers going home to Tel Aviv at the week's end from their duty stations. Many were asleep, with their M-16s cradled across their laps. We disembarked in Arlozoroff Station, the main train station in Tel Aviv.

Nir loves history and so he took me for a walking tour through the old Jewish cemetery in Tel Aviv. It was a walk through Israeli history, with the graves of such notables as the early Zionist leader Max Nordau, the great Hebrew poet Chaim Nachman Bialik, and Tel Aviv's first mayor, Meir Dizengoff. Nir commented that most of the streets in Tel Aviv were named after people who are buried in this cemetery.

From there we walked to Dizengoff Square, where the once-a-week outdoor collectors' flea market was in full swing. Sheltered from the hot sun, rows and rows of tables displayed items of interest for all types of collectors. The wares ranged from the usual collector items (stamps, coins, postcards, hunting knives, old Yiddish books) to the not-so-usual (old farm tools, antique scales, Russian army officers' uniforms). Nir stopped at a table displaying Russian emblems commemorating the sixtieth anniversary of the end of World War II. After a quick inquiry about the price, he walked away. "He's asking too much," said Nir. "I got the fiftieth anniversary emblem for half that price."

We stopped for a mid-morning snack at the only surviving 1950s bakery in Tel Aviv. It reminded me of a soda shop in the U.S. from the same era. Round stools lined a long formica-topped

243

counter and fresh baked goods were periodically lowered by rope down a dumbwaiter from the second-story bakery. The cranberry and cheese pastries were delicious.

Finally, we arrived at his friend Kobi's stamp and coin shop on Ben Yehuda Street. Nir introduced me to his group of collector friends, who gathered at this shop every Friday at noon. Like Nir, they all collected Israeli bank notes. But they also collected many other things, including stamps, coins, medals, and dies for medals.

Perhaps the most unusual collection was maintained by Nir's friend Efi, a forty-two-year-old air force reserve officer. He collected the usual things (e.g., bank notes), but also collected printed bills that had been used as money in World War II concentration camps. (Many camps had their own currency, which was used by non-Jewish camp laborers.)

I quickly learned why Nir and his group of friends were all single. When I commented that it was curious that all but one of the men in this group were single, they laughed as Efi responded: "Of course we are! If we were married, our wives would have long ago thrown us out for spending every penny we have on our collections. Wives and collections just don't mix."

Nir and I took a quick trip to a second stamp shop to buy the Israeli stamp that bore the photograph from the front cover of my father's book. It was very rewarding for me to finally see and own this stamp. Nir was excited too.

We returned to Pardes Chana just before the Sabbath began. Nir's parents, Dvora and David, were sitting in the living room with Nir's brother, Ziv, and Ziv's wife, Ayelet. Since my visit last year, Ziv and Ayelet's family had expanded. Their son, Noam (22 months old), was now joined by a little sister, Roni (10 months). Ziv still worked in the local police force as a member of their bomb squad.

Nir's sister, Sigal, was also there with her boyfriend, Ofer. Sigal had just passed the Israeli bar exam and so was in a relaxed mood. Ofer, a doctoral candidate in electrical engineering at Tel Aviv University, had a professional conference in Australia scheduled for next month. Afterwards, he and Sigal planned to meet in Hong Kong and travel through China for two or three months. Sigal said she would look for a job when they returned, but she knew it wouldn't be easy; Israel has an over-abundance of lawyers, making jobs in her field very hard to find.

A short nap prepared me for the delicious, multi-course dinner that Dvora had prepared for us. The family always came together for Friday night dinner. This was a beautiful family tradition and contributed to the fact that the babies were as comfortable with their grandparents as they were with their parents.

In the middle of dinner, Ziv took a call on his cell phone. His police dispatcher sent him to the house of Israeli Finance Minister Benjamin Netanyahu in nearby Caesaria. Apparently, someone had noticed something suspicious on the premises and had called for the police bomb squad. About forty-five minutes later, Ziv returned to finish his dinner and report that there were no bombs at the Netanyahu home that night.

After dinner, we watched the television news. It focused on the difficulties facing those Israelis who were being forced to leave their homes and businesses in the Gaza Strip. Some of these people were complaining about the temporary housing into which the government was moving them. I asked Ayelet why they had waited so long to move out when the government had given them notice over a year ago that they would have to leave. "These people never believed that Prime Minister Sharon would carry through on the withdrawal," she replied. "He is from the political right and they had voted for him, so they couldn't believe he would do such a thing. Also, the rightist leaders of the Israelis in the Gaza Strip kept telling their people to stay put and assuring them that the withdrawal wouldn't happen, and the people had listened to their detriment."

Ayelet and I understood the pain these people were going

through, but we did not have a lot of sympathy for them. They had made a poor choice by not believing the clear messages issued by their government. We had much more sympathy for the soldiers who had died protecting these people in the past, and the large number of soldiers who were now deployed in the south to move them out.

In the midst of the difficulties facing the Israeli army, keeping protestors out of the Gaza Strip and persuading Israelis to evacuate that area, the Palestinians decided to add to the turmoil. Palestinian terrorists launched a Kassam rocket at Sderot, which was still crowded with protestors. The plan backfired. The rocket missed Sderot and instead landed in a nearby Arab village, killing one Israeli Arab.

In the meantime, the Palestinian Authority leadership made threats of further belligerence towards Israel. One of the PA cabinet ministers gave a speech claiming that the withdrawal represented a Palestinian victory and a defeat for Israel. He promised to keep attacking Israel until they had achieved a complete victory and destroyed Israel: "Today Gaza, tomorrow the West Bank, and soon it will be Jerusalem." Apparently Prime Minister Abbas made no effort to restrain his cabinet minister.

SATURDAY, AUGUST 6, 2005

Today I embarked with David and Dvora for a full day of outings. First they drove me to the park surrounding the nearby Hadera power plant. By law in Israel, the power company is required to invest a percentage of its revenue in the neighboring communities. In addition to beautifying the park surrounding the plant, the Hadera power company had decided to restore an extinct agricultural settlement established in the 1920s called Heftzibah. The settlement had been built along the banks of the small river now bordering on one side of the power company's facility. We drove through the restored colony, with its huts rebuilt and its fields replanted with orchards. Heftzibah is now an educational site for school children learning about the history of their country.

From Heftzibah, we drove to David's favorite place: his tractor restoration club at Kibbutz Ein Shemer. I was impressed with the progress that had been made since my previous visit. The barn where they restored and displayed the tractors now had an air ventilation system and lights to shine on the completed tractors. In front of each tractor was a poster explaining its history, and on the walls were posters explaining the history of farming in Israel. Picnic tables in the middle of the barn were set up with paper and crayons for visiting school children.

On the way home, we stopped to visit Ziv and Ayelet at their home in Pardes Chana. The benefits of grandparents living near their grandchildren were evident as soon as we walked in the door. Noam gave a big shriek and came running to hug his grandparents. David had been bringing Noam with him to Kibbutz Ein Shemer on Saturdays and had clearly hooked Noam on tractors. Noam kept calling out "Tractor, tractor!" to encourage David show us pictures of Noam sitting on various restored antique tractors. It was one of the first words that Noam learned.

This evening, David turned on the television to catch the local news. The focus was still on the Israeli extremist who had killed four Arab Israelis on a bus in Shefaram. He committed these murders in the hope that this would trigger widespread Arab riots, which in turn would force the government to stop the withdrawal from the Gaza Strip. His plan failed. Many Israeli Jews had come to visit the Arab families of the victims to express their outrage at these killings and extend condolences to the families. And the government announced it would pay 100,000 shekels ($22,000) to each of the Arab families of the four victims, as an act of official condolence. In contrast to Yasir Arafat and Saddam Hussein, who had paid the families of Palestinians suicide bombers as a reward for terrorist acts against Jews, in this case the Israeli government paid the families of Palestinian victims of a Jewish terrorist.

Instead of worrying about Palestinian violence against Israelis, now the police were focusing on protecting Israeli Arabs from Jewish extremists committing similar acts. In the small West Bank settlement of Tapuach, the police arrested friends of the killer who had harbored him as a deserter. Apparently, they knew he was heading out with his rifle to kill Arabs and had done nothing to stop him; they were therefore charged as accessories to the crime.

SUNDAY, AUGUST 7, 2005

The taxi ride from Pardes Chana to Betzet Tira took only thirty minutes. By 9:00 A.M. I was back on base and in uniform. Work today consisted of outdoor painting. With five or six volunteers painting together, we covered a lot of ground. Our only delay was the fact that Gal would periodically stop by and insist we take a break to drink. He usually brought a couple of bottles of juice or soda and cups.

While the painting crew toiled away, another team of volunteers was busy nearby planting olive trees under the blazing sun. Under Paola's direction, Paul and Adrian dug a series of holes in the ground on the side of the mess hall, carefully spacing them far apart. Since the ground was hard and unforgiving, Paul and Adrian alternated with a pick and shovel, removing the dry loose rock from the holes and replacing it with good planting soil. By the end of the day, a number of young olive trees had been firmly situated in this soil.

Olive trees had a particular significance on this base. When the base was first built, the only original vegetation that was not paved over were the three ancient olive trees that adorned the central area between the mess hall and the soldiers' bunks. Last year, we constructed brick perimeters to protect each of these trees. Olive trees could survive for hundreds of years and so were treated with respect by the soldiers. Paola, Paul, and Adrian planted many other kinds of vegetation near the mess hall, but the olive trees received their special care.

Before the day's end, we heard that Benjamin Netanyahu had resigned his post as Finance Minister in Prime Minister Sharon's cabinet. Netanyahu's resignation was in protest over the Gaza Strip evacuation. It appeared that Netanyahu was setting himself up to run for the post of prime minister if Sharon dissolved his coalition government and called for new elections. That possibility seemed a likely scenario in light of the intense debate within Israeli society over the Gaza withdrawal.

MONDAY, AUGUST 8

There were very few soldiers in the mess hall this morning or at flag-raising. More of the base personnel had been sent to the Gaza Strip to help with the disengagement as the August 15 deadline approached. Gal pointed out a big truck that backed into one of the warehouses to pick up more supplies for the navy contingent assembled in the south to help with this effort.

After work and a quick dinner, we listened to a presentation by Stuart Palmer, a retired gentlemen originally from London who made aliyah with his family twenty-four years ago. He and his wife Hadassah had three children and fifteen grandchildren in Israel.

Stuart's passion in his retirement was teaching people how to be advocates for Israel. He distributed various handouts that separated myths from facts about the Middle East conflict. He especially highlighted the anti-Israel bias in the media, particularly at the BBC, where his brother had worked and confirmed that bias. He encouraged people with whom he spoke to review their local press stories about Israel and be proactive in correcting factual misstatements in them.

He also emphasized the fact that Palestinian schoolbooks educate Palestinian children to hate Jews. This had to change if the Palestinians ever wanted to have peace. But he warned that the public posture of the Palestinians was not a peaceful one, no matter what they said to the press. Both Article 15 of the Palestinian Authority Charter and Article 17 of the Hamas Charter currently called for the destruction of Israel. Although Prime Minister Abbas called for the cessation of violence against Israel in February

2005, the number of terrorist incidents had in fact increased after a temporary hiatus in February. The only good news on this
score was that the security fence was working. The number of attempted Palestinian attacks had not declined, he pointed out, but
the number that had been thwarted greatly increased.

This evening, as we sat around our picnic table, the new volunteers commented on various things they had observed on the base.
Marcelino was struck by how many of the "problem" soldiers assigned to the base viewed their lives and futures negatively, despite
the valuable skills they possessed. He cited as an example one soldier, a Russian immigrant, who was very negative about his future
prospects, without realizing that his fluency in four languages was
a valuable skill that could serve him well.

Marcelino, a high school advisor in a Chicago suburb, was an
eternal optimist and saw the best in people, especially these young
soldiers. He felt a need to counsel and motivate these youngsters
by injecting them with a sense of optimism about their future. At
the same time, he told them frankly that the road to success in
any field required hard work.

Other volunteers talked about their backgrounds and shared
why they had come. Paul, from Stuttgart, mentioned that he was
a "Jew by choice." His parents were German Christians from the
eastern part of Germany before World War ii. After the Allied
victory, a readjustment of borders gave that part of Germany to
Poland. His parents, along with all the other ethnic Germans in
the region, were forced to leave and move back to Germany. I
commented that, given this history of dislocation, his parents
might be bitter and be strongly opposed to Paul's conversion to
Judaism. "Not so," he said. "My parents were rather neutral about
it and didn't give me any problems."

Paul had served on a ship in the German navy and was
thrilled to be assigned to an Israeli naval base, albeit one without
ships. He seemed to relish being back in uniform again. Drawing
upon his previous naval service, he joked, "In the German navy,

if something moves within five minutes we salute it; if it doesn't move after five minutes we paint it." While the Israeli navy was devoid of saluting, it certainly required lots of painting and Paul didn't seem to mind it. In fact, he really painted with gusto.

Spending part of his summer vacation on an Israeli military base was an exciting break from Paul's teaching routine. At the vocational college where he taught electrical engineering in Stuttgart, his students seemed unmotivated and often skipped classes; they were rarely serious about their studies. Although he tried to encourage high standards, their lack of motivation frustrated him.

Adrian, a Dutch Jew in his early forties, was the tallest volunteer in our group at six feet five inches and had a very strong build. He was physically fit from a life of manual labor and had striking sky-blue eyes. Adrian's brother and his brother's family lived on a kibbutz in northern Israel, so he spent many of his weekends there. He did not seem to have strong roots back in Holland. Adrian described Holland as a land of increasing insecurity for its Jewish population, due to the growing Muslim immigrant community and the increasing militancy of that immigrant population. He made no secret of the fact that he was considering making aliyah and that he hoped to find a wife to settle down with in Israel.

We shared stories until relatively late that night. Huston and I were in our beds by 11:30. However, as was often the case, Marcelino stayed out later. He liked to walk around at night to talk with the sentries and the other young soldiers who were awake.

TUESDAY, AUGUST 9, 2005

Our morning was spent painting metal doors and beams with outdoor lead paint. We went about the work so diligently that at one point an officer in a nearby office called together the five volunteers on this project for a break. As we put down our brushes and rollers and came over to him, he handed out cups of juice to the five of us. "Thank you for brightening up our base," he said. "You do a great service for volunteering and we appreciate it."

Our team of five finished the painting job at noon and went

to lunch. Marion suggested that the olive oil set on the tables might be the only effective way to get the lead paint off our hands and arms. So while others used the oil on the tables to dip their bread in, Marion, Adrian, and I rubbed it on our hands and arms. It worked.

Going into the shower room after lunch, I learned how strict the Israeli army was about its rule that soldiers have their weapons with them at all times. A soldier had entered the shower room in full uniform, stripped it off to shower, and had laid his gun on the floor close to the entrance. I almost tripped over the M-16 as I entered the shower room.

After work we were joined by a group of twelve Sar-el volunteers from Italy for a tour of the old city of Acre. Our guide was a Sar-el educator named Eldad, who had given us an earlier lecture. Since the Italians spoke neither English nor Hebrew, Paola translated Eldad's running commentary from English to Italian. The tour covered the Old Crusader fortress part of the city. What impressed me the most was how much garbage the Arab residents throw on the ground where they live in the old city. With a bit of clean-up, that city could be transformed into a much more desirable tourist attraction.

One of the Italians, Giuseppi, spoke some English. He told us that his base was Cordanni, located in a grimy industrial area of Haifa. No soldiers remained on the base after work hours except for a few sentries. They had no madricha. Consequently, they had no lectures or programs to make their experience an interesting one. From Giuseppi's account, we appreciated even more how fortunate we were to be assigned to Betzet Tira.

After the Acre tour, the bus dropped us off at a large Haifa mall for dinner and shopping on our own. The mall was crowded – an encouraging sign that the Israeli economy was recovering from the twin blows of recession and the Intifada. But Angela and Marion mentioned on the bus ride back to the base that one of the mall employees had told them that there had been a bomb scare that morning, forcing everyone to leave the building while bomb-sniffing dogs had combed the complex. While an "all-clear" had allowed people back inside, the crowds were thinner than usual as a result of this incident.

This evening there was a commotion over the sentries' behavior. I happened to walk over to the front gate at about 10:30 P.M. to fill up my canteen at the cold water fountain. I saw that two officers had lined up eight or ten of the sentries. Apparently, the officers were not satisfied with their state of readiness. One of the officers had his clipboard out and recorded the deficiencies he had found as he "read the riot act" to the sentries standing at attention. Afterwards, a number of sentries were seen running through fire drills and simulated attack drills, presumably to sharpen their state of readiness.

WEDNESDAY, AUGUST 10, 2005

Today, Marcelino and I spent the day at Betzet Kishon to work in David's pipes warehouse again. I was very curious about why Marcelino, a fifty-five-year-old Hispanic Christian, had volunteered to work on an Israeli army base. During a work break, he was happy to satisfy that curiosity. He explained his hard work formula for success, which he espoused to his high school students in Chicago and to the soldiers on the base. Spending time in Israel as a young man, he told me, may have played a part in his adoption of that formula.

As Marcelino described his experience growing up in a tough Chicago neighborhood, it sounded like he had a lot in common with the "at-risk" youngsters on the base. By happenstance, during his four years at a local teachers' college, he was given an opportunity to spend a semester in Israel living on a kibbutz. Marcelino described his time there as a life-defining experience. The hard work and collective spirit of kibbutz life matured him. He returned to Chicago a changed young man – highly motivated for the first time in his life. Marcelino was proud of the fact that he had passed his work ethic on to his own children, all of whom were successful, educated professionals. One of Marcelino's goals while in Israel was to find "his" kibbutz and visit his "adopted parents" there, to say "thank you" for the experience that had transformed him for the better.

On the ride back to Betzet Tira, our driver Moran mentioned a report she had heard on the news: it said that dangerous language was being used by the religious rightists to vilify Prime Minister Sharon for authorizing the forced evacuation of the Jewish inhabitants of the Gaza Strip. They called him "an evil, ungodly man" and "an enemy of the Jewish religion." In tone and verbiage, the language was similar to that used by the rightists in condemning former Prime Minister Yitzhak Rabin prior to his assassination in 1995. The theme of the radio news report was that the inflammatory language currently being used against Sharon might be perceived as a "green light" from the extremist rabbis to kill him too. Therefore, Sharon's security detail was focused not simply on protecting him from the Palestinians, but on protecting him from Jewish religious extremists. By authorizing the Gaza evacuation, Sharon had put both his political and physical life on the line.

For dinner tonight, a bunch of the volunteers walked to Hof Ha-Carmel, the beautiful beach south of Haifa. Since Judy, Rachel, and Angela were leaving our group tomorrow, Marion made the excellent suggestion that we eat at the beach. We got a seaside table at a beach restaurant and had a fun evening talking about Sar-el and the other bases we had experienced.

The long walk to Hof Ha-Carmel gave me an opportunity to talk with Angela before she returned home. An attractive divorcée with a very quiet-spoken manner, Angela had spent her time on the base toiling over her gardening work in the hot sun. Her Hebrew was excellent and I was curious how a London grandmother had acquired such a fluency in Hebrew.

Angela's background was not that of a typical Londoner. Her parents had immigrated to Israel from Central Europe before World War II. Her Hebrew was that of a youngster born and raised in Israel. When she was a young girl, her parents moved the family to London. When her parents decided to return with the family to Israel, Angela remained behind in London where she married, raised her children and, eventually, enjoyed her grandchildren.

Now her parents were elderly and their ability to live independently in their Jerusalem home was in question. Luckily, Angela's brother lived in nearby B'nei Brak. Over time, he had been drawn to Orthodoxy and fit into the very religious community there. While in Israel on her Sar-el stint, Angela spent a weekend in B'nei Brak celebrating the bar mitzvah of one of her nephews.

Angela split her time between her family in London and her family in Israel. She expressed her love of the land of Israel and her feeling of comfort whenever she was there. She was quite candid that, despite the fact that she was going home to her children and grandchildren in London, she was sad to be leaving. As she spoke, I could sense that she experienced an internal turmoil as to where "home" really was. She clearly had not lost the attachment to the home she knew as a young girl. My guess was that Angela would continue to split her time between London and Israel, even after her parents were no longer her excuse for coming here.

I was usually the last one to get to bed in our bunk of three volunteers, because I stayed up late to update my journal. I stayed up tonight until 12:45 A.M. and Huston had still not yet returned. I didn't know how he occupied himself so late. I got some idea the next day when a very attractive female guard opened the gate to allow us to leave for the weekend; she walked up to Huston, gave him a big, slow kiss on the lips and said in a low sexy voice, "Bye-bye, Huston. See you soon."

THURSDAY, AUGUST 11, 2005

Today was a half-day of work because the workweek on the base ended at lunchtime. We finished another painting job in the morning. The painting team consisted of five guys – Adrian, Paul, Marcelino, Huston, and me – and Marion. I admired Marion; barely five feet tall, she kept up with the guys and in fact acted as the foreman of the job. She clearly enjoyed the camaraderie and humor of the team, but she was also serious about getting the job done.

After lunch, I took a cab south to the home of Dr. Bella Gutterman, the publications director of Yad Vashem, Israel's Holocaust Institute. She had arranged for the publication of my father's book in Hebrew. I came to her house in Ramat Hasharon to meet her and to thank her for what she had done.

Bella, who worked from home two days a week, explained how the Israeli postal authorities decided to put the photograph from the cover of my father's book on a recently issued stamp commemorating the sixtieth anniversary of the end of World War II. She had just edited a large photographic book on the Holocaust and, in the chapter on Jewish resistance, she included the picture from the cover of my father's book. The Israeli postal authorities came upon Bella's book and decided to use the photograph of my father's partisan group.

I told Bella my own story about the photograph: In 1943, a group of Russian soldiers spent a few days with my father's unit in German-occupied Poland. One of the soldiers, a military photographer, took a picture of my father with a few members of his unit. My father forgot about this incident until he came across the picture in the *Forward* (a Yiddish newspaper) in 1964. The newspaper was commemorating the anniversary of the Warsaw Ghetto Uprising and reprinted the picture with the caption: "Unnamed Jewish partisans in Occupied Poland." My father subsequently wrote to the editor of the *Forward* to supply the names of the pictured partisans. Years later, in 1991, I contacted the *Forward* to get a copy of the photograph. The *Forward* referred me to the YIVO Institute for Jewish Research in New York, which had a copy in their archives.

Bella's job was to read and consider memoirs of Holocaust survivors for possible publication. She admitted that this work can be very depressing; the stories were often violent and heart-wrenching. Her three children often chided her about spending so much time reading about the Holocaust.

She told me her interest in pursuing the field of Holocaust studies (she had a doctorate in it) derived from her family's past. Her parents were from Zamosc, a town in southeastern Poland near Lublin. When World War II broke out in 1939, the Russians initially occupied that part of Poland. Like many Polish Jews who retreated with the Russians, Bella's parents eventually found themselves in Uzbekistan; Bella was born near Tashkent. After the war, they returned to Poland, but seeing the hostility still exhibited by Poles against the few surviving Polish Jews, they immigrated to Israel in 1950.

Given her background, Bella was deeply committed to publishing first-person accounts by Holocaust survivors. She also produced age-appropriate materials to introduce this subject in the Israeli public schools. As our pleasant visit concluded, Bella promised to keep in touch about my father's book and arranged a cab for me to Tel Aviv.

It was not a good day to travel to Tel Aviv. The religious rightists had called for a mass demonstration in protest of next Monday's deadline for the removal of all of the Jewish inhabitants of the Gaza Strip. The demonstration was slated for Rabin Square in downtown Tel Aviv and tens of thousands of people were headed there in the late afternoon. The protestors had chosen the color orange to symbolize their cause. In the streets, people walked to Rabin Square in large groups, wearing orange shirts, scarves, bandanas, or belts and carrying Israeli flags draped with orange streamers. Many streets were cordoned off by police to accommodate the crowds of protesters.

I finally reached an address in Tel Aviv where I had arranged to meet Nir, to give him the Keren Kayemet (Jewish National Fund) box I had forgotten to give him the previous weekend. Many American Jewish families had these blue and white metal boxes for charity, and this one belonged to my wife. Nir stepped out of his monthly meeting of a collectors' association to greet me. He was glad to receive the box to add to his collection of Keren Kayemet boxes.

SATURDAY, AUGUST 13, 2005

I spent the weekend with my cousin Ruchama in Netanya. On Saturday morning, Ruchama drove to the same Netanya shopping center she had taken me to two years before. Two years ago, her car had to be checked just to enter the parking lot of the shopping center. This time there were no security guards at the entrance to the parking lot, only the usual guards at the entrance of the shops and restaurants. This loosening of security was a sign to me that the Intifada, although not over, was less of a threat.

Over lunch, I read a headline from Friday's *Maariv* newspaper, which Ruchama translated and fleshed out for me. It reported that the authorities were cracking down on relatives of the Gaza Strip settlers who had moved in with the settlers in an attempt to block the evacuation next Monday. Previously, the authorities had barred anyone from traveling to the Strip for fear they would stay to swell the number of Jewish inhabitants who would have to be evacuated. An exception from this prohibition was permitted to allow for family visits, but the exception had been exploited by the religious rightists to move more people into the Strip ahead of the August 15 evacuation date. When the authorities eliminated the exception, family members continued to try to move in. Now, the authorities were prepared to deal harshly with these family members.

In the middle of lunch, Ruchama suddenly turned to me and, referring to the tension over the impending Gaza disengagement, asked: "Isn't this the worst time for you to be in Israel, during all this *balagan*?" (a Yiddish term for chaos or confusion). Actually, I felt this was a good time for the volunteers to be in Israel. My base, like the other navy bases, had been stripped of personnel who were sent to the Gaza Strip. The volunteers were especially needed on the bases now, to fill in for the absent soldiers. "No," I said firmly, "I'm glad to be here now."

Sunset would mark the beginning of Tisha B'Av, the Jewish holiday commemorating the destruction of the First and Second Temples. Since it is a serious day of fasting in Israel, all shops and restaurants would be closed at sunset. Tomorrow would be an optional workday for all people in the country.

SUNDAY, AUGUST 14, 2005

Just before leaving Ruchama's apartment to take a cab back to the base, I turned on the CNN (Europe) news. On a half-hour program covering worldwide news, there was a segment commemorating the eighteenth anniversary of the death of Iran's Ayatollah Khomeini. The reporter for the segment was a veiled and robed Muslim woman and she extolled the virtues of Khomeini. In a reverent tone, she called him a great and holy man who was beloved by all Muslims. I knew that Khomeini was not so beloved by all Iranians, especially younger ones, and I thought that the report was a very biased piece. As I continued to watch, I noticed that other reports were also by Muslim reporters. At the end of the segment was a disclaimer to the effect that these reports had not been prepared by CNN journalists. It seemed to me that allowing these independent reporters to report the news enables bias and subjectivity to be injected in the news in a way that Americans would not tolerate. But the European CNN permits this, and this is what Europeans and Israelis see if they listen to the CNN news.

Back at the base, Huston reported that he had spent part of Saturday night at the Western Wall of the Temple in Jerusalem. In observance of Tisha B'Av, thousands of religious Jews had packed the plaza in front of the Western Wall and sang songs and read from the Bible all night. They even brought pillows, intending to sleep overnight in the plaza.

Marion brought me Friday's English version of the *Jerusalem Post*. It reported that the mass demonstration of protesters at Tel Aviv's Rabin Square last Thursday evening had been the largest in recent Israeli history. The police estimated the crowd to be 150,000; the rightists claimed double that number had attended. So many people had been packed into downtown Tel Aviv that cell phone coverage crashed.

The headline articles in the *Jerusalem Post* warned that, due to the tension over the Gaza disengagement, a nationwide state of emergency would exist in Israel beginning on Sunday (today). All police vacations were cancelled. The military acknowledged they were considering sealing off the entire southern part of Israel and restricting the public's freedom of movement in that area. The purpose would be to block further infiltration of religious zealots into the Gaza Strip. The nationwide state of emergency would last until after the disengagement. The *Jerusalem Post* also reported that 63 percent of the Gaza Strip settlers had agreed to leave voluntarily.

In the evening after work, Shy Davidi joined us for dinner. I asked him: "What will happen tomorrow?" Shy replied: "August 15 is the deadline for the disengagement. But all that will happen tomorrow is that local Israeli army commanders will personally deliver a letter to each community that has not evacuated. The letter will officially direct them to leave. This will be followed by two days in which we will be very soft and sensitive with them to encourage them to leave. Starting on Wednesday, this will be followed by two days when we will be very hard with them and move out the ones who have not left. So any forcible evictions will not occur until Wednesday."

"What if some of the settlers fire on the soldiers?" I asked. "We hope that will not happen," he replied. "The soldiers will not be armed, in order to avoid bloodshed."

It remained unspoken that if fighting broke out between soldiers and settlers, Israel would face a defining moment comparable to the *Altalena* incident in 1948. At that point, the Irgun, the radical Jewish militant faction in Israel, refused to accept the leadership of David Ben-Gurion and his new government. During the War of Independence, the Irgun attempted to land a ship called the *Altalena* loaded with arms for its own militia forces. Ben-Gurion directed artillery fire on the *Altalena*, blowing up the ship off the coast of Tel Aviv, and establishing that there would be only one government and one army in Israel. This painful incident of "Jews fighting Jews" still evokes bitter feelings among Israelis who remember it.

If the Gaza settlers opened fire on the unarmed soldiers, Prime Minister Sharon would be faced with the same type of decision that the *Altalena* incident had posed to Ben-Gurion. He would have to decide whether to respond with military force against the Gaza settlers in order to enforce the evacuation authorized by the government of Israel. Would Sharon have the political fortitude to order Israeli soldiers to fire on their fellow Jews? This was the unspoken question on everyone's mind in Israel at this tense moment.

Shy confirmed that 60–70 percent of the 7,500 residents of the Gaza Strip had agreed to accept monetary compensation to evacuate. The problem was that right-wing religious zealots, mostly young men, had infiltrated into the Gaza Strip from Israel. These zealots, who sneaked into Gaza by hiding in car trunks or walking through fields, numbered about 2,000. Shy said that these people were expected to pose the biggest problem to the military.

Changing the subject, Shy mentioned that he had read a portion of my father's book and found the story to be very compelling. It inspired him to speak with an Israeli newspaper reporter he knew, who wanted to interview me about my father's story and about my service in Sar-el, but the timing might not work out. Like all Israeli journalists, she was in the south of Israel covering the Gaza disengagement this week, and I would be leaving Israel on Thursday. I was pleased but surprised that he had found the time to look at my father's book.

MONDAY, AUGUST 15, 2005

At flag-raising, only twenty-eight soldiers appeared – about half the normal contingent. A large number were in the Gaza Strip for the disengagement scheduled to start today.

Sergeant Gal made a few cautionary remarks to the assembled soldiers. He reminded them that when they are off the base, they shouldn't congregate in crowded places and shouldn't travel alone. He also reminded the female soldiers that the Palestinians continue to try to abduct Israeli women in the army, so they should always carry pepper spray if they don't normally carry a weapon off base.

At the conclusion of the ceremony, we trooped over to Shy's office to present him with a bottle of wine and thank him for the tremendous support and time he had given to our group. We chose to catch him at this point because we assumed that he would be in the Gaza Strip with his troops for the remainder of the week. Shy allowed us to barge unannounced into his office and thanked us for our service at this tense time in Israel's history.

In the car ride this morning to Betzet Kishon, we were joined by another passenger. Jenya was a diminutive female officer who had been in the navy only eight years. Despite her relatively junior status, she was slated to replace Gilad as commander of Betzet Kishon when he retired. We soon realized why this impressive young woman had been selected for this responsibility.

Jenya was from Dnepopretrovsk in the Ukraine. She had immigrated to Israel by herself and eventually she brought over her parents and younger sister to Israel. Jenya spoke four languages (Russian, Ukrainian, Hebrew, and English) and was very patriotic. During her vacations, she volunteered to travel with Russian teenagers visiting Israel for the first time through the Birthright Program. On these trips, she explained to these teenagers what life was like for new immigrants to Israel. Because she was young, (and looked even younger), her words carried great weight with her teenaged audience. Despite her friendly smile and baby-face, Jenya could be very tough with soldiers when necessary.

Work at Betzet Kishon was hot and very physical today. David's only soldier in the pipes warehouse, Oz, was away for a day in the Gaza Strip for the disengagement. In our absence, David would have had to move and carry everything by himself, with the help of his forklift. For one person, it is a backbreaking job – and David did it for ten hours a day. For this reason, we were happy to be able to pitch in and take some of the load off of him. At the beginning of our volunteer stint, Marcelino and I had to overcome David's reluctance to give heavy work to people who were, in his words, "my father's age." Gradually we showed him that we could handle the work and he had come to rely on us.

We took a last look around at the vast array of naval supplies stored at the base on the way to lunch. As opposed to Betzet Tira, the naval supplies at Betzet Kishon were large items – massive diesel engines designed to power naval ships, gun mounts for 50-caliber machine guns, rocket launchers for the missile boats, and enormous tires for large aircraft. The equipment alone gave us a sense of the seriousness of the place.

As she had for many afternoons, Lee, the female soldier on sentry duty, came over to socialize with us. She surprised Marcelino and me by giving us each two CDs of music by Eyal Golan and Sarit Hadad. Luckily, we had brought her a present as well (Ahava skin products), so we were able to reciprocate.

This evening, we watched a recently made Israeli movie called *Turn Left at the End of the World*. It described two groups of Jewish immigrants, one from Morocco and one from India, who were settled together in a new community established in the middle of the Negev in 1968. The movie was funny and entertaining but also highlighted the strains and clashes between the two immigrant cultures and the hardships faced by all new immigrants to

Israel. Against this backdrop, the story focused on the friendship that developed between two teenaged girls, one Moroccan and one Indian, in this development town.

Shortly after the movie, Gal drove all the volunteers to his favorite ice cream shop in the nearby town of Tirat Karmel. He insisted on ordering the place's specialty for all of us – Belgian waffles, coated with honey and covered with ice cream, chocolate sauce, and whipped cream. He was very animated in encouraging us to eat and it clearly made him happy to watch us enjoying his favorite dessert.

We brought one soldier to the ice cream shop with us – Tzila, the nineteen-year-old soldier who previously had gone off for "Gaza training." Tzila previously had told us she had no home and never mentioned her parents; she lived on the base and on the weekends traveled to visit friends. She was a very large and physical girl, having earlier on knocked down the metal fence separating the men's and women's sides of the barracks. She was also very physical in how she interacted with people. She was aggressive in tone and would grab and shake the male soldiers when speaking with them – to the point that many were afraid of her. They joked that Tzila was the perfect Gaza disengagement soldier because she didn't need a weapon to be able to intimidate the settlers out of their homes. But deep down she was a sweet girl and just craved attention. Consequently, she hung around the volunteers' area and did her best to converse with us in her broken English.

Gal had brought her to tears the previous week by telling her that she needed to learn to be less argumentative and physical with people. Until he spoke with her, she had not realized that her manner had been intimidating to the other soldiers. However, towards the volunteers, she had been one of the friendliest of the soldiers. As a parentless teenager, she needed attention, and we obliged. We were pleased to invite her to join us on one of our last outings.

TUESDAY, AUGUST 16, 2005

Flag-raising ceremony was longer than usual this morning. Uncharacteristically, a podium and microphone were set up in front of the flagpole. After the Israeli national and Israeli navy flags were raised, Shy Davidi took the podium and addressed the assembled group. He read an announcement from Dani Chalutz, the head of the Israeli army, concerning the Gaza Strip disengagement. The gist of the announcement was that the army had a special job to do – to take all of the Jews out of the Gaza Strip. It read: "We can cry with them and feel their pain, but we must carry out our mission. The government's decision must be carried out. But don't forget that we are all Jews and we are all brothers." The soldiers listened somberly to these remarks and when Shy finished, Gal dismissed the assembled group.

Shy came over to greet us one last time. "Thank you again for coming. This will be the last time we will see each other before you leave on Thursday. I must be in the Gaza Strip for the rest of the week. I hope to see you next year." Then he was gone.

As we were walking from flag-raising, Azam, the old Druze villager who volunteered as a gardener on the base, stopped by to greet the volunteers as he often did. What was distinctly different this time is that he used a Yiddish expression to say goodbye to us: "*Azay gezunt*," meaning "Be well." It was incongruous to hear Yiddish spoken by a Druze villager, and very endearing.

Today's work at Betzet Kishon was heavy, but fun. The heaviest pipe that David and I lifted without a forklift weighed 89 kg (196 lbs). I commented to David that this was a very heavy pipe. He agreed, but added: "What do you think I do when the volunteers and my soldier are not here to help me? I would lift it myself." And he then proceeded to lift it himself to prove his point.

We filled numerous orders for pipes. Marcelino and David's soldier assistant, Oz, worked as one team and David and I were the other team. David operated his forklift outside the warehouse and I walked alongside (fast, to keep up with the forklift), assisting him. Shortly after lunch, David asked me, "Would you like to learn to use the forklift?" Having driven a tractor as a teenager, I was up to the challenge. After a few minutes of instruction, I was able to use it to pick up and fill orders.

David and I switched roles for a while. Now I drove the forklift and he walked alongside. We turned the heads of David's colleagues as we passed the open doors of nearby warehouses. The soldiers' wisecracks did not make a dent in David's pride. He was showing off how well he had trained "his volunteer" and he enjoyed the surprised stares of the soldiers.

The afternoon passed quickly because David liked to talk while we worked. At one point, David said to me: "I'm so happy that you volunteers are here. I feel very strongly for my country and I am pleased that you have come to show support for us. Even if you did absolutely no work, just your presence would make me happy."

David went out of his way to show his gratitude. For example, when I heard a familiar Israeli song on the radio that I liked, I asked him who was the singer. "Wait a minute," he said. Sitting atop his forklift, he called a friend of his on his phone, and spoke for a few minutes. "There. It is done," he said. "What do you mean?" I asked. "My friend has downloaded the CD which contains this song and you will have it before you leave on Thursday," he replied. After that, I had to be careful about what I said to him, for fear he would order yet another new CD for me. I had already received five CDs – three from David and two from Lee – and this new one would make six.

We all walked to the local convenience store in Tirat Karmel after dinner to buy snacks. As we were leaving, Marcelino went back into the store to look for raisins. The storeowner gave him a big bag of raisins and said: "It's on the house. Thank you for coming to Israel to volunteer."

When we returned to the base, we gave a present to Tzila, who had come over to talk with the volunteers again and practice her English. The present (Ahava) was a big surprise to her and she was clearly moved by it. As we broke up for the night, one of the soldiers in a bunk opposite ours opened up with his electric guitar attached to a speaker. He was an excellent musician and played a wide range of familiar songs, ranging from "Stairway to Heaven" to "Hatikvah." It was an excellent way to end the evening.

WEDNESDAY, AUGUST 17, 2005

Early this morning, I went for a quick workout in the fitness center. While there, I watched the television local news about the Gaza withdrawal. Israel is a democracy with a free press. Just as American journalists were embedded in American army units at the outbreak of the Second Gulf War, Israeli journalists were embedded in the Israeli army units assigned to remove the Jewish residents from the Gaza Strip. The news cameras were rolling as hundreds of soldiers walked through the streets of a particular Gaza village. The streets were quiet and nearly empty. Some residents were still there. A few paraded arm-in-arm in a line down a street, carrying banners protesting the evacuation. One woman harangued a group of soldiers who were taking refuge from the hot sun in the shelter of some trees. The troops were unarmed, which must have felt strange to soldiers who normally carry their M-16s everywhere. A soldier standing next to me in the fitness center, who was also watching the news, commented that the army hadn't yet started physically carrying people out of their homes. "When will that happen?" I asked. "Later today," he replied. "That's when the trouble may start."

Despite the tensions of the day, we had to get ready for the *keness* (gathering) for all the volunteers in Israel. Last year, Sar-el held a *keness* in Jerusalem for all of its volunteers while I was there in August. This year, the event would be held at a water park in Holon.

We took a bus to Holon together with the twelve Italian

volunteers based at the Cordanni base in Haifa. At the massive water park, we joined 350 other volunteers of all nationalities. Marcelino was especially happy to meet the Mexican group and speak with them in Spanish. We also met up with another English-speaking group based at Batzop, my former base in Ramle. We spent the day in and out of the water under the hot sun. Luckily, Paul had enough sunscreen #30 for everyone in our group.

At 4:00 P.M., all of the volunteers and madrichas assembled under a large netting (essential shelter from the sun) for a short program. Then General Aharon Davidi was called to the podium. We gave the founder of Sar-el a standing ovation. Speaking softly, General Davidi gave his remarks in Russian, French, and English. He thanked us for volunteering, especially for showing support for Israel during the tension of the Gaza withdrawal. He character-ized it as one of the most difficult times in Israel's history, because it pitted Jew against Jew.

We listened intently to the radio news on the bus ride back to Betzet Tira. According to a government spokesperson, the Gaza evacuation was going according to plan. Today soldiers started physically removing people from their homes. No violence was encountered and the government said that the evacuation might take less time than planned because a large percentage of the resi-dents had left before the soldiers moved in.

Back at the base, both volunteers and soldiers crowded around the television in the *moadon* to hear the news of the day's historic events. CNN confirmed what we'd heard on the bus radio. Resistance to the forced evacuation was lighter than expected, al-though some residents were being forcibly evicted. Prime Minister Sharon had made a public appeal to the residents not to hurt the soldiers: "Don't hurt these young people. They are simply carrying out my orders," he said. "Please don't hurt them. Instead, direct your criticism and blame at me."

The government's decision to send in unarmed soldiers had been a masterful move. It served to de-escalate the confrontation between the soldiers and the Gaza residents, especially after two days of persuasion. The operation was expected to be completed within a week, instead of the three weeks previously anticipated.

Nonetheless, there was still strong opposition to the evacuation. One woman, a Gaza Strip resident, set herself on fire in protest. A large group of religious zealots had barricaded themselves into a Gaza Strip synagogue and refused to come out. And a frustrated religious zealot in the West Bank settlement of Shilo grabbed an Israeli guard's gun and killed three Palestinians who had done nothing to provoke him.

The local Israeli news broadcast pictures of emotionally overwrought Gaza residents. Some of the residents were weeping as they were being forced out of their homes. Others were screaming as they were being carried out. Some of the mothers expressed their opposition to the evacuation by sending their children to stand out in front of their homes. Although the young soldiers carried out their duties very professionally, the next day's *Jerusalem Post* reported that this work took an enormous emotional toll on the soldiers. Many of them at some point broke down in tears. The *Post* carried photos of soldiers hugging and consoling Gaza residents being led away, as well as soldiers hugging each other in sadness.

One poignant moment caught by the television cameras broadcast a young man in his early twenties who opened his door in response to a soldier's knock. Standing in his doorway, the young man told the soldier that he could not understand why the Israeli army was forcing him to leave his home. At that point, the young man got so choked up he could not speak. Instead, he began to cry and the soldier hugged him saying, "I love you. I understand you are hurting. Let's go and talk some more." The young man cried on the soldier's shoulder for a while because he was so overcome by sadness. Then they both slowly walked away. It was such an emotional scene that some of the soldiers among us seemed close to tears. The volunteers remained silent, out of respect for the emotion in the room. The pictures broadcast on the television were traumatic for all Israelis, whether or not they supported the withdrawal.

THURSDAY, AUGUST 18, 2005

Last night, Noa triggered a near-revolt among the volunteers when she informed us that we would not be working this morning. Most of the volunteers were leaving in the afternoon and had assumed, as in the prior two weeks, that we could get in a morning's work before our three-week stint ended. However, Noa told us we would need the morning to close up.

Noa was right. After flag-raising, we turned in our uniforms, boots, and sheets. After completing our packing, we cleaned our rooms and washed the floors. We had to leave our bunks in as clean a condition as we had found them three weeks earlier. By the time we finished everything, it was close to noon.

In the middle of the morning, David appeared at our bunk. Gilad had given him permission to leave his warehouse at Betzet Kishon to drive down to Betzet Tira in order to say goodbye to Marcelino and me. David came bearing gifts. First, he gave me the CD he had promised. Then he brought a package of the strong coffee he made every morning in the warehouse for Marcelino. Finally, he brought us each a bottle of Israeli wine from a winery in the Golan Heights. I felt guilty taking all these gifts because I knew it cost David a significant sum in relation to his low salary.

Marcelino had already left when David appeared. He had gone in search of the remote kibbutz where he had spent a four-month stint during his college years. While I could not ship the bottle of wine to him, I promised David I would send Marcelino the package of the coffee he liked so much.

Marion and I were scheduled to take the same flight to New York at 1:00 A.M. Friday morning. Rather than simply hanging around the base the rest of the day or spending the afternoon in Ben-Gurion Airport, we decided to take advantage of the free afternoon to tour the sights of Haifa. The Haifa Tourist Office gave us a map and a recommended walking tour, which started us at Mercaz Ha-Carmel, near the highest point of the city. For the next three hours, we hiked the streets of Haifa, heading generally downward towards the sea. We walked through the immaculately maintained grounds of the gold-domed Bahai Temple where we saw a beautiful, bejeweled bride in her wedding gown posing for pictures. Throughout our walk, we enjoyed spectacular views overlooking Haifa's half-moon harbor, bordered by the brilliantly blue Mediterranean.

At the Stella Maris Monastery, we climbed into a cable car that took us down the steep slope to sea level. The cable car deposited us near the Yotvata Restaurant (part of a chain of Israeli dairy restaurants), where we ate a light dinner at the water's edge. I had just completed my fourth stint in Sar-el, Marion her fourteenth. We had come to make a contribution to Israel with our work; we left richer for all the personal relationships we had made here.

POSTSCRIPT

Why do thousands of people volunteer each year to work on Israeli military bases? Why would grown men and women give up three weeks of their precious time and pay their way to and from Israel in order to work very hard there?

First and foremost, the volunteers are motivated by a desire to show Israelis that they are not alone and that the world has not abandoned them. The mere presence of volunteers in Israel should have been enough to accomplish this, but we went out of our way to make this point. We did this in the many conversations we had with the soldiers while working side-by-side with them, over meals, and in casual encounters on the base. We also made this point during our free weekends, talking to relatives and friends, shopkeepers, and taxi drivers.

In addition to a desire to show Israelis we are with them, many volunteers felt a need to connect with and support Israel in a personal way – with a greater sacrifice than simply giving money. That greater sacrifice was our time, our sweat, our inconvenience in living in soldiers' quarters and being away from our homes. In turn, a greater sense of connection with Israel resulted from our labor – the products that we produced or repaired, and the bases that we physically improved and helped to operate.

Here is one small example: Bernie and two other volunteers in Batzop worked on testing batteries the entire three weeks there. (These are large, heavy batteries used in military equipment such as tanks, not the small batteries used in flashlights.) It was a repetitive and boring job, but it had to be done. And Bernie took great satisfaction in the amount of money he and his teammates saved the IDF. They tested about 400 batteries apiece each day and about half were found to still be usable. Each usable battery would have cost the IDF about $40 if it had had to be replaced with a new one. And each of the three volunteers worked about twelve full days on battery testing. If you do the calculations, the three of them saved batteries worth $288,000. The math is compelling; they saved the IDF a lot of money. And if you project similar savings to the antennae we built, the radios and radio bases we rebuilt, and the tank helmets we refurbished, our group of forty-four volunteers at Batzop saved the IDF a great deal of money – most likely more than the combined amount we could have collectively contributed.

In addition to the economic value of what we produced, our greater connection with Israel came from the lasting physical improvements we brought to the bases. These improvements could be seen in a variety of things, including painting guardhouses and gates, planting trees, building sidewalks, and organizing and cleaning army warehouses that hadn't been cleaned "since the British." And, hopefully, Philip's magnificent painting of the Sar-el emblem will continue to grace the entrance to our Batzop compound to greet future volunteers for years to come.

An even greater connection grew when we saw the things we worked on being used by IDF soldiers. It gave Bernie a thrill when soldiers from a tank unit would show up at his workplace because they needed batteries. Gary and Kathy felt proud when they saw "their" antennae used in radio backpacks by soldiers guarding the Lebanese border. And I remember my talk with Mrs.

Ross' daughter, whose son used "our" helmets in the Tank Corps. Knowing that the fruits of our labor went directly to the frontlines provided a direct connection with Israel and a great sense of personal satisfaction.

There was a third common theme that I heard regarding the volunteers' reasons for participating in Sar-el. It was a generational theme that was stated in different ways by different volunteers, but can be distilled as follows: The volunteers feel a very strong connection to Israel for a variety of reasons – and they want to impress that feeling of connection upon their children and grandchildren through their personal example. I share in this motivation as well.

I also came to realize that many volunteers were on a personal journey in which service to Israel filled deep-seated needs. Some volunteers were looking for a new start and hoped to establish roots and a new life in a new country. Others were on a spiritual journey to find more meaning in life, express their faith commitments, or strengthen their connection to Judaism and the Jewish people.

I can trace my own motivation to the strong Zionist background that my father instilled in me and my brothers. This background includes the credo "Never Again," meaning Jews should never again allow themselves to be placed in the helpless and hopeless situation they faced prior to and during the Holocaust. Volunteering is my way of practicing that credo.

My wife Arlene suggested that my motivation went beyond Zionism. It was tied to the great respect I had for my father as a resistance fighter during the Holocaust. To me, he was a "larger than life" hero, and I was proud of my father for "fighting back." Perhaps in some small measure, volunteering on military bases was my way of emulating my father and acting on my commitments, as he had.

But there are other things I have gotten out of this experience, many of which can be generalized to the other volunteers as well.

First, there is the friendship and camaraderie among the volunteers. When you work and sweat together, derive satisfaction from your efforts together, suffer inconvenience together, and laugh over it together, you build a durable connection to a community of volunteers. The common bond of experience made us feel part of a special family and often this bond lasted beyond our time in Israel.

Second, our experience allowed us the opportunity to get to know a broad range of Israeli soldiers. Talking with Elena in the quartermaster's warehouse, and with Sivan as she sped us through the streets of Haifa, gave me a better understanding of how young Israelis view their service in the army as well as their futures after the army. And working with the older *miluim* soldiers, the army reservists coming in for their annual four-week duty, gave me more of a sense of how tough it is to live in Israel, with its high unemployment and economy challenged by terrorism. Listening to Raz, and to the officers on the navy ships, increased my appreciation and admiration for the *esprit de corps* of the Israeli combat units. And meeting new immigrants, like Ilya, brought home the challenges facing the soldiers who are new to the country and without family in Israel.

Most importantly, living with the soldiers impressed upon us how young and vulnerable they are. The great bulk of them are eighteen to twenty-year-old youngsters who, without their uniforms and weapons, could easily be mistaken in the U.S. for high school twelfth-graders. They kid around like teenagers, dress like teenagers, and socialize like teenagers. In many cases, the volunteers had children as old or older than these youngsters. And for that reason, we felt very protective towards them, even though they were the ones with the guns. The attack on Avigail in Ramle impressed upon all of us how vulnerable these youngsters are and how real the dangers are that they face every day.

Finally, from my conversations with the soldiers and my weekend discussions with my Israeli cousins, I gained a better understanding of the way in which many Israelis view the Israeli-

Palestinian conflict. By reason of their geography, Israelis view this conflict through a different prism than do Americans or other Westerners. Israelis are reminded every day, in the form of random Palestinian violence, that they are potential targets of terrorism. For this reason, security must be their foremost priority and this justifies offensive military actions to preempt terrorist attacks.

My own thinking about the Israel-Palestinian conflict has been influenced by my volunteer experiences. I had been a strong supporter of Barak's 1999 peace overture to the Palestinians. The Palestinians' violent response has moved me from the left to the right, like most of the Israel populace. I have seen that offering concessions is viewed in the Arab world as a sign of weakness and provokes more Arab violence intended to extract even greater concessions. Therefore, I have become more hawkish in my view of the conflict, although I still support further Israeli withdrawal from the Palestinian-populated areas of the West Bank. And I share the concern of many Israelis that a significant portion of the Palestinian populace is more focused on destroying Israel than on creating a Palestinian state to peacefully co-exist with Israel. When the Israelis withdrew from the Gaza Strip, they left intact most of the extensive agricultural infrastructure (e.g., nurseries, irrigation systems) in the emptied Jewish settlements. Instead of seizing this golden opportunity to build a strong economic base in a new Palestinian state in Gaza, Palestinian mobs celebrated the Israeli withdrawal by destroying this agricultural infrastructure. Then the Palestinians launched a series of Kassam rocket attacks from the Gaza Strip into Israel. I read a news report that a Kassam rocket, launched from the now deserted Jewish settlements in the northern tip of the Gaza Strip, struck an army base in Israel just north of the Gaza Strip and injured five soldiers. I later found out that the base was Zikim.

Would I recommend this experience to others? Definitely not to everyone. But for people who do not require five-star hotels and meals, who are reasonably fit, and can live like Boy Scout or Girl Scout campers, Sar-el does provide an unforgettable experience.

For those people, I recommend this program, especially if they have patience and a sense of humor. These attributes are helpful because this is an army experience and the bureaucracy of the Israeli army is similar to the bureaucracy in other armies.

In sum, this is a remarkable program for people who can "hack it." It takes you out of your comfort zone. In so doing, it satisfies valuable needs for both Israel and for the volunteers. As for me, my stints on Israeli military bases have been a thoroughly rewarding experience that expanded my horizons and further strengthened my connection with Israel. And I hope that, by describing that experience, I have offered a new option for people to explore and strengthen their own connection to this special place.

ABOUT THE AUTHOR

M ark Werner is an attorney in Raleigh, North Carolina. A
graduate of Haverford College, he received his law degree
from the University of Pennsylvania. He is the son of a Holocaust
survivor.

Mr. Werner has been actively involved in United Jewish
Communities (UJC) and the American Israel Public Affairs
Committee (AIPAC). He spends a part of his summers volun-
teering on Israeli military bases through Sar-el, also known as
Volunteers For Israel.